# Ethnic Nationalism
# and Regional Conflict

# Ethnic Nationalism and Regional Conflict

## The Former Soviet Union and Yugoslavia

EDITED BY

## W. Raymond Duncan
## and G. Paul Holman, Jr.

Westview Press

BOULDER • SAN FRANCISCO • OXFORD

Maps, except where otherwise noted, provided courtesy of the United States Central Intelligence Agency

This Westview softcover edition is printed on acid-free paper and bound in library-quality, coated covers that carry the highest rating of the National Association of State Textbook Administrators, in consultation with the Association of American Publishers and the Book Manufacturers' Institute.

Published in 1994 in the United States of America by Westview Press, Inc., 5500 Central Avenue, Boulder, Colorado 80301-2877, and in the United Kingdom by Westview Press, 36 Lonsdale Road, Summertown, Oxford OX2 7EW

A CIP catalog record for this book is available from the Library of Congress.
ISBN 0-8133-8813-9

Printed and bound in the United States of America

The paper used in this publication meets the requirements
of the American National Standard for Permanence of Paper
for Printed Library Materials Z39.48-1984.

10    9    8    7    6    5    4    3    2    1

# Contents

# Preface

As this book goes to press, ethnic nationalism's impact can be seen throughout the former Soviet Union and Yugoslavia. When President Boris Yeltsin dissolved Russia's parliament in September 1993, many of its members and outside supporters—some xenophobic Russian nationalists, others left-over communists or monarchists—joined ranks to destabilize Yeltsin. In early October, the ensuing street violence between such parliamentary backers and Yeltsin's riot police brought the city of Moscow to its most extreme instability since the 1917 Revolution. Anti-Yeltsin turbulence—led by a core of armed parliament defenders with far-right Russian nationalist credentials (volunteers from the Russian National Unity movement)—ended only when Yeltsin called for military reinforcements to crush the rebellion.[1]

In the former Soviet Union, Georgia's leader, Eduard Shevardnadze, narrowly escaped death in late September 1993 when the key Georgian provincial city of Sukhumi fell to nationalist Abkhazian forces. Shevardnadze blamed Russian military groups for backing Abkhazian separatists, vowing to avenge the defeat. Indeed, it appears that Russian forces supplied tanks and other military equipment—including "volunteers"—to Abkhazian rebels who drove Georgian Government forces backing Shevardnadze from Sukhumi.[2] As part of this drama, ethnic Russian military officers have shown great antipathy toward the Georgian leader—formerly Mikhail Gorbachev's foreign minister—whom they blame personally for the collapse of the Soviet Union and withdrawal of Soviet troops from Eastern Europe.[3] Russian military forces have also supported anti-government forces in at least two of the former Soviet republics: ethnic Russians and Ukrainians in Moldova's break-away "Trans-Dnestr Republic," as well as ethnic Armenians in Nagorno-Karabakh, who have been promoting a self-determination movement against ethnic troops from Azerbaijan.[4]

Not surprisingly, the Russian Foreign Ministry has called for expanded United Nations help in peace-keeping in the troubled ethnic conflicts of the former Soviet Union.[5] However, in the rump state of Yugoslavia, Russia has shown a distinct tendency to identify more closely with ethnic Serbs, led by President Slobodan Milosevic, than have other members of the United Nations Security Council. It was only when the U.S. and its major allies in the UN backed

Yeltsin in his showdown with the Russian parliament in October that Russia's leader abruptly dropped his opposition to a U.S.-supported plan to increase pressure on Milosevic to end ethnic civil war in Croatia.[6] War-torn former Yugoslavia, meanwhile, remained in turmoil—without an agreed-upon peace plan to end ethnic conflict and showing signs of increasing fragmentation as nationalist leaders like Milosevic and President Alija Izetbegovic of Bosnia faced emerging rivals who would complicate peace negotiations even more.[7]

These and other ethnic conflicts examined in this volume indicate how turbulent the world has become in the post–Cold War era—and how difficult it has been to craft western security policies to address the turmoil. North Atlantic Treaty Organization (NATO) allies have been tragically unable to orchestrate an effective policy to quell the violence in the former Soviet Union and Yugoslavia, as our case studies on these regions, especially former Yugoslavia, so vividly illustrate. The future of western security policies is blurred, despite the Clinton Administration's acknowledgment that a major aspect of the current era is, as Anthony Lake, National Security Adviser, has stated, "an explosion of ethnic conflicts."[8] Indeed, even future UN peace-keeping efforts have been marked by the western powers' reluctance to engage militarily in Bosnia—and by emerging constraints on U.S. participation in UN peace-keeping efforts born by months of frustration and setbacks in Bosnia, Haiti, and especially in Somalia. Although President Clinton's early statements were extremely positive, the deaths of U.S. servicemen in Somalia in early October 1993 produced a chilling effect on the President's views and on public support for joint peace-keeping under UN auspices.[9]

We hope our studies of ethnic conflict will shed light on the regional dynamics unfolding in the former Soviet Union and Yugoslavia and stimulate new thinking about international security. The issue clearly affects U.S. foreign policy as America sorts out its primary and secondary priorities in the post–Cold War world, especially given its past quagmires in Vietnam and Lebanon.

*W. Raymond Duncan*
*G. Paul Holman, Jr.*

## Notes

1. See *The Christian Science Monitor*, October 4, 1993, p. 3.
2. *The New York Times*, October 7, 1993, p. A9.
3. Conversation with Professor Melvin Goodman, National Defense University, October 1, 1993. Professor Goodman is coauthor of a forthcoming biography on Shevardnadze (with Lyn McGiffert Ekedahl).
4. *The New York Times*, October 7, 1993, p. A9.
5. *The New York Times*, September 29, 1993, p. A11. The appeal was made by Andrei V. Kozyrev, Russia's Foreign Minister.

6.    *The New York Times*, October 5, 1993, p. A12.

7.    *The New York Times*, October 7, 1993, p. A15.

8.    Anthony Lake, "From Containment to Enlargement," speech at Johns Hopkins University, School of International Studies, September 21, 1993.

9.    On emerging constraints to U.S. participation in regional peace–keeping, see President Clinton's address to the 48th session of the UN General Assembly, September 27, 1993.

# Acknowledgments

This study is the product of a conference held at the Naval War College, Newport, Rhode Island, in April 1993. The authors would like to thank RADM Joseph Strasser, president of the Naval War College, for his unstinting support in organizing this conference, as well as all the professors, staff, and students in the National Security Decision Making Department (NSDM) who participated in conference planning and discussions. In this group, Christine Anderson, NSDM Department, stands out for her superhuman efforts in organizing the April conference.

We are especially grateful to a number of individuals in the NSDM Department for their comments on the manuscript during its various drafts, notably Col. D.T. Buckwalter, Col. J.J. Sullivan, Col. Allan Ricketts, Capt. Bill Calhoun, Col. Chris Eyler, Gary Misch, Bobby Childress, and Michael Corgan. We also are pleased to thank Dr. Melvin Goodman of the National Defense University in Washington, D.C., for his insight, Cathy Stanmeyer for reading parts of the manuscript, and Norman Frisch for his outstanding work on the maps. Responsibility for the final chapters naturally remains the authors'.

The staff of the Document Preparation Center, State University of New York, College at Brockport, devoted enormous time and effort in preparing the manuscript for publication. Jeanne Saraceni was especially helpful, as was Lori Lingg, and Pamela Rowles. Without their efforts, we surely would have been lost in terms of getting the manuscript published in a reasonable length of time.

Finally, we want to express our appreciation to three individuals who helped bring this project to fruition. Rebecca Ritke, senior editor at Westview Press, and her assistant, Carol Jones, expedited the manuscript in a professional manner, and Ann Goodman of the Central Intelligence Agency made heroic efforts in locating suitable maps for the book.

*W.R.D.*
*G.P.H.*

# Introduction: Ethnic Nationalism in the Post–Cold War Era

## W. Raymond Duncan
## and G. Paul Holman, Jr.

Nationalism is not necessarily a negative phenomenon in contemporary world affairs. By forging identity with "a people" as the central focus of loyalty, nationalism can serve as a basis for collective solidarity to legitimize governing institutions and stimulate economic growth.[1] In nineteenth-century England, France, and America, as one observer notes, national identity and nationalism offered "roads to modernity."[2] Indeed, post–World War Two West Germany and Japan illustrate how patriotic devotion to one's country unifies and mobilizes individuals for remarkable economic and political development. In short, nationalism is inherently neither good nor bad, but a fact of life that shows a capacity for both good and evil.

Still, when one nation glorifies itself at the expense of others—as in national chauvinism, jingoism, xenophobia, fascism and other doctrines—it becomes a negative force in world politics. Nationalism in Germany and Japan during the inter-war period and World War Two, with its xenophobic feelings of superiority vis-à-vis other national groups, illustrates the point. Although not an evil in and of itself, then, nationalism has the potential to stir up trouble.

Our aim in this book is not to indict nationalism, cultural pluralism, or pride in one's heritage. Certainly the self-esteem gained from one's cultural and national roots has its place in modern society, for as Arthur M. Schlesinger, Jr., reminds us, "nationalism remains, after two centuries, the most vital political emotion in the world—far more vital than social ideologies such as communism or fascism or even democracy."[3] Our focus is rather on one form of nationalism that has become increasingly pronounced in recent years: *ethnic nationalism*, by which is meant individual loyalty to a particular ethnic group.

Our goal is to explore the nature and impact of ethnic national identity on regional stability as it seems to be playing out in the post–Soviet/communist world. In some arenas—as in Yugoslavia and the Transcaucasus—chauvinistic, exclusionary, and xenophobic brands of ethnic nationalism have invoked supposed past glories to redress presently perceived injustices.  Such activities have generated disturbingly high levels of conflict.  Indeed, Samuel P. Huntington argues that

> World politics is entering a new phase. ... The fundamental source of conflict in this new world will not be primarily ideological or primarily economic. The great divisions among humankind and the dominating source of conflict will be cultural. Nation states will remain the most powerful actors in world affairs, but the principal conflicts of global politics will occur between nations and groups of different civilizations.[4]

## The Former Yugoslavia

Yugoslavia's break-up graphically illustrates the dark side of ethnic nationalism and how, in the words of one observer, "animosity among ethnic groups is beginning to rival the spread of nuclear weapons as the most serious threat to peace that the world faces."[5]  Certainly this view applies to former Yugoslavia. There, xenophobic ethnic nationalism—rooted in a turbulent Balkan past, unresolved border disputes, and collapse of the multinational Hapsburg and Ottoman empires—shipwrecked the Yugoslav state from 1991 onwards.[6]  Wars broke out between Croatians and Serbians, Croatians and Bosnian Muslims, and Serbians and Bosnian Muslims—with Serbians engaging in a gruesome, systematic "ethnic cleansing" of Bosnian Muslims in quest of expanded territory.[7]  While ethnic conflict is no stranger in the Balkans, few observers anticipated the scale of ethnic nationalist violence that exploded as communism collapsed in the former Yugoslavia from 1990 onwards.

In pressing for a "Greater Serbia," Serbians became famous for a Nazi look-alike brand of "ethnic cleansing" in Bosnia, while conducting their tribal war in Croatia.  By Christmas 1992, over 128,000 were dead, 500,000 refugees had fled the country into neighboring states, around 3 million Bosnians were driven from their homes, and nearly 1.7 million were at risk of starvation in the approaching winter.  Xenophobic ethnic nationalism spread through former Yugoslavia like a debilitating virus, creating what one observer has termed a kind of "Jihad" of ethnic strain, or Lebanonization within the fledgling states.[8]  Such conditions hardly foreshadow stable political rule in former Yugoslavia's new states, nor do they form a basis for regional stability.

## The Former Soviet Union

In the former Soviet Union ethnic national tensions have escalated dramatically since its break-up into the Commonwealth of Independent States (CIS) in 1991.  Such tensions stem from the collapse of Communism and centralized control, weak political institutions incapable of managing conflict, and political elites all too ready to exploit ancient feuds to advance personal agendas. Yet it should be noted that ethnic national conflict in a region so complex and mixed as the former Soviet Union is not axiomatic.[9] Whether ethnic nationalism produces conflict or instability is a function of other phenomena, such as the roles played by political elites, social conditions and economic factors.[10]

What we can say about ethnic nationalism in the new republics is that they have inherited multiple crises that were at work in the former Soviet Union before it collapsed.[11] These crises—*economic, irredentist–territorial,* and *political* in nature—have been passed on to the newly independent republics, spawning intensified ethnic identities and regional tensions. The *economic* crisis, for example, is illustrated by the former Soviet Union's declining growth rates and high inflation, the former running around 14–15 percent annually, the latter at 5–8 percent. Declining productivity after the break–up was matched by a 25–30 percent rate of inflation a month in Russia, with similar patterns in Ukraine and elsewhere.

A *national* crisis—in the sense of centrifugal ethnic national forces spawned by a territorial irredentism in Russia and the other new states where ethnic minorities abound—is another historical inheritance, kept alive in part by economic conditions. Russia has the largest number of ethnic minorities—over 100 non–Russian ethnic groups in Russia and twenty areas with large non–Russian ethnic concentrations, numbering over 27 million non–Russians residing within the Russian Federation. Expressed another way, about 40 percent of the former Soviet Union's minorities live in Russia.[12] Outside Russia, in the new states of the former Soviet Union, live 25 million Russians. Russian politicians play up this issue—primarily on the platform of protecting the human rights of those 25 million Russians who have become minorities in foreign countries.[13]

*Territorial* and *political* crises add to the heavy baggage and formidable challenges faced by the newly independent countries of the former Soviet Union. The territorial problem springs from disputed borders; of Russia's sixteen borders, twelve are disputed. Of Ukraine's seven borders, five are disputed. The large numbers of minorities living within other states, like the Armenians inside Azerbaijan, not surprisingly exacerbate such territorial disputes. Finally, a number of countries in the former Soviet Union are experiencing a political struggle between democratic and authoritarian forces—a fourth crisis that magnifies the others. Especially pronounced in Russia, where democratically elected Boris Yeltsin faced those who would turn back the clock, the political crisis has its versions in Ukraine and other republics.

The consequences of these inherited crises have been expressed in multiple forms—from Estonian, Latvian and Lithuanian opposition to a Russian presence in the Baltic region to ethnic national wars in the Caucasus and Central Asia.

In Latvia, for example, anti-Russian nationalists have demanded the removal of Soviet Army soldiers' remains from a military cemetery in Riga, because their presence was offensive.[14] In Nagorno-Karabakh in the southern Caucasus, under the rule of Azerbaijan but populated mostly by ethnic Armenians, a five-year undeclared war between Armenian separatists and Azerbaijanis has raged, taking about 3,000 lives, while Abkhazians and Ossetians inside Georgia have battled Georgians for self-rule.[15] Communal violence in Tajikistan has led over 50,000 to flee for their lives.[16]

Ethnic tensions mark Russia's political landscape, with secessionist movements in Tatarstan, Bashkortostan, Sakha, Tuva, Chechenya, and Northern Ingushetia becoming more vocal in resisting central control. In some cases, such movements want control of natural resources, such as in the vast Siberian republic of Sakha, rich in gold and diamonds; or oil in Tatarstan and diamonds and natural gas in Siberia. Strong independence movements, however, are offset by long association with Moscow and the costs of national security for regions that house co-existing ethnic groups. Nevertheless, one possible future in Russia, as David Shipler notes, is civil war.[17]

Russo-Ukrainian tensions are especially worrisome, given the nuclear weapons that remain in the possession of the two states. Russian politicians advocating protection of Russian-speaking minorities outside Russia naturally alarm Ukraine and other republics, for they raise the specter of Russian imperialism. Russia's new military doctrine assigns to Russia's armed services the mission of defending Russia's citizens, as well as defending "Russian speakers" living in those newly independent states bordering Russia; and Russian military forces reportedly have engaged in action in four former Soviet republics—Moldova, Georgia, Tajikistan, and Azerbaijan.[18] In this regard, worth noting is President Yeltsin's Security Council declaration of November 1993 that highlighted Russia's main source of military danger as no longer any nation or alliance, but small local wars and conflicts—a danger the Security Council saw as "constantly growing."[19] Lenin was right when he called Czarist Russia a "prison house of nationalities," and while the Soviet Union's totalitarian rule may have slammed shut the prison doors temporarily, the fall of the Soviet empire has opened the cell doors again.[20]

## Definitions and Concepts

In assessing the nature and power of nationalism in the post-Cold War era as it operates in the former Soviet Union and Yugoslavia, we should distinguish between states, nations and nationalism. All too frequently observers inappropriately treat "states" as if they were "nations." To regard the two as synonymous is to miss key distinctions between them and to ignore the emotive passions of nationalism. Because sovereign states, national identity, and nationalism remain major forces in international politics, it is worth reminding ourselves of their nature and definition.

A *state's* basic characteristics are easily described: (1) a geographically bounded entity with an identifiable population; (2) a recognized authority structure that has the ability to make laws, rules, and decisions, and to enforce such laws, rules, and decisions within its boundaries; and (3) a territorial association of people recognized for purposes of law and diplomacy as a legally equal member of the system of states—otherwise known as a state's *sovereignty* within the international legal system. The size and power of individual states may vary greatly, but their capacity to act on an equal basis in international politics is generally understood, acknowledged, and protected by law and convention. Former Yugoslavia, therefore, was a "state," while Croatians, Slovenes, and Serbs were national groups inside the Yugoslav state.

A *nation*, by contrast, need not necessarily be either geographically bounded or legally defined. A nation is best understood as a grouping of *people*, who individually identify themselves as linked together in some manner. A nation is as much a *psychological association* as anything else. Groupings of people who consider themselves to be ethnically, culturally, or linguistically related may thus be considered a nation—such as Serbs or Croats in the former state of Yugoslavia, or Estonians, Latvians, Lithuanians, Abkhazians, Ossetians, Tajiks, Kazakhs, Uzbeks, Russians or Ukrainians in the former Soviet Union.

Of special significance today is the psychological and perceptual link between ethnic identity and national identity. As more than one observer has noted, the standard criterion of what constitutes a nation today and what translates into a claim for self-determination (meaning the establishment of a territorial nation-state) is ethnic-linguistic. Here it is important to underscore that language typically symbolizes ethnicity.[21] As Eric Hobsbawm notes,

> Every separatist movement in Europe that I can think of bases itself on 'ethnicity'.
> ... That is to say on the assumption that 'we'—the Basques, Catalans, Scots, Croats, or Georgians are a different people from the Spaniards, the English, the Serbs or the Russians, and therefore we should not live in the same state with them.[22]

Slovene, Croatian and Bosnian Muslim separatism from Serb-dominated Yugoslavia—and Serbian breakaway movements from inside newly independent Croatia and Bosnia—illustrate self-determination drives that spring from separatist ethnic national identity.[23]

Today's ethnic claims to nationhood—and the right to a separate territorial state for separate ethnic groups—should be distinguished from 19th-century versions of nationhood. "Nationality" as viewed typically in the 19th century did not consider either language or ethnicity as necessarily essential to "national" consciousness.[24] Ethnicity, by this definition, was not mandatory for the original "American" revolutionary nationalism which inspired the formation of the U.S.—nor have ethnic differences in the U.S. thus far led to explosive separatist movements as they have in the Balkans and former Soviet Union.[25] Indeed, when President Woodrow Wilson proclaimed the notion of "self-determination" of nations, his Secretary of State, Robert Lansing, worried that the idea was "loaded with dynamite" and might make the world more dangerous.[26]    From Lansing's perspective, "It will raise hopes which can never be realized. It will, I fear, cost thousands of lives. ... What a calamity that the phrase was ever uttered! ... What misery it will cause."[27]

Yugoslavia and the Soviet Union were the two great communist showcases of how ethnic–linguistic loyalties might be superseded by working class solidarity and ultimately transmuted into a new form of patriotism in a multi–national state. The collapse of the old political and ideological order—and planned economy and social security—in Yugoslavia and the Soviet Union help explain intensified and violent identity with ethnicity and language as one's final, unshakable, or "bottom–line" guarantee. This fall–back on ethnicity at a time of social, economic and psychological upheaval has resurrected separatist nationalism and ancient territorial claims in regions now occupied by ethnic national groups different from those making the claim. Serb territorial claims in Kosovo, where the population is ninety percent Albanian, illustrate the point. Because no sizeable state is ethnically "pure," the possibilities for break–up, ethnic national self–determination, and movements either to form a new state or to join with fellow "ethnic nationalists" already occupying another state boggle the mind. Armenians in Nagorno–Karabakh, wishing to join fellow Armenians in Armenia, or Serbs in Bosnia wanting to join with Serbs in Serbia illustrate the point, as do Tatars in Russia and Ossetians in Georgia.

The emergence of many new states—or autonomous self–governing regions inside states—on the global chessboard may not in and of itself bring an end to conflict.    If those new states are weak—unable to govern or feed themselves—then there is the danger of further breakdown into anarchy, created by sub–national groups, factions, and clans in competition with one another for power and control of resources, as in Afghanistan, Colombia, Ethiopia, Haiti and Somalia—and parts of Central Asia in the former Soviet Union. It may well be the case, as Amitai Etzioni argues, that self–determination movements, "a major historical force for more than 200 years, have largely exhausted their legitimacy as a means to create more strongly democratic states."[28]

Let us put it another way. Xenophobic ethnic nationalism, with its wake of destruction vividly illustrated in the Balkans, may be yet another version of what Barbara W. Tuchman so eloquently described in her book, *The March of Folly: From Troy to Vietnam*.    Ms. Tuchman's study asks why high–ranking policy–makers "so often act contrary to the way reason points and enlightened self–interest suggests?"[29]    One reason they do so stems from nationalist attitudes and perceptions, personified by leaders like Slobodan Milosevic of Serbia. As Joseph Campbell captures so well in his book, *The Power of Myth*, myths identify the individual with a particular local group rather than with humankind occupying the planet.[30]

Ethnic nationalism, if carried to its xenophobic extremes—focusing on feelings of group centrality, as if one's group were the center of everything, indeed the center of the universe—operates as such a myth.[31]  When W.G. Summer first introduced the term "ethnocentrism" in 1906, he described it as the "view of things in which one's own group is the centre of everything, and all others are scaled and rated with reference to it."[32]  In all its mythical connotations, which can give rise to the types of instability we see in the Balkans and parts of the former Soviet Union, ethnic nationalism's characteristics, in the words of Ken Booth, entail

> strong identification with one's own group and its culture, the tendency to see one's own group as the centre of the universe, the tendency to perceive events in terms of one's own interests, the tendency to prefer one's own way of life (culture) over all others (seeing it as involving the best and right ways of acting), with an associated bias against other groups and their ways of acting, and a general suspicion of foreigners, their modes of thought, action and motives.[33]

When carried to extremes—as by Serbians in the Balkans—chauvinistic ethnic nationalism can be used by political leaders to unleash wars of the most violent dimension, including the maiming of women and children as a means of psychological intimidation and the obliteration of entire communities—thus setting up conditions for future retaliation.[34]

## U.S. Security Implications

The conflagration of ethnic national conflicts flaring up across the former Soviet Union and Yugoslavia have raised a host of national security questions for the United States and the West.  The collapse of the Soviet threat and the chaotic international environment after the Cold War have left U.S. diplomacy "without a clearly defined purpose," as one newspaper editorial put it in early 1993, at the start of the Clinton Administration.[35]  Nor did the new U.S. Secretary of State, Warren Christopher, disguise the challenge for American security after its "victory" in the Cold War—namely to develop "a new set of foreign policy precepts" comparable to the containment strategy developed after World War Two.[36]  At his confirmation hearings before the Senate Foreign Relations Committee, Christopher cited the "surfacing of long-suppressed ethnic, religious and sectional conflicts" in the world.  He said that the task of heading off such rivalries would be the primary objective of the United States.[37]  Christopher called for "preventive diplomacy" to keep the conflicts from spreading.[38]  By November 1993, however, after months of grappling with local conflicts in former Yugoslavia, Somalia and Haiti, Christopher had redefined priorities for America's foreign policy, which did not include ending the war in Bosnia.[39]

Given the post–Cold War transformation of the international system—with its rising warfare among ethnic national, communal, religious and sub–national groups, conflicts across state borders, and break–down of sovereign states—developing new foreign policy precepts comparable to the containment doctrine is likely to prove difficult at best.[40] Matters have not been helped by enshrining President Wilson's proposals for self–determination in the UN Charter after World War Two. As Senator Daniel Patrick Moynihan (D–NY) has stated, "The defining mode of conflict in the era ahead is ethnic conflict. It promises to be savage. Get ready for 50 new countries in the world in the next 50 years. Most of them will be born in bloodshed."[41]

The end of the Cold War is one of the major driving forces in unleashing ethnic wars. In the view of Francis M. Deng, a former Sudanese Foreign Minister and now a senior associate at the Brookings Institution, "Once you remove the Cold War factionalism, there is the euphoria of freedom, everyone asserting the identities that were previously suppressed. ... We are now witnessing the desire of people to fall back on that which is authentic to them."[42] For Madeleine K. Albright, U.S. representative to the UN, "The international community is at a crossroads of the concept of what is a nation–state."[43]

Numerous security–related questions come to mind when observing how ethnic nationalism and regional conflicts in the former Soviet Union and Yugoslavia have transformed the international system. They arise from the simple fact that the post–Cold War world likely will be characterized by competition between the amalgamating forces of "integration"—such as the European Community and North American free trade area, global information network, and worldwide financial networks—and the tumultuous forces of "fragmentation"—as we now see occurring in Central Europe and the former U.S.S.R.[44] Indeed, high–level spokespersons for the U.S. Central Intelligence Agency (CIA) point to the problem of Russia and the other republics as the biggest American security concern for decades to come—especially with widespread crime and violence, the absence of a concept of private property, a disunified currency system, political infighting and danger of hyperinflation.[45] Such forces exacerbate ethnic national conflicts.

The questions are many. Is Yugoslavia a prototype of the future? When, how, and in what ways do ethnic conflicts impinge on American and Western national interests? Is it true, as some observers argue, that today's "strategic" thought, rooted in a Clausewitzian world paradigm of states engaged in acts of aggression against states is no longer valid in a world of ethnic national and religious groups battling against counterparts inside and across state boundaries?[46] How high a priority should be assigned to the maintenance of global and regional stability? Under what conditions should the United States and the West use force to address such conflicts? What kind of force? Should diplomatic, economic, and political tools of influence take priority over military force? Is Desert Storm—the U.S.-led coalition that ejected Saddam Hussein from Kuwait—a model for dealing with future ethnic conflicts? Do cases like the Balkans resemble more the Lebanon model, where U.S. ground forces walked into a raging civil war that left 241 marines dead from a truck bombing? What problems does the UN encounter in attempting peace-keeping operations in a situation like the Balkans?

Considerable debate has emerged concerning the use of force in the turbulent new international system in the context of U.S. national security decision-making. In a West Point valedictory address in January 1993, President Bush warned that the U.S. must not be drawn by its new dominant position into assuming a role as "the world's policeman."[47] Bush argued that force was justified only "where and when force can be effective," "where its application can be limited in scope and time," and "where the potential benefits justify the potential costs and sacrifice."[48] Former Chairman of the Joint Chiefs of Staff, Colin Powell, has argued that the U.S. is obliged to lead in the post-Cold War period, because no other country on earth has the power possessed by the U.S.[49] For Powell, this obligation emphasizes the importance of U.S. military power. Yet he stresses the need for clear political objectives when using military force and the impossibility of establishing a fixed set of rules for the use of force—to create ambiguity in the minds of potential adversaries.[50] While Powell has been disinclined to use violent force in the Balkans, others—Ronald Reagan, Margaret Thatcher, George Shultz, Henry Kissinger, Jeanne Kirkpatrick, and Zbigniew Brzezinski—have been more enticed by the lure of military solutions.

Much of the debate over the use of military force has focused on the Balkans. At first reluctant to do much of anything except point to the European Community (EC) to take the lead in addressing the crisis, the Bush Administration gradually became more and more involved—pressing for UN resolutions to support "all necessary measures" to back humanitarian aid, and for a "no-fly zone" over Bosnia, and identifying a number of Serb leaders as potential "war criminals." Yet the U.S. eschewed deployment of ground forces. The incoming Clinton Administration—including President Clinton, Secretary of State Christopher, Secretary of Defense Les Aspin, and U.S. Ambassador to the UN Albright—tilted more strongly toward the use of military force, yet demonstrated great caution in identifying the type that would be required. No one wanted a repeat of Lebanon or Vietnam, and few if any spokespeople advocated putting U.S. ground forces into Bosnia, unless they were to be part of a multilateral force backing a peace plan. Certainly not the Chairman of the Joint Chiefs of Staff, Colin Powell.[51] Indeed, for some time—dating back at least to 1982 when Defense Secretary Caspar Weinberger opposed placing U.S. forces in Lebanon without a clear mandate and political objective, as opposed to Secretary of State George Shultz's stronger commitment to the use of U.S. troops—the U.S. Defense and State Departments frequently have taken opposing views on this key subject.

## West Europe and Security in the Post-Cold War Era

From the West European perspective, ethnic nationalism and regional crises have proved difficult arenas in which to mobilize effective, coordinated action. For example, as Yugoslavia unravelled, the European Community (EC), despite its prediction that it could handle the problem and despite U.S. urging, was preoccupied with the fall of Communism in East Europe, German reunification, and a number of internal matters. Among these were economic recession, signs of resistance to European unification, and nascent right-wing nationalism in Germany owing to economic difficulties and refugee problems. Nor have NATO, the Conference on Security and Cooperation in Europe (CSCE), and West European Union (WEU) solved the Balkan crisis. Complicating NATO and CSCE security decisions is the unanimity rule, while the WEU does not have an effective military mechanism for peace-keeping.

When the EC has paid attention to the Balkans, there has been little consensus on how to handle the spreading conflict. The EC's watershed decision was probably to emphasize humanitarian relief over some type of direct armed action, because that decision created a mindset that precluded military intervention in Bosnia, despite Serbian "ethnic cleansing." Still, the EC—along with the WEU and CSCE—launched a number of peace-keeping activities, trying to arrange political negotiations to end the conflicts. In addition, the West European countries and the U.S. imposed an arms embargo on Yugoslavia and froze economic aid. The EC also helped evacuate refugees and backed UN resolutions on humanitarian aid and the "no-fly zone." Despite such activities, the Balkan war raged on, virtually out of control.

The big fear for Western Europe—and the U.S. as George Bush made clear to Slobodan Milosevic—lay in the possibility of a "spill over" of conflict into Serb-dominated Kosovo. Ninety percent of Kosovo's population is Moslem and Albanian, and civil war there could trigger mass refugee flows toward Greece, Greek intervention, and Greek-Turkish war. Russians would likely back the Serbs. Trying to stave off a Kosovo scenario replicating events in Bosnia, President Bush in his last month in office threatened unilateral action against Serbia to deter the spread of fighting into Kosovo. In a letter delivered in late December to Milosevic and his Yugoslav army chief, General Zivota Panic, Bush declared that "in the event of conflict in Kosovo caused by Serbian action, the U.S. will be prepared to employ military force against the Serbs in Kosovo and in Serbia proper."[52] The letter was vetted with president-elect Clinton before it was sent.[53]

## International Dimensions of Security–Seeking

In its efforts to safeguard international peace, the UN has run into serious difficulties in the Balkans and elsewhere, which point toward its ongoing limitations in the arena of peace–keeping activities. To begin with, when the UN enters a civil war, it gets shot at, and lives could be lost, as has occurred in former Yugoslavia. UN peace–keeping is likely to work best when it has the cooperation of all parties, when its efforts are tied to a permanent settlement or ceasefire agreement, and when contending parties are disarmed, confined to bases, or separated.[54] Limiting factors in UN peace–keeping in places like the Balkans are:[55]

- Ambiguous or unclear mandates.
- Civil war and lack of central authority.
- Lack of clear cease–fire lines.
- Poor terrain and deployment in cities.
- Mismanagement and administrative problems.
- High availability of weapons to opposing forces.
- Chain–of–command problems for the peace–keepers.

Among the problems associated with UN peace–keeping must be cited lack of cooperation within the complex UN bureaucracy, language barriers and rules of engagement among UN forces, and unfamiliarity with military operations, rules of engagement, and roles and missions at the senior levels of the UN. In addition, peace–keeping has been manipulated by UN members to advance political agendas. Most importantly, it should be pointed out that in many cases civil wars have made peace–keeping virtually impossible and could lead to intra–UN conflict. Yet in the coming era of ethnic and religious wars, where the U.S. and West Europe will find it extremely difficult to contain battles, the UN may be the only game in town. As such, it merits more attention from the U.S. and Western Europe to make it mobilize and project power more effectively, despite the obstacles.

The UN Security Council (UNSC) has become stronger with the end of the Cold War—although one cannot predict for how long. U.S.–Soviet cooperation in the UN Security Council helped make Desert Storm possible in the Gulf War against Iraq—aided by the personal friendship between Secretary of State James Baker and Soviet Foreign Minister Eduard Shevardnadze. A more cooperative Security Council also provided the international legal framework and coalition–building possibilities for the Restore Hope humanitarian aid operation in Somalia in 1992-93. The U.S. and West Europe, moreover, have used the UN umbrella to press for humanitarian aid, economic embargo and the "no-fly zone" in Bosnia, attempting to end that region's brutal hostilities. Still, questions remain. How would U.S. national security decision-making operate in the context of a stronger UN?  How would U.S. troops take part in a force under the command of the UN?  Obvious constitutional problems arise for the U.S. should it move more closely into some type of permanent UN military organization.

Many observers now point to a more empowered UN as the key intergovernmental organization that can play a major role in peace–keeping in settings like those discussed in this book.  As Secretary General Boutros–Ghali writes, the new era has brought new credibility to the UN, and peace–keeping has become the most prominent UN activity.[56]  Perhaps the time has come to think about how a standing UN force might be created and maintained, including a UN Navy with U.S. participation, coupled with a more centralized UN focus on intelligence.  The U.S., for its part, began to study several options of some new kind of force under UN auspices as the Clinton Administration got to work early in its term.  These options include a permanent force assigned to the UN for peace–keeping and other emergency interventions, the short–term designation by various countries of their own forces as needed by the UN, and volunteer forces for the UN.[57]

Yet the UN faces great challenges in coping with the savage ethnic and religious conflicts that have erupted within and between new states.  Making the UN work in ethnic wars will be far more difficult than coping with a hegemon like Saddam Hussein in a region where many states clearly perceive their national interests at stake.  The basic problem is trying to make collective security work to deal with sovereign states and civil wars, when most Western states are unwilling to place any part of their sovereign forces under UN collective security control.  Nonetheless, it seems clear that the international community eventually will have to come to grips with the emerging era of hostile ethnic conflict.  For its part, the U.S. had begun to ask tough questions about its role in UN peace–keeping missions as U.S. casualties mounted in Somalia during September–October 1993.  In his September 27, 1993, speech to the 48th session of the UN General Assembly, President Clinton made clear that the U.S. would ask a number of questions about proposals for new peace–keeping missions:

> Is there a real threat to international peace?  Does the proposed mission have clear objectives?  Can an end point be identified for those who will be asked to participate?  How much does the mission cost? ... The United Nations simply cannot become engaged in every one of the world's conflicts.[58]

## Crisis Prevention in the Future

How does the U.S., the West, and other factors deter ethnic, sectional, and religious conflicts—the driving forces in future regional wars.  The obvious question is, how do we achieve crisis prevention? In addressing that fundamental question, two alternatives come to mind. First, the U.S. might choose to apply unilateral force early in a regional conflict to prevent what it does not want to occur. The U.S. clearly chose not to follow this route in Croatia in 1991 and Bosnia in 1992. Second, the U.S. could opt for participation in some type of multilateral force to keep a conflict from spreading. This might have been pursued in Croatia through, say, NATO. The U.S. eschewed this second option in Yugoslavia by tossing the ball to the Europeans.[59]

Of the two alternatives, multilateral force may be the more desirable approach, because it establishes broader international legal legitimacy for preventive actions and lessens the costs and burdens on any single actor in the international system. To make it work, however, there are at least two preconditions: (1) a willingness of multilateral force partners to get involved early, before a crisis expands, and (2) a readiness of the partners, including the U.S., to use force in ways that entail costs and risks in the short run that are greater than the U.S. and the West were prepared to accept in Yugoslavia. The whole idea of crisis prevention is that such short-run costs and risks will be less than higher long-run costs and risks associated with not deterring the conflict.[60]

Yugoslavia is a compelling case of what can happen when crisis prevention is not at the outset of a conflict. It illustrates how swiftly ethnic national conflict can spread, resulting in chaos, savagery, environmental devastation, and mass refugee migrations. If the U.S. and the West cannot translate force into crisis prevention in Yugoslavia at a time when this messy world may produce more "Yugoslavias," then one wonders whether institutions can be crafted to cope with future ethnic wars.[61] U.S. entanglement in Somalia is especially significant in this regard, for as the loss of U.S. lives mounted in that war-torn region, critical voices to U.S. participation in that country's peace-keeping efforts mounted in the press and congress. By early October 1993 it appeared as if the U.S. might be losing its affection for UN peace-keeping efforts, owing to mounting casualties, lack of clear mission, and the sense that Somalia was beginning to look like Vietnam in the perceptions of some American observers.[62]

The central challenge of the future arguably is the former Soviet Union, with its ethnic mixes inside new states, historic animosities, ethnic tensions, regional instability, flow of arms, border conflicts, and territorial irredentism.[63] In terms of future crisis prevention, the former Soviet Union presents every type of challenge the international community will face. If the international community can deal with that range of issues—despite its failure to stop the late twentieth-century Balkan wars—then it should be positioned to deal with chauvinist brands of ethnic nationalism elsewhere in the world.

## Framing the Analysis

Toward establishing a comparative setting for our readers to think about security problems associated with ethnic nationalism, our chapters examine key issues as applied to specific regions in the former Soviet Union and Yugoslavia. They include:

- Historical roots of ethnic conflict.
- Dimensions of national identity and political expression of nationalism.
- Impact of the international community in managing regional conflict.
- Lessons learned about managing regional conflict spawned by nationalist tensions.
- Policy and strategy alternatives for muting ethnic tensions in the region.

We hope this study will contribute to an understanding of the nature and implications of ethnic nationalism and how its effects on regional conflict might be prevented or managed. Our overall goal is to provide insight regarding the debate about ethnic nationalism—and how to achieve security in what has become an increasingly turbulent international system.

## Notes

1. See Liah Greenfield, *Nationalism: Five Roads to Modernity.* Cambridge: Harvard University Press, 1992; also Hans Kohn, *Nationalism*, New York: D. Van Nostrand Co., Inc., 1955.

2. Greenfield, *Op. Cit.*

3. See Arthur M. Schlesinger, Jr., *The Disuniting of America: Reflections on a Multicultural Society*, New York: W.W. Norton and Co., 1992, p. 47.

4. Samuel P. Huntington, "The Clash of Civilizations?" *Foreign Affairs,* Vol. 72, No. 3 (Summer 1993), p. 22.

5. Charles William Maynes, "Containing Ethnic Conflict," *Foreign Policy,* No. 90 (Spring 1993), p. 5. As Donald L. Horowitz, a student of ethnic nationalism, notes, "The importance of ethnic conflict, as a force shaping human affairs, as a phenomenon to be understood, as a threat to be controlled, can no longer be denied." See Donald L. Horowitz, *Ethnic Groups in Conflict,* Berkeley: University of California Press, 1985, p. xi.

6. See Robert D. Kaplan, "A Reader's Guide to the Balkans," *The New York Times Book Review*, April 18, 1993, pp. 29 ff. Kaplan is author of *Balkan Ghosts: A Journey Through History*.

7. For a detailed look at the siege of Sarajevo, continuing blockade of humanitarian assistance, terrorizing of Banja Luka's 30,000 Muslims, forcible imprisonment, inhuman mistreatment and willful killing of civilians at detention camps, massacre of Muslims, and mass executions of Muslims, see Secretary of State Lawrence Eagleburger's statement at the International Conference on the Former Yugoslavia, Geneva, December

16, 1992, "The Relentless Agony of Former Yugoslavia," *Foreign Policy Bulletin*, January–April 1993, pp. 57–75.

8. Benjamin R. Barber, "Jihad vs. McWorld," *The Atlantic Monthly*, March 1992, pp. 53–63. Lebanon erupted in civil war in 1975, as various factions of Christians, Syrian–backed Moslems, and Palestinians battled for territory and political power. The U.S. was drawn into this conflict during 1982–1984, when 241 marines lost their lives in a terrorist truck bombing of their position at Beirut's international airport in 1983, and 17 Americans were killed earlier that year in a bombing of the U.S. Embassy. See Thomas L. Friedman, *From Beirut to Jerusalem*. New York: Anchor Books, 1989. Roger Thurow and Tony Horowitz argue that the Balkan wars greatly resemble the Middle East. See their essay, "History's Lessons," in *The Wall Street Journal*, October 7, 1992, p. 1.

9. Our thanks to Dr. Robert Legvold, former Dean and currently Professor, the Harriman Institute, Columbia University, New York City, for his observations, which led to this and several points immediately following. Conversations with Dr. Legvold, March 31, 1993.

10. For background reading on this point, see Seyom Brown, *International Relations in a Changing Global System*, Boulder: Westview Press, 1992, pp. 20 ff.

11. Ibid.

12. See *The Christian Science Monitor*, April 14, 1993, p. 19.

13. Ibid.

14. *The New York Times*, February 3, 1993, p. A6.

15. *The New York Times*, April 7, 1993, p. A3. See also "Lessons from Central Asia—Nagorno Karabakh and Afghanistan Considered," *United States Institute of Peace Journal* (June 1992), pp. 1–3.

16. See Molly Moore, "Tajiks Trade One Nightmare for Another," *The Washington Post*, January 19, 1993, p. A15.

17. *New York Times Magazine*, April 4, 1993, p. 28.

18. Ibid. See also *The New York Times*, April 15, 1993, p. A9, for a report on Russia's entanglement in the fighting between Armenia and Azerbaijan over Nagorno–Karabakh.

19. *The New York Times*, November 3, 1993.

20. See Adam B. Ulam, "Looking at the Past: The Unraveling of the Soviet Union," *Current History*, Vol 91, No. 967 (October 1992), pp. 339–346. The global sweep of ethnic nationalism is truly monumental—well beyond the former Soviet Union and Yugoslavia. Geographic regions across the globe are experiencing nationalist upheavals. In Western Europe, nations like the Danes, British, and French resist economic and political unification in the European Community (EC), while Basques and Catalonians fight for independence from Spain. In the Middle East, stateless Kurds resist Turkish and Iraqi domination, while Palestinians struggle for their own homeland. In Africa, ethnic national (tribal) wars are waged inside states, as in Nigeria, Rwanda, Burundi, Kenya, Angola and Ethiopia—while the Zulus of Inkatha in South Africa make their wishes violently clear. In South Asia we see the face of Tamil and Sinhalese nationalism in Sri Lanka and new forms of Hindu and Sikh nationalism in India.

21. See Eric Hobsbawm, "Whose Fault-Line is it Anyway," *New Statesman and Society*, April 24, 1992, pp. 24–26.

22. Ibid., p. 23.

23.  The concept of national self-determination espoused by Woodrow Wilson during World War One is especially noteworthy, because it gave international prominence to the force of nationalism.  National self-determination provided a concept that groups defined as "nations" have the right to form territorial states, such as the new East European states that emerged with the fall of the Hapsburg and Ottoman empires after the First World War.  National self-determination produced still more sovereign states carved from the former British, French, Belgian, German and Portuguese empires in the post–World War Two period.  The government of the former Soviet Union—ruling over one hundred nationalities—was forced to deal with economic and political pressures generated by its national groups from 1917 onwards, despite a tightly centralized system of political rule.

24.  See William Pfaff, "The Absence of Empire," *The New Yorker*, April 10, 1992, pp. 59–69.  Pfaff points out that the original "nations" of Western Europe had no unitary ethnic base, but rather based "national identity" more on cultural and political perceptions which constituted what it meant to be British or French, German or Dutch or Spanish.  Ibid., p. 60.

25.  Hobsbawm, *Op. Cit.*, p. 23.  The "primordialist" theory of ethnicity as the basis of nationhood—while not the root of national identity and nationalism in West European or immigrant nations of the old "white Commonwealth" of Canada, Australia, and New Zealand—nevertheless for historical reasons has seized the minds of the peoples of Central and Balkan Europe as well as those inside the former Soviet Union.  Ibid.

26.  Robert Lansing, *The Peace Negotiations: A Personal Narrative*. Boston and New York: Houghton Mifflin Co., 1921, p. 97.

27.  Ibid., p. 98.  Lansing points out that "self-determination" as Wilson used it meant substantially the same thing as "the consent of the governed," which had been accepted for over three hundred years but never uniformly applied.  By making "national" self-determination a moral precept, something to be desired, but impossible of practical application, Lansing feared world peace would be severely menaced in years ahead as one ethnic group after another would pound on the doors for its own sovereign state so that it could be self-governing. Ibid., pp. 96–97; 103–104.

As it turns out, national self-determination was violated in the World War One peace treaties.  See Lansing, Ibid., pp. 98–99.  Wilson's thinking about the concept of "nation," seemed to equate the ethnic melting-pot concept of an "American" nation with those more strictly ethnic-based as in Western and Central Europe.  See Woodrow Wilson, *War and Peace: Presidential Messages, Addresses, and Public Papers (1917–1924)*. New York and London: Harper & Brothers Publishers, 1970, p. 180.  On the complicated nature of applying the national self-determination concept, see Edward Mandell House and Charles Seymour, ed., *What Really Happened at Paris: The Story of the Peace Conference, 1918–1919*.  New York: Charles Scribner's Sons, 1921, especially pp. 204 ff., which discusses the protection of minorities, and pp. 429 ff. on the issue of boundaries and self-determination.

28.  Amitai Etzioni, "The Evils of Self-Determination," *Foreign Policy*, No. 89 (Winter 1992–93), pp. 21–35.  Nationalism, Etzioni points out, used to be a way to gain one's own flag, national hymn, and other symbols of selfhood, but, perhaps "even more important, as a way to lay the foundations for a responsive government." p. 22.  Not so today.  "The romantics of self-determination must pause before the prospect of a United Nations with thousands of members." p. 28.  See also Gerald B. Helman and Steven R.

Ratner, "Saving Failed States," Ibid., pp. 21–35. See also Joel S. Migdal, *Strong Societies and Weak States: State–Society Relations and State Capabilities in the Third World*, Princeton: Princeton University Press, 1988.

29. See Barbara W. Tuchman, *The March of Folly: From Troy to Vietnam*. New York: Alfred A. Knopf, 1984.

30. See Joseph Campbell, *The Power of Myth*, with Bill Moyers, New York: Doubleday, 1988, p. 24.

31. See Ken Booth, *Strategy and Ethnocentrism*. New York: Holmes and Meier Publishers, 1979, pp. 14–15.

32. As quoted in Booth, *Op. Cit.*, p. 5; from W. G. Sumner, *Folkways*. Boston: Ginn, 1906, p. 13.

33. Booth, *Op. Cit.*, p. 15.

34. On the rape of Bosnian women, see "Krieg Gegen Die Frauen," *Stern*, November 26, 1992, pp. 20–25.

35. *The New York Times*, editorial, January 24, 1993. The international environment, as it turns out, is an interesting example of a chaotic system—using some of the newer concepts of chaos theory. See Stephen R. Mann, "Chaos Theory and Strategic Thought," *Parameters*, Vol. XXII, No. 3, pp. 53–69.

36. Ibid.

37. See *The New York Times*, February 7, 1993, p. A1. "If we don't find some way that the different ethnic groups can live together in a country, how many countries will we have?" he said. Ibid., p. A1.

38. Ibid.

39. *The New York Times*, November 5, 1993. New priorities included supporting reform in the former Soviet Union; renewing the NATO alliance; promoting markets and democracy in Asia; securing a comprehensive peace in the Middle East; and nonproliferation of nuclear and other dangerous weapons.

40. See Martin van Creveld, *The Transformation of War*. New York: The Free Press, 1991.

41. Ibid., p. 14. See also Daniel Patrick Moynihan, *Pandemonium: Ethnicity in International Politics*, New York: Oxford University Press, 1993; also Paul Kennedy, *Preparing for the Twenty-First Century and the End of the Modern Age*, New York: Random House, 1993.

42. Ibid.

43. Ibid.

44. See John Lewis Gaddis, *Foreign Affairs*, Spring 1991, pp. 102–122. As Gaddis argues, the most serious source of instability in world politics will probably be the political, economic and social fragmentation that is already developing where communism has collapsed.

45. See Elaine Sciolino, "Senior CIA Analyst Admits Discord Over Russia," *The New York Times*, February 4, 1993, p. A12. At the outset of the Clinton Administration, the CIA was locked in debate over how best to reform Russia and promote its nascent democracy.

46. Van Creveld, *Op. Cit.*

47. Michael Wines, "Bush, in West Point Valedictory, Offers Principles on Use of Force, *The New York Times*, January 6, 1992, p. A1.

48. Ibid.

49. Colin Powell, "U.S. Forces: Challenges Ahead, *Foreign Affairs*, Winter 1992/93, pp. 32–45.

50. Ibid., pp. 37–38.

51. Powell granted an interview to *The New York Times*, September 28, 1992, p. 1, during which he argued that military force is best used to achieve decisive victory. For the first time, he publicly explained his reluctance to intervene in Bosnia. Powell assailed the proponents of limited military intervention to protect the Bosnians.

52. See Don Oberdorfer, "A Bloody Failure in the Balkans," *The Washington Post*, February 9, 1993, p. 1.

53. Ibid.

54. CIA study, dated July 29, 1992, p. 2.

55. Ibid.

56. Boutros–Ghali, "Empowering the United Nations," *Foreign Affairs*, Winter 1992/93, pp. 89–102.

57. Ibid.

58. President Clinton's UN address, *Associated Press Release*, September 27, 1993.

59. Conversation with Dr. Robert Legvold, Columbia University, for this line of thought. Interview, Winchester, Massachusetts, February 22, 1993.

60. Ibid.

61. Ibid.

62. See President's Clinton's address to the nation, October 8, 1993, when he implied that the UN had not provided effective leadership in Somalia and that the U.S. might have no choice but to go it alone in crafting a policy in that country. *The New York Times*, October 9, 1993, p. A7.

63. Ibid.

# 1

# Yugoslavia's Break–up

## *W. Raymond Duncan*

Of all the regional conflicts in the former Soviet Union and Yugoslavia, the Balkans' ethnic savagery from 1991 onwards most vividly seized the attention of America and the West. By the time President Bill Clinton took office in January 1993, Yugoslavia had collapsed as a sovereign state. Ravaged by ethnic brutalities in Croatia and Bosnia–Herzegovina (referred to as Bosnia henceforth), with a similar fate threatening Serb–dominated Kosovo, Yugoslavia became the scene of bloodbaths on a scale not seen in this part of the world since the Nazi atrocities of the 1930s and 1940s. American policy–makers in President George Bush's Administration initially tossed the ball to the Europeans to deal with the escalating conflicts. They in turn attempted one cease–fire after another, arms and aid blockades, humanitarian efforts, and feverish, ill–fated political negotiations to try to end the ethnic wars.

Yugoslavia's break–up consisted of not one, but several ethnic wars, some of which erupted in 1989–1990, all of which complicated conflict–management efforts by the outside world:

- Slovenes clashed with Serbs over Slovenia's drive for independence throughout 1989 and 1990, culminating with Ljubljana's withdrawal from Yugoslavia in June 1991 and subsequent battles with the Serb–dominated Yugoslav People's Army (JNA).[1] With Slovenia exiting Yugoslavia, Croatia followed suit, thus setting up conditions for more battles with Serbia.

- In Croatia, war erupted in part as a result of ethnic frictions between a militant Serb minority scattered inside Croatia and Croatian nationalists, and in part from Serbian President Slobodan Milosevic's territorial expansion toward a "Greater Serbia" when Croatia declared its independence in June 1991.[2] UN peace–keeping efforts failed to prevent a renewed Croatian offensive in Serb–held areas in early 1993.

- Despite the evidence of what was happening in independent Slovenia and Croatia vis-à-vis the Serbs, Bosnia declared its independence in 1992. At this point three wars erupted: (1) a battle for territory between Bosnian Serbs and Bosnian Croats,[3] (2) a fight for territory between Bosnian Serbs and Bosnian Muslims throughout Bosnia, with Bosnian Serb militias led by Radovan Karadzic, backed by Milosevic and the JNA,[4] and (3) a struggle for land between Bosnian Croats and Bosnian Muslims.[5] By the spring of 1993, beleaguered Bosnian Muslims faced not only Serbian "ethnic cleansing," but also a renewed battle against Bosnian Croats in a broad arc of territory north and west of Sarajevo that featured the kind of brutality often associated with the Serbs.[6]

Largely because American and West European policy makers were unprepared to deter the spreading battles by preemptive military intervention during the early stages of Yugoslavia's break-up, hostilities gathered momentum as Slovenia and Croatia declared independence in June 1991. Bosnia's independence on March 3, 1992, added fuel to the flames. By December 1992 Yugoslavia's tragedy included around 128,000 dead, over 500,000 refugees who had fled from the country, and three million Bosnians driven from their homes. At that time nearly 1.7 million people were at risk of starvation in Bosnia in the coming winter, and over 20,000 Bosnian women reportedly had been systematically raped in special camps where they were held. In the absence of taking early steps toward crisis prevention, America and the West ultimately faced the task of crisis management—which proved futile in deterring the carnage.

Serbian "ethnic cleansing" of Bosnian Muslims—with its pattern of prison camps, mass killings, systematic rape of Bosnian women and other atrocities—especially shocked the Western world from 1992 onwards.[7] The media's daily coverage of the fratricidal mayhem—newspapers, magazines and television heightening public awareness—added pressure to stop the blood bath, notably in the U.S. during a presidential campaign. In reacting to the Balkan atrocities, Bill Clinton as presidential candidate advanced the idea of arming the struggling Bosnians and bombarding Serb artillery in places like Serb-besieged Sarajevo.[8] Once in office, however, he emphasized the "quagmire" aspects of Bosnia, about which little could be done.[9] Still, by April 1993, the Clinton Administration had backed a UN-European Community (EC) peace plan sponsored by Cyrus Vance and Lord David Owen, named a special envoy to the peace talks, and pressed for greater enforcement of a "no fly zone" over Bosnia and for tightened economic sanctions against Serbia.[10] U.S. efforts included a UN-sanctioned parachute drop of food and medicine into remote areas of Bosnia.[11]

Given former Yugoslavia's importance as a possible prototype of future ethnic wars, its recent history in terms of American and European efforts to manage its conflicts, and the lessons it offers in regard to crisis prevention, the purposes of this chapter are threefold. Our analysis: (1) explores the historical roots of Yugoslavia's explosive ethnic conflict; (2) examines how, and in what ways, America and the West reacted to escalating tensions in the region; and (3) suggests some implications of this record for future U.S. national security decision making.

Toward these ends, we focus on:

- Yugoslavia's legacy of the past.
- Role of political elites in spawning national tensions.
- U.S., UN and West European security decision-making.
- Security lessons learned about Yugoslavia's break-up.

Because Yugoslavia arguably is the model of future ethnic wars, this chapter also looks at the U.S. and European national security decision making process as it unfolded in the Balkans. Our hope is to gain insight into how future leaders might attempt to craft crisis prevention measures before they reach the scale of another Yugoslavia. In the Balkans, as we shall see, America and the West did too little too late, failed to coordinate early deterrence efforts, and did not bring force to bear at a time when it probably would have done the most good.[12]

## Yugoslavia's Legacy of the Past

What historic factors help account for former Yugoslavia's violent turmoil? At least three stand out: (1) Years of ethnic national tensions, (2) the presence of ethnic minorities inside Croatia and Bosnia-Herzegovina when they declared independence, and 3) forces reenforcing ancient ethnic antagonisms and hindering cooperative problem-solving as tensions escalated—such as poor economic conditions, Serbia's hard-line resistance to political liberalization in Yugoslavia's other republics, and competing republic ties with other countries.[13]

### Historic Ethnic National Tensions

The legacy of ethnic national tensions in "Yugoslavia"—a term which means the land of the South Slavs (Croats, Bosnian Muslims, Macedonians, Montenegrins, Serbs, and Slovenes)—is best captured by key historical milestones. The Paris Peace Conference created the multinational state of Yugoslavia in 1918 out of elements of the empires of Austria-Hungary and Ottoman Turkey following World War One.[14] The Serbs were the largest national group in Yugoslavia—which initially was called the Kingdom of Serbs,

Croats, and Slovenes.[15]   The Serbs, who won independence from Turkish domination in 1878, constituted about 36 percent of the new state's population, while the Croats, the second largest group, comprised about 20 percent.[16]

The Kingdom of the Serbs, Croats, and Slovenes changed its name to Yugoslavia in 1929. It comprised a patchwork of seven separately-identifying ethnic groups whose ethnicity had crystallized into national consciousness during the nineteenth and twentieth centuries: Serbs, Croats, Albanians, Slavic Muslims, Slovenians, Montenegrins, and Macedonians—as well as over a dozen other distinguishable ethnic national groups.[17] In effect, then, Yugoslavia was a sovereign state containing many separately-identifying national groups.[18] Each brought to Yugoslavia its own legacy of the past—including perceived adversaries and defining characteristics of nationhood.  Table 1.1 illustrates multi-ethnic national groups inside Yugoslavia.

The histories of Yugoslavia's nationalities were remarkably distinct, despite a common South Slav origin.[19]  Slovenia and Croatia in the north—the most prosperous regions—were part of the Hapsburg Empire, influenced by centuries of close contact with Austria, Hungary, and Italy, adoption of Roman Catholicism, use of a Latin alphabet, and orientation toward Western and Central

TABLE 1.1
Yugoslav Population by Nationality in 1981

| Nationality | in 1000's | Percent |
|-------------|-----------|---------|
| Serbs | 8,140 | 36.3 |
| Croats | 4,428 | 19.8 |
| Muslims | 2,000 | 8.9 |
| Slovenians | 1,754 | 7.8 |
| Albanians | 1,730 | 7.7 |
| Macedonians | 1,340 | 6.0 |
| Montenegrins | 509 | 2.6 |
| Hungarians | 427 | 1.9 |
| Turks | 101 | 0.4 |
| Others | 481 | 2.1 |
| Undeclared | 1,291 | 5.7 |
| Unknown | 153 | 0.7 |
| Total: | 22,425 | 100.0 |

Source: Statistical Yearbook, Belgrade, Modern Administration, 1987, p. 6, as published by Bogomil Ferfila, "Yugoslavia: Confederation of Disintegration?" *Problems of Communism* (July–August 1991), Vol. XL, p. 20.

Europe.[20] Serbs, Macedonians, Montenegrins, and Bosnians were ruled by the Ottoman Turks for over 500 years under repressive autocratic control. The Christian majority in these regions—like the Serbs—is Eastern Orthodox in contrast to Roman Catholic, uses the Cryllic alphabet, and remains least economically developed.

Islam became strong in Bosnia and Kosovo in southern Serbia.[21] Serbs in particular retain bitter memories of Muslim domination, and many view the Bosnian Muslims as Slavs who "sold out" to Ottoman rule. Note, however, that by the 10th century, Slavs in Bosnia already had adopted a form of Christianity that stressed the human aspects of Jesus, first known as Manichaeanism, later as Bogomilism. Roman Catholics and Orthodox Churches denounced it as heretical, while the Muslim Turks treated Bogomilism with greater tolerance. Indeed, after the Turks crushed the Serbs at Kosovo, and the Ottoman hordes surrounded Bosnia, the Turks offered the Bogomils military protection, secure titles to their lands, and religious freedom if they would adopt the Muslim faith and not attack Ottoman forces. Bosnian Bogomils accepted this plan, which allowed a sort of free Slavic state within the Ottoman empire, with special autonomy and immunities, and which angered Serbs and Russians.

The ethnic tensions plaguing Yugoslavia are underscored by persistent ethnic stereotyping. One study finds that in 1971 Croatian self-images emphasized their love of justice and peace, thousand year-old culture, and "Westernness." Serbian self-images, in contrast, focused on the heroic character of the Serbs and their role as guardian of Yugoslavia. Croats perceived Serbs as expansionist and arrogant, while Serbs saw the Croats as passive, timid, and inclined to collaborate with foreign and subversive elements. Slovenes viewed themselves as superior (love of order, efficiency at work, and cleanliness), viewing other ethnic groups as inefficient. Slovenes were viewed by other ethnic groups as unsociable and unfriendly.[22]

Historic tensions among Yugoslavia's nationalities came in different forms. The more prosperous Slovenians and Croatians grew mistrustful of Serbs, for example, whom they viewed as having a less industrious work ethic.[23] The Slovenes in particular resented what they saw as lack of political reforms and economic productivity in the rest of the country. About the time Slovenia decided to break away from Yugoslavia in 1991, it represented only eight percent of the population, yet produced 20 percent of Yugoslavia's national product and 25 percent of its exports, while paying around 4 1/2 times more in federal taxes to subsidize the "backward" underdeveloped southern republics than it received in federal finance programs.[24]

Conflict between Croats and Serbs intensified as separate historical cultural and political identities grew into modern national consciousness during the nineteenth century.[25] Croat nationalism is a case in point. Ante Starcevic, founder of the Party of Croatian Rights in the late nineteenth century, became a vocal advocate of xenophobic Croatian nationalism. He included all Serbs in the Croatian nation if they were ready to scuttle their own national consciousness and become Croats, because for him Serbs were an inferior and evil race.[26] As the father of modern Croatian nationalism, Starcevic unfortunately set in motion a force leading to xenophobia, which in the words of one observer, "aimed to suppress and perhaps exterminate all those who had a different national consciousness."[27]

This version of extreme Croatian nationalism was the predecessor to the *Ustasha* independence movement during the 1930s and into the World War Two period. The *Ustasha* was notorious for a passionate and aggressive hostility against the whole Serbian nation. The *Ustasha*, which borrowed heavily from European fascist movements and during World War Two formed the Independent State of Croatia (NDH), allied itself with the Germans and killed thousands of Serbs—estimated from 200,000 to as high as 750,000.[28] The Serbs retaliated against Croatia, forming irregular bands called *Chetniks*. Ultimately, as one observer notes, "as many as a million Yugoslavs died at the hands of their own countrymen."[29]

Serbian nationalism and authoritarianism are rooted in centuries of violence and struggle against foreign oppression. Serbian dreams of a "Greater Serbia," for example, date back to the 14th century, when Serbia enjoyed empire status and fought the Battle of Kosovo against the Turks in 1389. That holiest of days in Serb folk mythology commemorates not a great Serb victory, but the defeat that led to Ottoman domination over the Serbs for almost five hundred years. Despite the Kosovo defeat, Serbs see the battle as a proud and fierce resistance to domination—not unlike the Balkan Wars against the Turks during 1912–1913, which spawned epic poems and ballads.[30]

Serbian nationalists seem consumed by the aura of defying overwhelming odds, which springs from centuries of struggle and uncertainty, and a history of hopes for expansionism. Worth noting in terms of the Serbian national image is its kingdom status during the 12th century, complete independence from the Ottoman Empire by 1878, and extension of its territories to the southern borders of present-day Macedonia by 1914.[31] In modern Yugoslavia under the leadership of Josip Broz Tito—who was of mixed Croat and Slovene ancestry—Serbs dominated the officer corps in the Yugoslav military, the civil service and secret police; Belgrade was Yugoslavia's power center.[32]

Bosnian Muslim national identity was spawned not in the nineteenth century as occurred with other Balkan nations, but much later—during the period between World Wars One and Two.[33] Bosnian Muslim identity became increasingly pronounced under Tito's rule, owing to his ambitious educational program and development of a Muslim intelligentsia able to articulate the needs of a distinct Muslim community inside Yugoslavia.[34] Most Bosnian Muslims are Slavs-Croats and Serbs who converted to Islam during the five centuries of Ottoman rule.[35] The Slav Muslims—a nation nominally identified by its religion, not by language or ethnicity—received recognition as an official

Former Yugoslavia

Yugoslav nation in the Constitution of 1974, although it had received formal recognition on the 1971 census forms.[36] Keep in mind, however, that when Bosnia–Herzegovina declared its independence from former Yugoslavia in March 1992, the Muslims made up 44 percent of the population, Serbs 31 percent, and Croats 16 percent. Thus, recognition of Muslim nationality led Bosnian Croat and Serb leaders to feel threatened by a new nationalist force, a sentiment undoubtedly perpetuated by Muslim factions eager to press the issue.[37]

### The Ethnic Mix Inside Yugoslavia's Separate Republics

The Balkan wars that erupted in 1991 stem from the ethnic mix inside Yugoslavia's separate republics, illustrated by Table 1.2. Ethnic minorities—

especially the widely dispersed Serbs living inside Croatia and Bosnia—were powder kegs ready to explode once Croatian and Bosnian leaders determined to declare independence for their Croat and Bosnian Muslim populations. Serb irredenta made up 30 percent of the population in Bosnia, 17 percent in Croatia, 55 percent in Vojvodina and 10 percent in Kosovo. Wars exploded not only due to underlying ethnic tensions among the various groups—such as Serbs and Croats in Croatia and among Serbs, Croats and Muslims in Bosnia. The inattention Croat and Bosnian leaders gave to the complexity of the Serbian societies living within their borders as they moved toward independence became another major source of war.[38]

Croatia's leader, Franjo Tudjman, in the view of one observer, for example, simply failed to realize that the passive and adaptable, modern, urban Serbs living in the Croatian cities were not like those Serbs living in the countryside.[39] Outside Zagreb, in the region around Knin—a case in point—lived militant Serbs with a warrior consciousness and strong affinity with weaponry.[40] Similarly, Tudjman's Croat representatives living in the republic's extremities harbored strong antipathy toward Serbs, sentiments hardly like the laid-back Croat academics drafting Tudjman's policies in Zagreb.[41] All this constituted a recipe for violence.

For Serbs living in the Knin district (Krajina), the victory of Franjo Tudjman and ascendancy of the ruling Croatian Democratic Union (HDZ) in April–May 1990 revived the Serbs' fear of Croat extremist nationalism and memories of atrocities committed against them by the fascist *Ustasha* movement during the Second World War.[42] The rural Serb answer was a call to arms, demands for a "Serb autonomous region" comprising those districts where they were in the majority, and ultimately the creation of the "Serbian Autonomous Region of Krajina" (comprising municipalities in Croatia with a majority Serb population) which declared itself a separate entity inside Croatia in February 1991.[43] In making clear their desire to unite with Serbia and Montenegro and the Serb population of Bosnia, Croatia's Serb populations provided the green light for escalating conflict between Croatian authorities and Serb militants—exacerbated by the intervention of the Serb-dominated Yugoslav National Army (JNA) and Serbia's Stalinist-turned-nationalist, Milosevic, who was all too pleased to pursue a "Greater Serbia" policy.[44]

Next door in Bosnia, several problems lay in waiting for Bosnian Muslims when they declared independence from Yugoslavia in March 1992. First, Bosnia had never existed as an independent state since the medieval kingdom. It lacked the political culture and experience of independent governance. Second, Bosnia had survived historically by virtue of a protective shield from the Yugoslav state or its predecessors, the Austrian or Ottoman empire.[45] Third, in addition to its internal stability being guaranteed by an external power, it broke for independence without consulting its minority national populations—notably the Serbs—at a time when the state had no overarching

## TABLE 1.2
### Breakdown of Ethnic Groups in Yugoslavia

| SLOVENIA | | VOJVODINA | |
|---|---|---|---|
| Slovenes | 90% | Serbians | 56% |
| Croats | 3% | Hungarians | 21% |
| Serbians | 2% | Others | 23% |
| Others | 5% | | |

| CROATIA | | SERBIA | |
|---|---|---|---|
| Croats | 75% | Serbians | 65% |
| Serbians | 12% | Albanians | 20% |
| Others | 13% | Croats | 2% |
| | | Others | 13% |

| BOSNIA-HERZEGOVINA | | KOSOVO | |
|---|---|---|---|
| Muslims | 40% | Albanians | 90% |
| Serbians | 33% | Others | 10% |
| Croats | 18% | | |
| Others | 9% | | |

| MONTENEGRO | | MACEDONIA | |
|---|---|---|---|
| Montenegrins | 68% | Macedonians | 67% |
| Muslims | 13% | Albanians | 20% |
| Albanians | 6% | Serbians | 2% |
| Serbians | 3% | Others | 11% |
| Others | 10% | | |

political party spanning the three national communities inside Bosnia.[46] Yet the dilemma for Bosnian Muslim president Alija Izetbegovic, was that Croatia's and Slovenia's declared independence and world recognition forced him to do the same, because Muslims would not accept life in a smaller Yugoslavia dominated by Milosevic and the Serbian political elite in Belgrade, against which they would have little protection.[47]

Bosnia's declaration of independence from Yugoslavia, as might be expected from Croatia's experience, led to vicious clashes between Bosnian Serbs and Muslims. Xenophobic Serbs portrayed Izetbegovic as the mastermind of a drive to create an Islamic state in Bosnia.[48] That Izetbegovic indeed had published his "Islamic Declaration" in 1970, calling for "the creation of a united Islamic community from Morocco to Indonesia," did not ease Bosnian Serb fears.[49] In any case, by the end of April an estimated 350 people had been killed and

420,000 left homeless.[50]   In Bosnia, Milosevic moved fast in support of Bosnian Serbs and Serb militia units.   Serb-sponsored "ethnic cleansing" of Bosnian Muslims led to legions of stories of Serbian atrocities committed against defenseless Muslims, and  by May 1992 the Serb-led JNA and Serbian militias controlled about 70 percent of Bosnia's territory.[51]

The complex ethnic mix in Bosnia which lay at the heart of the tragedy is well captured by Misha Glenny, Central Europe correspondent of the BBC's World Service:

> Driving across Bosnia in 1990 just prior to the elections afforded me a brief glimpse into the republic's miserable future.  One village drowning in a sea of green crescents, which proclaimed the (Moslem) Party of Democratic Action (SDA), would give way to another, where the *sahovnica* (denoting the Croatian Democratic Union-Bosnia and Hercegovina, HDZ-BiH) was sovereign, or where every wall was covered with the four Cs and the acronym SDA (the Serbian Democratic Party).  In some villages, the western half was green while the eastern half was red, white and blue (Serbian) while in many towns it was easy to identify the predominantly Croat, Serb or Muslim districts.  Many doomed settlements were a jumble of all three.[52]

This ethnic mix resulted in the revival of old ethnic conflicts and vendettas that played out at the local level in some of the most gruesome fighting seen since the Nazi atrocities of World War Two—including the slaughter of innocent women and children, forced imprisonment of civilians, and mass rape of women.[53]

### Economic and Political Forces

A combination of economic and political forces intensified ancient ethnic antagonisms from 1990 onwards and hindered cooperative problem-solving as tensions escalated.   These included underdeveloped and uncompetitive economies, with the exception of Slovenia; Serbia's neo-Stalinist resistance to political liberalization elsewhere, as in Slovenia; and competing republic relations with the outside world.  In terms of economic conditions, it seems fair to conclude that former Yugoslavia's deteriorating economic conditions stimulated an oppressive and intolerant form of nationalism.  A primary reason for the rise of Slovenian nationalism and drive for independence, for example, which triggered parallel drives by Croatia and Bosnia-Herzegovina, lay in the Slovene view that they had little economic future in the state of Yugoslavia.[54]

Serbia's hard-line resistance to political liberalization and increased republic autonomy greatly contributed to escalating ethnic tensions.   The problem stemmed from what had become a Serb-dominated, centrally controlled Yugoslav state after World War Two, when other groups desired more autonomy in a looser political structure.[55]  Not surprisingly Serbia's leaders, notably Milosevic, were distinctly displeased with multiparty elections in Slovenia and Croatia in April and May 1990—Yugoslavia's first contested multiparty elections in 51 years. When victories went to the opposition over ruling communist parties, with the victors putting forward manifestos featuring demands for greatly increased autonomy for Yugoslav republics, tensions mounted between Serbs, on the one hand, and on the other, Slovenes and Croats.[56] Subsequent formation of non-communist governments—and establishment of multiparty political systems introduced by means of constitutional changes in Slovenia and Croatia during 1990—aroused Serbia's ire even more. As Slovenia and Croatia moved toward more democratic forms of government, Serbia remained in the authoritarian hands of neo-Stalinist leadership, namely Milosevic.

Competing republic ties with the outside world created additional barriers to inter-ethnic harmony in Yugoslavia. Slovenia and Croatia, which ceased to be socialist republics in April and May 1990, tended to ally with Germany and Austria as tensions rose. Serbia's natural ties lay with Russia, and Bosnia-Herzegovina's Muslims received support from such Islamic countries as Turkey, Saudi Arabia, and Iran. Given the persistence of hatred and memory locked up in ethnic national perceptions, such external ties became strong obstacles to conflict resolution insofar as they bolstered those parties engaged in war.

External ties complicated conflict-management in several respects. Croatia's links with Germany revived for militant Serbs the prospect of a new German-Croat alliance—a revived, once Nazi, puppet state controlled from Zagreb.[57] Croatian nationalists in turn perceived Milosevic's hard-line, Serb-inhabited Belgrade as a neo-Bolshevik administration fighting against Croatia's brand of a Western free-market democracy.[58] As one observer notes, "The underlying causes go back to business left unfinished by both the Second and First World Wars," and one might add, to the different international ties of Yugoslavia's separate republics as inter-ethnic tensions escalated. Islamic support for Muslims, Russian backing of the Serbs, and Germany's early lead in recognizing Slovenian and Croatian independence exacerbated adversarial perceptions locked in the past.[59]

Religious battle lines, drawn along the same ancient divide that separated the Byzantine Empire in the east and Roman Empire in the west have added to the external dimensions of Balkan conflict. Some observers see the region's conflicts as essentially religious wars linked to ancient outside ties. As a prominent Serbian historian, Slavenko Terzic, states the problem, "On the one hand there are the Croats representing the age-old Catholic and German front of Central Europe opposed to the Orthodox Serbs whom they see as Byzantine barbarians. On the other, there is Bosnia's Muslim President, Alija Izetbegovic with his vision of introducing an Islamic state into Europe.[60] Izetbegovic's authoring of the Islamic Declaration, the 1970 tract calling for the moral renewal of Islam throughout the world—which led to his incarceration by the Yugoslav communist government in the early 1980s—was hardly designed to soothe Orthodox Serb emotions, especially as Islamic states declared support for beleaguered Muslims.[61]

## Role of Political Elites in Spawning Nationalist Tensions

Political elites have played an enormous role in spawning nationalist tensions, which brought about the collapse of and violent wars within the former state of Yugoslavia. Simply put, the Yugoslav tragedy would not have occurred without elite leadership politics. This conclusion rests upon several assumptions and sources of evidence.

First, strong leaders with powerful personalities traditionally have played major roles in Balkan politics, given the region's authoritarian political culture, lack of democratic traditions, and competing belief systems. Tito, whose role in holding post–World War Two Yugoslavia together despite its fissiparous tendencies, is well known. Tito, the seventh of 15 children of a poor peasant family, whose father was a Croat, his mother a Slovene, broke from the Soviet bloc, proclaimed the equality of all national units in Yugoslavia, abandoned the Soviet system of centralized planning, and gave increasing power to workers' councils. Tito, unique among communist leaders, early on recognized and adapted to the power of ethnic nationalism. In 1953 he pressed for a constitution that created a relationship between the Yugoslav Federation (a joint, equal community of all nationalities in Yugoslavia) and the republic (the five major Yugoslav nationalities, each constituting a sovereign Socialist republic) based on two essentially equal and mutually dependent social and political communities.

Strong-man leaders like Serbia's Milosevic and Croatia's Tudjman—and others in lower echelons of power—follow in this authoritarian tradition. Men of extraordinary personality who possess the kinds of skills that work best in the Balkan setting, Milosevic and Tudjman, one-time, true-believing Bolsheviks, traded communism for nationalism, without losing faith in the political uses that can be made of ideology. They have demonstrated skill in crafting an *ideology of nationalism*—with its vision of the national past, present and future; pin-pointing of outside enemies; opposition to control over internal policy by outside national groups; blueprint for redistributing jobs and opportunities; and transformation of national institutions and benefits—all placed in service to achieve political ends.

Manipulated by strong personalities and political elites like Tudjman and Milosevic, a nationalist ideology of the Croat or Serb people has served numerous political ends. They include first, legitimizing Tudjman's and Milosevic's power—that is, forging popular compliance and support of a regime's policy decisions without exclusive reliance upon the threat or use of coercive force.[62] Legitimizing power in turn makes it possible for the strong leader to remain in office, despite pressures that may be working to force the leader out. Another aim of the nationalist ideology is to mobilize the masses for participating in new national institutions. "Institutionalizing" change is one way to try to achieve new national goals through maximum political participation. Such nationalist policies, however, typically occur at the expense of other minority groups inside the state, such as Serbs in Croatia.

Second, that political elite behavior has been a major source of violence in the former Yugoslavia is illustrated by a central fact of life in the Balkans. Many Croatians, Serbs, and Muslims lived peaceably side-by-side in numerous towns and villages in Croatia and Bosnia-Herzegovina—that is, until political leaders became obsessed by the national question, driven by religion and territory, and by their own views of ancient history. When national leaders acted in ways to arouse latent ethnic passions, they dramatically undermined the capacity of Croats, Serbs and Muslims to live in relative inter-ethnic harmony. Tudjman's drive to create a state for the Croatian people relied on the excessive use of symbols, bunting, Croatian heraldry and stress on nationalist iconography—demoting Croatia's Serbs to a denigrated minority. As Tudjman's nationalist politics spread, other politicians in outlying regions intensified the nationalist game. As a result, Serbs and Croats in cities like Vukovar found their friendships transformed into merciless mutilation of each other.[63]

Similarly, Milosevic's turn from Marxism to nationalism led him to use the rhetoric and symbolism of nationalism in ways that aroused nationalist passions of Serbs in Croatia and Bosnia. As a consequence, once-peaceful communities of Serbs, Croats, and Muslims living side by side in Bosnia erupted into staggering levels of violence.[64] In extending his personal power beyond the borders of Serbia, as Glenny so well observes, Milosevic:

> widened the nationalist debate to include the Serbian masses, a move fraught with incalculable danger for the Balkan peninsula. He organized a series of demonstrations in Serbia, in Kosovo and in the northern Autonomous Province of Vojvodina, where a substantial Hungarian minority lives. These were bizarre manifestations which perfected the fusion of communist, Serbian and Orthodox Christian iconography. Above all, the hundreds of thousands of Serbs who came to worship at this movable temple gave homage to Milosevic, whose stern but flap-eared visage and shaving-brush hair-style became the central artifacts in this new religion.[65]

Third, Serb and Croatian nationalist leaders have acted in ways to keep the violence going, demonstrating only weak interest in seeking *peaceful* resolution of conflicts. Time and again during 1991-1993 Milosevic disingenuously promised to abide by EC-brokered peace accords, only to turn around the next day and break the commitment. And in January 1993, Tudjman launched a surprise offensive to oust Serb forces from Croatian territory under UN supervision (UN Protection Force, UNPROFOR)—which brought in Serb reinforcements under much more hard-line Serb commanders than previously.[66] Integrity was distinctly not the name of the game. Tudjman, for his part, has surrounded himself with emotive symbols of the past stressing violence rather than peace in Croatian history.[67] Milosevic, rather than working with the UN to bring peace to the Balkans, campaigned for the Serbian presidency in December 1992 by whipping up traditional Serbian defiance toward foreign pressure. Instead of cooperating with the UN and the West, Milosevic said, "People in capitals across the wide world are trying to tell us how to behave in our land. In our land, we will behave as a free people behaves and not according to the dictates of world politicians."[68]

Fourth, the leadership styles and operational codes of men like Tudjman and Milosevic have set the tone of acceptable leadership principles and values for others below them, leading to the scale of violence we have witnessed since 1991. In identifying Serbians and others as possible war-crimes defendants, then Secretary of State Lawrence S. Eagleburger included a number of Croatian and Serbian leaders who clearly took their cues—as well as support—from their heads of state. Such individuals included Borislav Herak, a Bosnian Serbian who has confessed to killing over 230 civilians; Zeljko Raznjatovic, leader of the Tigers, a Serbian paramilitary force, accused of the deaths of up to 3,000 civilians in Bosnia; Vojislav Seselj, leader of the Chetniks, a Serbian paramilitary group accused of atrocities in Bosnia; and Radovan Karadzic, leader of the self-proclaimed Serbian Republic of Bosnia and Herzegovina, reportedly masterminding the siege of Sarajevo.[69]

Sarajevo under the Serbian siege symbolized the violence and atrocity in Bosnia during the winter and spring of 1993. As artillery shells daily pounded the city, elderly residents froze to death in old-age homes. Nearly 400,000 people tried to survive the winter with little food, water, heat or electricity—dodging exploding shells, carrying daily water supplies on sleds through snow storms, chopping down city trees, and collecting scraps of wood in the cemeteries. Still, it would be a mistake to assume that all Serbs in Serbia agreed with Milosevic's support for "ethnic cleansing"; many Serbs opposed Milosevic and his repression at home and abroad.[70] Belgrade Serbs more than once during 1992–1993 turned out to protest Milosevic's policies.

Fifth, in arousing uncompromising nationalist passions in the violent quest of nationalist aims, Balkan leaders have proven adept in using the dominant tools of Balkan politics: "deception, corruption, blackmail, demagoguery and violence."[71] Such traits undoubtedly stem in part from the authoritarian political cultures of the societies over which these men ruled, the mutual slaughter of Croats and Serbs during the Second World War, and the personal histories of men like Tito, Tudjman and Milosevic.

Not least in shaping the character of Tudjman and Milosevic was their family histories. Tudjman was a dogmatic young Marxist, nineteen years old, when Hitler's blitzkrieg rolled through the Balkans; he joined Tito's communist guerrillas, while his father retained membership in Croatia's nationalist groups. He and his family endured a war of incredible violence and terror.[72] Shortly after the war both of Tudjman's parents were shot to death, and while a mystery still hangs over the affair, a number of investigators believe they committed suicide.[73] Curiously enough, Milosevic's parents also committed suicide, which may help explain his character. Milosevic's calculated use of nationalist ideology, according to one observer, is paralleled by his almost total lack of passion, regard and affection for the masses who provide him with political support.[74] In character with his neo-Stalinist personality, Milosevic launched a purge in February 1993 of those Serbian intellectuals who opposed him, firing the Rector of Belgrade University and the directors of the Modern Art Museum, the National Theater and Belgrade's biggest hospital.[75] In Croatia, Tudjman's government maintained tight control over major industries, the press and the security forces—an intimidating situation for anyone who might disagree with the country's authoritarian nationalist leader.

## U.S. and West European Security Decision Making

While neither the U.S. nor West Europe applied direct military power to stop the fighting, the Europeans early on tried to negotiate cease-fires. Such efforts by the European Community (EC), Conference on Security and Cooperation in Europe (CSCE) and Western European Union (WEU), however, proved ill-fated.[76] While Slovenia was able to defend its territory after a short war with the JNA, Serbian militiamen and the JNA had seized control of a third of Croatia by the end of 1991.[77] When Bosnia declared its independence in March 1992, Bosnian Serb and Croatian land-grabs led to intense fighting with Bosnian Muslims, and by the end of 1992, Serbia had captured 70 percent of Bosnia—despite UN-imposed sanctions enforced and monitored by NATO, WEU and the CSCE, and peace-negotiating efforts by the EC.[78]

Bosnian Serbs defied international peace efforts in early 1983 that would require them to give up nearly 40 percent of that territory and restrict Bosnian Serb political control to just three of 10 semiautonomous provinces that would in effect be divided among Bosnian Serb, Croat and Slavic Muslim "constituent peoples."[79] In May 1993 delegates to the self-styled Bosnian Serb parliament voted to reject a peace plan devised by the international mediators Cyrus R. Vance and Lord Owen.[80] Days later, tens of thousands of Bosnian Serbs similarly rejected the plan in a two-day referendum.[81]

Whether or not a massive U.S. and West European military or combined military/economic/diplomatic effort in the early stages of the game—through UN legitimizing resolutions *a la* the Gulf War of 1991—could have stopped the escalation of fighting will long be debated. Many U.S. State Department officials believe the U.S. and NATO should have acted more persuasively as early as 1990 when the signs of crisis were clear.[82] Indeed, the Central Intelligence Agency (C.I.A.) predicted in a National Intelligence Estimate (NIE) in October 1990 that Yugoslavia would break apart in 18 months, with a high probability of triggering a bloody war.[83] The main culprit, the report said, would be Serbian President Milosevic.

U.S. and West European decision makers failed to coordinate military, political and economic power in ways that might have stopped the fighting at the outset for several reasons:

- U.S. determination to stay on the sidelines during the early stages of the crisis, because, (a) Secretary of State James Baker tended to see the Balkans as a "no win" situation, and (b) top U.S. officials believed the Balkans should be handled by the Europeans given the region's geopolitical proximity to Europe.
- U.S. preoccupation with other international events, such as Iraq's invasion of Kuwait in early August 1991, Desert Storm in January 1992, and later the Shi'ite and Kurdish problems in Iraq.
- U.S. attention on Gorbachev's mounting problems in Moscow, the collapse of communism and post-Cold War politics in Eastern Europe and the Soviet Union.
- EC lack of power in foreign policy, because national governments control Europe's foreign policy and any government can veto the Community's executive authority; the EC does not have a command system for joint military operations outside NATO.[84]
- EC attention to internal problems, such as recession and growing resistance to European unification. The EC also focused initially on the fall of Communism next door in Eastern Europe, German unification, and—like the U.S.—Iraq's invasion of Kuwait, rather than rising tensions in the Balkans.
- EC reluctance to exert military force, choosing instead diplomacy and humanitarian assistance. EC decisions lacked teeth. Emergency meetings, missions dispatched to Yugoslavia to supervise one ceasefire after another, peace conferences at the Hague, monitors on the ground to observe and report on the fighting, cancelled EC credits and assistance to Yugoslavia, and an arms embargo imposed in July 1991 (endorsed by the U.S.), failed to deter the Balkans' raging ethnic wars.

Weak and ineffective European responses—and tepid U.S. reactions at the outset of the crises—probably gave leaders like Tudjman and Milosevic the green light for aggression. As the crisis grew in intensity, like a brush fire turning into a forest fire, it became increasingly difficult to contain. As far as the U.S. and West European decision makers were concerned, when the crisis was in its early stages it did not appear important enough for the allies to act decisively—despite the NIE warning. By the time it had built up enough momentum to affect West European and U.S. interests—with mounting numbers of refugees in Central and West Europe; a widening regional destabilization; threat of spill over into Kosovo, potentially dragging NATO's Greece and Turkey into the struggle; and a potential impact on Russia's internal politics—it was harder to do something about it. The risks and complexity of the crisis had grown as the conflict escalated.

The difficulties of conflict resolution multiplied with time. One problem in the early stages of Yugoslavia's break-up was that the crisis flared and receded so often that decision makers got used to a kind of crisis brinkmanship. Another complicating factor in the early stages—at least from the U.S. perspective—was the foggy roles of the players. The U.S. did not always see the links between Belgrade and Serbian groups in Croatia and Bosnia. Situational and informational uncertainties made it difficult to generate effective U.S. and European leadership to deal with the expanding wars, perceive fundamental problems to be addressed, craft a viable policy to cope with fundamental issues, and amass appropriate power to enforce the policy. By January 1992, fifteen ceasefires had been arranged and broken.

West European countries have found various reasons for not taking the lead in stopping the Balkan wars with military force. Germany, Great Britain, and France all have expressed excuses for not exerting military force; the upshot has been a pronounced inability to act together with strength of purpose. Germany faced a serious recession, with refugees flooding in and huge costs associated with rebuilding former East Germany. Germany provided humanitarian aid, but avoided military might—at least until April 1993, when it took a historic step by allowing German airmen, who make up one-third of the crews of NATO's AWACS reconnaissance planes, to take part in NATO enforcement of the UN-mandated "no-fly zone" over Bosnia.[85]

Great Britain and France have their own reasons for avoiding a heavy military presence. Britain committed troops to UNPROFOR, but was reluctant to go beyond such a commitment. London, moreover, dragged its heels regarding enforcement of the UN's "No-fly zone" over Bosnia, fearing Serb retaliation against its UN contingents.[86] It should be noted that because Britain was already bogged down in a war in Northern Ireland, it had little interest in taking on a war against the Serbs. An added rationale for not committing British ground forces during 1991–1992 lay in history: Britain fought for the Serbs in World Wars One and Two. When asked if the British position amounted to appeasement, *a la* Prime Minister Neville Chamberlain with Hitler in the 1930s, British decision makers give a resounding "no."[87]

The largest UN contingent in former Yugoslavia has been France's. France wants to take a leading position in Europe and would like to keep NATO out of the former Yugoslavia because the U.S. plays so predominant a role within NATO. From a French perspective, the more NATO leads in the Balkans, the longer U.S. power is preserved in Western Europe.[88] France, however, has been active in UN operations in Bosnia; General Philippe Morillon, commander of the UN force in Bosnia, made a personal crusade of getting food into one Serbian town, Srebrenica, in March 1993.[89]

This is not to argue that Western Europe did little or nothing in the escalating fighting. Far from it. As noted above, the EC and CSCE went into action, struggling to negotiate ceasefires with the combatants. In July 1991 the EC imposed an arms embargo on Yugoslavia, endorsed by the U.S., and froze EC financial aid, even though EC members still differed over whether the European Community should recognize Slovenia and Croatia. France was active in pressing for UN action, and in September 1991 the UNSC adopted Resolution 713, calling for a complete arms embargo on Yugoslavia and immediate cessation of hostilities. About this time the Russians jumped in, when Gorbachev invited Tudjman and Milosevic to Moscow for talks, whereupon yet another ceasefire was signed—and immediately broken.

A whirlwind of European, UN and U.S. diplomatic and economic activity closed out 1991. The WEU provided naval ships to create "humanitarian corridors" for evacuating 3,000 refugees in Dubrovnik. The UN (rather than the EC) negotiated its first cease-fire—which broke down in a few days—and the UNSC unanimously adopted Resolution 721, requesting a report on the feasibility of sending peace-keeping forces to Yugoslavia. The U.S., for its part, announced trade sanctions on Yugoslavia, and Germany led the way in recognizing Slovenia and Croatia. Other countries, including the U.S., followed suit, while Serbia played its own diplomatic game by recognizing the Serbian Republic of Krajina inside Croatia! Throughout 1992-93 the Europeans—EC, CSCE, NATO, and WEU—tried to enforce their rules regarding crisis management as meetings followed meetings, missions went to the field and one EC peace conference session after the other met and arranged repeatedly broken cease-fires.

### U.S. and UN Conflict Management: The Bush Administration

Whereas West Europe initially carried the ball in trying to deal with the Balkan crises from 1991 onwards, the U.S. and the UN became much more active in 1992. In January the UNSC approved the deployment of 10,000 peace-keeping forces for Yugoslavia, with contingents from 30 countries, and in February it established UNPROFOR—with a mission to demilitarize and oversee civil administration in Croatia's UN protected areas. The UN became a major news item throughout 1992 in these and complementary efforts to deliver humanitarian food relief to beleaguered Bosnian Muslims. Table 1.3 indicates the range of UN efforts to manage the Balkan conflict during 1992.

As for the U.S., the spring of 1992 marked a transition in President Bush's and Secretary of State James Baker's passive disapproval of Serbian "ethnic cleansing" to a more forceful role in the Balkan crisis. They determined to ratchet up the pressure on Serbia, while still avoiding direct commitment of ground forces—probably because Lebanon and Vietnam were still on their minds. Like the Persian Gulf crisis, they used the UN as the mechanism through which to focus U.S. policy. Baker's State Department cancelled landing rights for the Yugoslav airline, withdrew U.S. military attaches from Belgrade, ordered the expulsion from the U.S. of their Yugoslav counterparts, and closed Yugoslav consulates in New York and San Francisco. UNSC Res. 757 of May 1992—with its severing of trade links to Yugoslavia, frozen government assets abroad, oil embargo, sporting and cultural ban, and cut air links—owed much to U.S. pressure.[90] Yet the fighting raged on.

Bureaucratic infighting among the various organizations involved in U.S. national security decision making on Yugoslavia had become routine during 1991–92 as Bush, Baker, State Department officials, the Pentagon, Joint Chiefs of Staff and Congressional leaders struggled to craft some kind of viable policy to stop the fighting without committing military forces.[91] The State Department pressed Baker and Bush to opt for military intervention, a position the Defense Department, especially General Colin Powell, Chairman of the Joint Chiefs of Staff, resisted.[92] Meanwhile, the media and numerous high–profile opinion makers, like ex–Secretary of State George Shultz, ex–National Security Adviser Henry Kissinger, and former U.S. Ambassador to the UN Jeanne Kirkpatrick, were pressuring U.S. officials for stronger action against Milosevic and the Serbs.[93] The presidential election campaign of 1992 added pressure on the Bush Administration to do something, because President–elect Clinton went out of his way to proclaim the need to respond to moral outrages in Bosnia.[94]

What evolved from these political and organizational struggles was a three–track U.S. policy: (1) vigorous efforts under UN auspices to get humanitarian aid into and protect Bosnian Muslims; (2) leadership in international opposition to Serbia's "ethnic cleansing" tactics—to the point of identifying Serbian "warcriminals" and advocating a Nuremberg–type War Trials; and (3) supporting economic sanctions against former Yugoslavia, yet not singling out the Serbs as culprits in all the problems. Still, Bush, Baker, National Security Adviser Brent Scowcroft, and Secretary of Defense Richard Cheney made clear they were not thinking of using military force to halt the conflict or get dragged into a quagmire of "internal civil war."[95]

Specific U.S. actions to bolster the Bush Administration's three–track approach included:

TABLE 1.3
1992 United Nations Security Council Resolutions on Yugoslavia

| Date | UNSC Resolutions |
| --- | --- |
| Feb. | 743 establishes UNPROFOR. |
| Apr. | 749 authorizes full deployment of 14,000 peace-keeping forces. |
| May | 757 calls for a comprehensive trade embargo. |
| Aug. | 770 authorizes "all measures necessary" to deliver humanitarian aid in Bosnia. |
| Aug. | 771 condemns "ethnic cleansing." |
| Oct. | 780 authorizing investigation of Balkan "war crimes." |
| Oct. | 781 adopts "no-fly zone" over Bosnia; does not authorize combat aircraft to enforce the ban. |
| Nov. | 787 widens existing sanctions against the Federal Republic of Yugoslavia; includes "all inward and outward maritime shipping." |
| Dec. | 798 condemns "acts of unspeakable brutality;" demands that all detention camps, particularly for women, be closed immediately. |

Source: *Keesings Contemporary Archives*, 1992.

- Pressure in the UNSC to pass Resolution 770, August 1992, authorizing "all measures necessary" to insure delivery of humanitarian aid.
- Similar pressure in September–October to pass UNSC Resolution 781 imposing a "no-fly zone" over Bosnia to protect delivery of humanitarian aid.[96] Resolution 781, however, had no enforcement clause.
- Orchestration of a UNSC resolution in November to tighten sanctions against Serbia and Montenegro with a military blockade by NATO and the WEU—passed in November 1992.[97]
- Attempts in November–December to persuade fellow Security Council members to back a resolution permitting U.S. and allied combat aircraft to shoot down violators of the "no-fly zone."
- Naming figures in December to be prosecuted over war crimes, which included Serbia's Milosevic, to be tried by a "second Nuremberg" tribunal.[98]
- Warning Milosevic in December 1992 that the U.S. was prepared to intervene militarily in former Yugoslavia if Serbia attacked the ethnic Albanians who lived in the republic's formerly autonomous province, Kosovo. This letter of warning was delivered in Belgrade to Serbian President Milosevic, and Gen. Zivota Panic, commander of the Serbian-controlled Yugoslav army.[99]
- Pentagon contingency operations for Yugoslavia in December, which entailed several options: (1) enforcing the no-fly zone over Bosnia with

U.S. and allied air power; (2) expanding the current 23,000 strong relief operation with protection from the air; (3) arming Bosnians, mostly by airdrops; using ground troops to deter attacks on ethnic Albanians in Kosovo province—this would breach Serbian sovereignty; (4) forming safe havens within Bosnia, which could be done, but only with ground forces.[100]

## The Clinton Administration's Approach to Bosnia

Whereas President Clinton had vowed to make domestic policy a top priority, the Balkan situation did not go away.  The day after the inauguration, Croatia began a military push in the Krajina region in an effort to retake territory formerly seized by Croatian Serbs.  Three days earlier, the State Department's annual report on human rights termed the carnage in Bosnia worse than anything seen in Europe since Nazi times.  Former Yugoslavia was the subject of the new Administration's first formal policy review, initiated by Presidential Review Directive (PRD) No. 1 in late January, and Yugoslavia was the subject of the first National Security Council's (NSC) Principals Committee meeting and later the President's first formal NSC meeting.

By January 1993 Lord Owen of Britain and UN representative Cyrus Vance had devised a sweeping settlement plan proposed by the UN and EC, calling for division of the republic into 10 quasi-autonomous provinces with a central government representing Serbs, Croats and Slavic Muslims.[101]  As Bosnia's bitter enemies wrangled over the plan—while "ethnic cleansing," Serbian blocking of UN food convoys, and Sarajevo's siege continued—the Clinton team moved from its initial nonacceptance to neutrality to positive endorsement of the Vance-Owen peace plan, probably realizing it was the only game in town.[102]  It marked the first time the U.S. had become directly involved in a mediation effort aimed at stopping the fighting that began in June 1991.  In backing the Vance-Owen formula, Clinton made clear the full weight of American diplomacy would be brought to bear, and the new President stated that he would be willing to use troops for enforcement of an agreement—a major shift in terms of putting U.S. prestige and power on the line.[103]

Clinton followed the new policy commitment with actions.  He appointed Reginald Bartholomew in February as envoy to cooperate on peace-making in the Balkans.  Bartholomew's first visit took place in Moscow, where Russian nationalists had signaled strong support for Russia's traditional Serbian ally and pressured Boris Yeltsin to oppose new moves against the Serbs.[104]  Secondly, Clinton called for a NATO role in the eventual enforcement of the Vance-Owen peace proposal—thus moving the U.S. into a stronger leadership position in applying collective defense measures than previously.[105]  The U.S. urged its allies to start preparing an international force to exceed 50,000 troops, which would be sent to Bosnia immediately after a peace settlement to enforce its agreement.[106] France, not surprisingly, was not especially pleased with such NATO planning. In addition, Secretary of State Warren Christopher urged tighter sanctions to force Serbian compliance and indicated that the no-fly zone should be enforced. As part of this stepped-up pressure on Serbia, the U.S. inaugurated airdrops of relief supplies to besieged towns in Bosnia in February.[107] By April the U.S. was able to gain UN approval of enforcement provisions for the "no-fly zone," and NATO forces began Operation Deny Flight on April 12.[108] At this point in time, then, it appeared that the U.S., UN and international community were on track in terms of coordinating policy to end the fighting.

Such hopes were short-lived. The Bosnian Serbs rejected the Vance-Owen peace formula, European leaders resisted deeper military involvement, and the U.S. quietly deferred taking strong initiatives on its own. By mid-April the Principals Committee of the NSC again was meeting to review U.S. policy. With Serbian forces approaching the town of Srebrenica, and fearing a possible massacre, President Clinton told reporters that the international community must now reconsider measures previously found unacceptable, although he specifically stated that introduction of U.S. ground forces was not an option.[109] The U.S. agreed, however, to support tightened UN sanctions against Serbia, to take effect if the Serbs did not accept the Vance-Owen formula, despite Russian objections.[110]

Debate within the Clinton Administration over what to do in Bosnia matched the bureaucratic in-fighting apparent during the Bush period. In late April, in an unusual revolt against American policy in the Balkans, the State Department's top experts on the Balkans sent Secretary of State Christopher an impassioned letter calling Western diplomacy a failure and recommending military action against the Serbs.[111] It should be noted that in 1991-1992, during the former Bush Administration high-ranking State Department officials had been pressing former Secretary of State Baker for months in much the same direction. Meanwhile, Madeleine Albright, President Clinton's U.S. representative at the UN, echoed this sentiment in a memorandum urging air strikes to protect the predominantly Muslim towns and cities under siege in Bosnia—a policy that Chairman of the Joint Chiefs of Staff Powell stated would not work.[112] Defense Secretary Les Aspin, in contrast, argued that Serbian forces might be overrated and that air strikes could be effective.[113] Bureaucratic infighting clearly has been at work on the subject of military force in Bosnia.

The nature of U.S. policy toward Bosnia became further clouded in May 1993, when Secretary Christopher visited Europe—a trip billed to rally support for military action against Bosnian Serb forces. A senior State Department official, Under Secretary Peter Tarnoff, the State Department's chief operating officer, stated later that the trip in fact was not to sell Clinton's military plan but to gather European ideas.[114] The West Europeans, according to Tarnoff, "were genuinely disarmed by the fact that he was there to consult. ... He did not have a blueprint in his back pocket. ... He had some things we favored."[115] Tarnoff pointed out that part of Christopher's goal was to set limits on American involvement, implying that as the Clinton Administration focused on domestic economic troubles, it expected to withdraw from many foreign policy leadership roles customarily undertaken by the U.S.[116]

The Tarnoff revelations led the Clinton Administration to rush to erase the impression that a new doctrine of reduced U.S. influence and leadership was in the offing for the post-Cold War period.[117]  In June, however, with the Vance-Owen plan dead and a new plan afloat to turn Bosnia into three ethnic ministates, Christopher took another step back from the war in Bosnia. He stated that the conflict "involves our humanitarian concerns, but...not...our vital interests."[118]  It was clear by then that the Clinton administration's approach to ethnic conflict in Bosnia would focus on limiting and containing the conflict—trying to keep it from spreading elsewhere.[119]  This approach was accentuated in late July when, as Bosnian Serbs were driving to take Sarajevo (a so-called, UN-designated "safe area"), U.S. officials seemed to have virtually ended their Bosnia effort, blaming Europe for the crisis.[120]

In resisting being drawn militarily into the Balkans, the Clinton Administration nevertheless agreed with Russia and key European allies on a policy of guarding safe havens for Muslim civilians besieged by Serbian nationalists.[121]  Such protection, not aimed at rolling back Serbian territorial gains, would require deployment of several thousand more UN troops in Bosnia in addition to the 9,500 already there.[122]  The UNSC passed this resolution June 4th, co-sponsored by the U.S., Russia, Britain, France and Spain.[123] The Bosnian Muslims at first refused to agree to the safe havens concept, but ultimately accepted it—given the lack of viable alternatives.  Serbian forces virtually ignored it.

## Lessons for Future Conflict
## Management in Former Yugoslavia

A close look at this ill-fated record of U.S. and West European efforts to stop the fighting in former Yugoslavia through diplomacy and economic sanctions—as opposed to direct military force—suggests several lessons. First, it illustrates how the collapse of the former Soviet Union and Yugoslavia—and demise of communism and the Cold War—has propelled the international system into a period of volatile transition.  The transition is fraught with xenophobic brands of ethnic nationalism, violent struggles for territorial and political control, intra-state conflict, and breakdown of sovereign states.  The result has been extraordinary numbers of refugees, mass migration, and terrorism—such as systematic rape and elimination of one ethnic group at the hands of another.

This has happened, in part, because a global recession exacerbated ethnic national animosities and undermined the West's resolve to stop the fighting early on.

Second, the scope and nature of turbulence in the former Yugoslavia has greatly complicated questions of when, where and how America and the West should apply military force in pursuit of national interests. Although America and the West had numerous important national interests associated with the widening war among Croatia, Serbia and Bosnia in the early stages of the conflict, Baker and Bush insisted that the Balkans conflict was peripheral to U.S. interests. The motto was "let the Europeans handle it." In retrospect, U.S. interests arguably included

- Encouraging the UN, EC, and CSCE to play a stronger role in guaranteeing international stability.
- Enabling NATO to fulfill its role as executive agent of the UN in the Yugoslav conflict.
- Preventing turmoil in Bosnia from spilling over into Kosovo and threatening Greek-Turkish entanglements and weakening NATO.
- Warning would-be imitators of Serbian actions in Eastern Europe and the former Soviet Union not to challenge the U.S. and NATO commitment to regional stability.
- Preventing the migration of millions of refugees from the Balkans to Austria, Hungary, and Germany and the exacerbation of these nations' problems.[124]

The obvious problem has been to craft a policy that applied sufficient power to attain such aims, without bogging down in another Lebanon.

How much more difficult is crafting a policy for intervention in an internal war than dealing with regional hegemony like Iraq's invasion of Kuwait. Situational and informational uncertainties in the Balkan wars have undermined a clear definition of such national interests and objectives. Ambiguity stems from unclear battle lines; ambiguous political/military control; lack of a single front line, as opposed to many pockets of fighting and ethnic mixes; no clear vital interests such as oil; and absence of aggression across sovereign territory, as in Iraq's invasion of Kuwait. Under such conditions high-level officials in the Pentagon—like former Chairman of the JCS, Colin Powell—have resisted commitment of ground forces and other forms of military involvement.[125]

Third, the confused nature of the Balkan conflicts created impediments to rational decision making. Rational decision making is difficult even under the best of circumstances—a sharply defined adversary, vital resources in jeopardy, and allied support for concerted action. The difficulty arises from our pluralist democratic system, which translates into competing organizational agendas and roles, political infighting and maneuvering; and from the thinking—attitudes, values and beliefs—of individuals at high levels of policy making. Volatile cases like the Balkans—with its uncertainties and challenges regarding how and when to use military power—tend to magnify organizational, political and cognitive frictions inside the democratic decision making processes. The new era has not lent itself to old definitions and concepts of rational behavior in terms of the use of force, associated with Cold War years.

Fourth, the media have played a huge role in pressuring the U.S. Administration to take decisive action in Bosnia to try to stop the killing. From reporting in such newspapers as *The New York Times* to ABC, CBS, and NBC news coverage of the conditions in Bosnia—from Serbia's "ethnic cleansing," to its prisoner-of-war camps and mass rapes—media reporting politicized the Balkan wars. Republicans like former Secretary of State George Shultz, former UN Ambassador Jeanne Kirkpatrick, and former National Security Adviser Henry Kissinger urged a more direct use of U.S. force. During the presidential election campaign of 1992, presidential candidate Clinton challenged incumbent President Bush to take more forceful action in Bosnia, and several U.S. Senators made it clear that televised images of brutality evoked memories of the Jewish Holocaust during World War Two. Bosnia's war images disturbed the American public's view of the world—urging some kind of pressure out of empathy for other peoples, concern with human rights violations, and belief in universal human decency.[126] At the same time, Americans are cautious about foreign involvement, believe strongly in dialogue and rarely favor the use of military force—which left Bush still in touch with basic American values when he eschewed use of U.S. ground forces in Bosnia, using instead diplomacy and economic sanctions.

Fifth, had America led in defusing the conflict during the early stages of the game, probably in the fall of 1991, instead of waiting for others to do so, the costs of the war in human and material terms probably would have been vastly lower.[127] A settlement in the interests of all parties was more likely before the fighting spread. If we learn anything from the Balkans it would be the importance of U.S. leadership in multilateral uses of force, through inter-governmental organizations such as the UN.[128]

Overall, we have witnessed in Yugoslavia's break-up the enormous capacity of ethnic animosities to generate violence, to the point that if external powers are unprepared to bring to bear overwhelming force or orchestrate another method to alleviate hatred, the fighting will continue. How to deal with the inter-ethnic hatred undermining sovereign states is one of the most perplexing questions facing the international community in the late twentieth century.[129] The UN's failure to resolve the Balkan wars—along with EC, WEU, CSCE and NATO inadequacies—suggests that in the face of such ethnic forces, much remains to be done in trying to determine what might work in trying to moderate ethnic conflict.[130]

## Notes

1. The government of Ljubljana held a referendum on independence from Yugoslavia in December 1990, which won an overwhelming majority. This brought the Slovenes into conflict with Serbia's chauvinist, neo-Stalinist president, Slobodan Milosevic and the Serb-dominated Yugoslav People's Army (JNA). As a consequence, fighting broke out between Slovenia and Serbia in June 1991. See *Keesings Contemporary Archives*, June 1991, pop. 38274-38275; also Carole Rogel, "Slovenia's Independence: A Reversal of History," *Problems of Communism*, Vol. XL, July-August 1991, pp. 31-40. Several factors pushed Ljubljana toward independence, such as Slovenia's relative economic prosperity and sensitivity to its negative image abroad by attachment to Yugoslavia, set against federal taxes going to Yugoslavia's less prosperous republics, Serbia's thwarting of economic reforms and the violation of Albanians rights in Kosovo. Rogel, pp. 35-36.

2. See Misha Glenny's insightful book, *The Fall of Yugoslavia* (London: Penguin Books, 1992), Chapters one and five. Glenny is the Central European correspondent of the BBC's World Service, based in Vienna. He toured and interviewed extensively in former Yugoslavia as it fell apart in regional wars.

3. The road to war, in retrospect, is quite clear on this matter, because on November 12, 1991, the Croatian Democratic Community (HDZ party) established the so-called Croatian Community of Bosnia Sava Valley in Bosanski Brod. Six days later, on November 18, 1991, leaders of 30 municipalities met in Grude to found the Croatian Community of Herzeg-Bosnia; this meeting was followed on January 27, 1992, by the creation of the "Croatian Community of Central Bosnia." See Dr. Milan Vego, "The Army of Bosnia and Herzegovina, *Jane's Intelligence Review*, February 1993, p. 63.

4. Milan Vego notes that between mid-September and mid-November 1991, Serbs in Bosnia-Herzegovina established six autonomous regions in the republic—independent from the government in Sarajevo. Then in November 1991, Serbs voted to establish an independent Serbian republic within the borders of Bosnia-Herzegovina, followed by a January 14, 1992, vote to declare the "Serbian republic of Bosnia and Herzegovina" to be a part of what was left of former Yugoslavia. See Vego, "Croatian Community of Central Bosnia," p. 63.

5. In the Sarajevo war, Misha Glenny observes that "about 90,000 Serbs remained in Sarajevo to face the devastation of their city side by side with their Moslem, Croat, Jewish, and Yugoslav neighbors. It is a struggle, above all, between the rural and the urban, the primitive and the cosmopolitan, and between chaos and reason." See Glenny, *The Fall of Yugoslavia*, Chap. 5.

6. *The New York Times*, April 9, 1993.

7. See Hearing Committee on Foreign Relations, U.S. Senate, "Civil Strife in Yugoslavia: the United States Response," Hearing before the Subcommittee on European Affairs, February 21, 1993, U.S. Government Printing Office, Washington, D.C., 1991; and U.S. Senate, Committee on Foreign Relations, A Staff Report, "The Ethnic Cleansing of Bosnia- Herzegovina," U.S. Government Printing Office, August 1992. Also Secretary of State Eagleburger's Statement at the International Conference on the Former Yugoslavia, Geneva, December 16, 1992, in the *Foreign Policy Bulletin*, January-April 1993, pp. 57-75.

8. See Don Oberdorfer, "Clinton: Enforce 'No-Fly Zone' in Bosnia," *The Washington Post*, December 12, 1992, p. A19.

9. See Thomas L. Friedman, "Bosnia Reconsidered," *The New York Times*, April 8, 1993.

10. Tom Post, *et. al.*, "Give Peace a Chance?" *Newsweek*, February 22, 1993, pp. 34–36. Also *The Christian Science Monitor*, April 19, 1993; and *The New York Times*, April 19, 1993; and *The Washington Post*, April 9, 1993.

11. Thomas L. Friedman, "Airdrop Proposal Gets Endorsement of the U.N. Chief," *The New York Times*, February 24, 1983, p. A1.

12. I am indebted to Professor Robert H. Legvold, Columbia University, for these thoughts. Interview, Winchester, Massachusetts, February 22, 1993.

13. Spyros Economides, "The Balkans and the Search for Security," *Arms Control: Contemporary Security Policy*, Winter 1992, pp. 122–124.

14. *Yugoslavia: A Country Study*. Area Handbook of Yugoslavia, Washington, D.C.: U.S. Government Printing Office, 1982, p. 12.

15. See John Zametica, *The Yugoslav Conflict*, Adelphi Paper No. 270, International Institute of Strategic Studies (IISS), Summer 1992, pp. 6–7.

16. Ibid., p. 13; See also Fred Singleton, *A Short History of the Yugoslav Peoples*. Cambridge: Cambridge University Press, 1985, Chapter five.

17. Ibid.

18. See Pedro Ramet, *Nationalism and Federalism in Yugoslavia, 1963–1983*. Bloomington: Indiana University Press, 1984, especially chapter two.

19. See Schevill, *Op. Cit.*, pp. 141–143.

20. Ibid.

21. Ibid.

22. See Ramet, *Op. Cit.*, p. 23.

23. See Misha Glenny's impressive *The Fall of Yugoslavia*. London: A Penguin Book, 1992, pp. 63–64.

24. See *Keesings Contemporary Archives*, April 1990, p. 37381. Also Ferfila, *Op. Cit.*, p. 23

25. Aleksa Djilas, *The Contested Country: Yugoslav Unity and Communist Evolution, 1919–1953*. Cambridge: Harvard University Press, 1991, pp. 4–5. Djilas notes that "Non-Slav observers did not distinguish between Croats and Serbs until the ninth century. ... The Croatian and Serbian tribes, though identical in ethnic and linguistic origin, developed distinct political organizations." Ibid., p. 4.

26. See Djilas, *Op. Cit.*, pp. 106–107.

27. Ibid., pp. 106–107. Djilas states that with Starcevic "there entered permanently into Croatian politics the idea that all those who have a different national consciousness, or those whose political ideas are a hindrance to the realization of complete Croatian sovereignty, expansion, and homogeneity are racially inferior and fundamentally evil beings. Mystical and fanatical, intolerant and violent, territorially expansionist and nationally homogenizing, Starcevic's ideology contained all the important elements of the ideology of extreme Croatian nationalism in the twentieth century." Ibid.

28. Ibid., Chapter four.

29. Zametica, *Op. Cit.*, p. 8.

30. See Fred Singleton, *A Short History of the Yugoslav People*, Cambridge: Cambridge University Press, 1985, pp. 47–48; and R.G.D. Laffan, C.F., *The Serbs: Guardians of the Gate: Historical Lectures on the Serbs*. Oxford: At the Clarendon Press, 1918, Chaps. 4–6.

31. Zametica, *Op. Cit.*, p. 20.

32. See Josef Joffe, "The New Europe: Yesterday's Ghosts," *Foreign Affairs*: America and the World 1992/93, Vol. 72, No. 1, p. 30.

33. Glenny, *Op. Cit.*, p. 140

34. Ibid., pp. 140–141.

35. Ibid., p. 139.

36. Ramet, *Op. Cit.*, p. 148. The 1971 census was the first in which "Muslim" was treated as a fully recognized nationality. Ibid.

37. Ramet, p. 148.

38. See Glenny, *Op. Cit.*, p. 3.

39. Ibid.

40. Glenny, *Op. Cit.*, pp. 3–6.

41. Ibid. See Chapter one.

42. *Keesings Contemporary Archives*, August 1990, p. 3766.

43. *Keesings Contemporary Archives*, February 1991, p. 38019.

44. Croatia's Tudjman retaliated by blaming Serbian nationalists and *Chetniks* (fascists) for trying to provoke military intervention to demolish Croatia and set up a "Serboslavia" or Greater Serbia. See *Keesings Contemporary Archives*, May 1991, p. 38203.

45. This key point is made by Misha Glenny, *Op. Cit.*, p. 143.

46. Ibid., p. 147.

47. Glenny, *Op. Cit.*

48. *The Washington Post*, August 11, 1992, p. A13.

49. See John Zametica, *The Yugoslav Conflict*, Adelphi Paper No. 270 (Summer 1992), p. 38.

50. *Keesings Contemporary Archives*, April 1992, p. 38848.

51. *The Washington Post*, May 27, 1992, p. A25.

52. Glenny, *Op. Cit.*, pp. 146–147.

53. Eagleburger Statement, *Op. Cit.*

54. By the late 1980s, when Communism began to fall elsewhere in East Europe, Yugoslavia already was in a debate over the merits of a genuine market economy and Western-type multiparty system. Meanwhile, economic conditions worsened with falling production, rising unemployment, increased indebtedness and growing inflation—forces which sparked ethnic national conflict. For background, see Zametica, *Op. Cit.*, Chapter one.

55. In part the Serbo-Croatian dispute stemmed not only from ethnic tensions *per se*, but also from the lack of parliamentary democracy to channel interests and influence, a Serbian view that the new Yugoslav state was perceived as a "Greater Serbia," and the Serbian belief that they should be appreciated for having liberated Croats and Slovenes from Hapsburg power. See Zametica, pp. 6–7.

56. See *Keesings Contemporary Archives*, April 1990, p. 37381.

57. See Glenny, the back cover of *The Fall of Yugoslavia, Op. Cit.*

58. Ibid.

59. For additional discussion, see Franz-Lothar Altmann, "Ex-Yugoslavia's Neighbors: Who Wants What?" *The World Today*, Vol. 48, Nos. 8–9 (August/September 1992), pp. 163–165.

60.  See Roger Cohen, "Cross vs. Crescent," *The New York Times*, September 17, 1992.

61.  Thomas Butler, "Centuries of Grudges Behind Today's Balkans Calamity," *Manchester Guardian Weekly*, September 13, 1992, p. 21.

62.  On the absolutely critical issue of creating and maximizing legitimate authority, see Norman H. Keehn, "Building Authority: A Return to Fundamentals," *World Politics*, Vol 26 (April 1974), pp. 331–52.

63.  See Glenny, *Op. Cit.*, pp. 18–19.

64.  Milosevic began this process in 1987 when, at the Seventh Session of the Serbian League of Communists' Central Committee, he passionately defended the Serbian and Montenegrin minority in the province of Kosovo. Glenny, *Op. Cit.*, p. 32.

65.  Glenny, *Op. Cit.*, p. 33.

66.  *The Washington Post*, February 21, 1993, p. A25.

67.  Above Tudjman's desk is a gold–framed painting of 10th–century Croatia's King Tomaslav dressed in battle armor and thrusting a sword into the air.  Downstairs in the lobby is another painting in which skeletons and severed heads of medieval Turkish Muslim victims lie strewn in the foreground while triumphant Croatian knights ride through a conquered village.  Floating angels carry a banner: "Glory and Victory," Steve Coll, "Franjo Tudjman, At War With History," *The Washington Post*, March 1, 1993, p. B 1.  "What Tudjman has not managed, however, is to find a version of the past—his own, his family, his nation's—that lends itself to peace." Ibid., p. B8.

68.  Chuck Sudetic, "Milosevic, Unfazed by Criticism, Rouses the Faithful Serbian Voter," *The New York Times*, December 16, 1992, p. A5.

69.  Elaine Sciolino, "U.S. Names Figures to be Prosecuted over War Crimes," *The New York Times*, December 17, 1992, p. A1.  Milosevic is also on the list.

70.  Over 100,000 Serbs demanded Milosevic's ouster in June 1992.  UN sanctions, plus hyperinflation, shortages and growing unemployment, appear to have jolted many Serbs to a realization that economic ruin could result.  In the wake of a rally on June 29, Milosevic used the state–run television and radio to portray members of opposition—including the Serbian Orthodox Church—as paid stooges of Serbia's alleged enemies, including the Roman Catholic Church, CIA and the German government. *The Washington Post*, June 30, 1992.

71.  Glenny, *Op. Cit.*, p. 36.

72.  During the Second World War, 1941–1945, Yugoslavia plunged into a prolonged, bloody, simultaneous civil war (the *Ustasha* and *Chetnik* affairs) and national liberation struggle.  Ethnic nationalism in the Balkans was made more complex by Josip Broz Tito, whose Partisans resist German occupation.  His Serbs, Croats and Bosnians, with the aid of Soviet weapons, threw the Germans out of Belgrade in late 1944.  Led by the victorious Tito, who had promised equality of nations inside Yugoslavia after the War, the country moved toward an uneasy mix of suppressed nationalists under a rigidly centralized bureaucracy and communist federation.  See John Zametica, *The Yugoslav Conflict*, Adelphi Paper No. 270 (Summer 1992), pp. 8–11.

73.  Coll, *Op. Cit.*, p. B8.

74.  Glenny, *Op. Cit.*, p. 31.

75.  Jonathan C. Randal, "Serbia's President Purges Intellectuals," *The Washington Post*, February 20, 1993, p. A16.

76.  See *Keesings Contemporary Archives*, September 1991, p. 38420.

77.  *The Washington Post*, May 25, 1991, p. A1.

78.  *The Washington Post*, December 15, 1992, p. A3.

79.  *The Washington Post*, May 4, 1993, p. A17.

80.  *The New York Times*, May 7, 1993, p. A1.

81.  *The Washington Post*, May 16, 1993, p. A1.

82.  Interviews with State Department officials, November 1992.

83.  Ibid.

84.  See the letter by Mark M. Nelson, Senior Associate, Carnegie Endowment for International Peace, Washington, D.C. to *The New York Times*, April 9, 1993, p. A26.

85.  *The Washington Post*, April 9, 1993.

86.  Significant sectors of the British media suggest the country is bogged down in a "Vietnam" in former Yugoslavia; they consequently want no part of deepening military entanglement, beyond those forces committed to UN operations.  Additionally, the British economy is in a long recession, which makes funding military action difficult. *Interview*, Tom Higgins, U.S. Foreign Service officer, February 26, 1993.

87.  Peter Jennings, ABC News special, March 18, 1993.

88.  Ibid.

89.  *The New York Times*, p. A10.

90.  A *Newsweek* interview with Secretary of State Baker's adviser indicated that Milosevic's advances on Croatia might be viewed as still trying to hold Yugoslavia together;  "But his aggression in Bosnia crossed a new threshold," says Baker adviser. Image after televised image of attacks on innocent civilians exposed Milosevic as an aggressor.  So Baker used every occasion to push sanctions imposed by UN under Chapter 7 of its charter, which also permits military action. "The pressure tactics worked," says *Newsweek*, "last week the EC voted a partial trade embargo and UN SC imposed more sweeping economic sanctions."  *Newsweek*, May 25, 1992.  Such sanctions arguably do not affect intolerant nationalism in the wisest way.

91.  In August 1992, the State Department official who was in charge of managing day-to-day U.S. policy toward the Balkans resigned from the Foreign Service to protest what he called the Bush administrations"s "ineffective" and "counterproductive" handling of the devastating Yugoslavia civil war.  In an interview George D. Kenney, 35, said U.S. policy had failed to deal with the growing crisis in the Balkans because "the administration at high levels in the State Department and White House did not really want to get involved."  Senior career officers, he added, "have chosen to take the safest course" by not challenging their superiors."  See *The Washington Post*, August 26, 1992, p. A18.

92.  On September 28, 1992, Powell delivered a resounding "no" on using limited force in Bosnia.  See *The New York Times*, September 28, 1992, p. Aa.  Powell argued that military force is best used to achieve decisive victory.  For the first time, he publicly explained his reluctance to intervene in Bosnia.  His remarks were the most recent and vivid example of behind-the-scenes debate in the Bush Administration over use of force.  The debate was joined by lawmakers and former Bush Administration officials who contend that the Pentagon had an "all or nothing" doctrine for using force, increasingly irrelevant to a world in which violent nationalism and ethnic conflict have taken the place of superpower hostilities and Cold War rivalry.

Powell assailed the proponents of limited military intervention to protect the Bosnians. He questioned the need to establish an air-exclusion zone over Bosnia like those the U.S.

had imposed over parts of Iraq, where the Pentagon saw less risk.  The U.S. and allies were then discussing such a zone.

Powell also angrily rejected suggestions by former PM Margaret Thatcher of Britain and others that the West undertake limited air strikes to deter the Serbs from shelling Sarajevo and continuing their attacks.  He said, "As soon as they tell me it is limited, it means they do not care whether you achieve a result or not.  As soon as they tell me surgical, I head for the bunker."  Powell's point is that you must begin with a clear understanding of what political objective is being achieved by the use of force.  The next step is to determine the proper military means, whether the objective "is to win or do something else.  Preferably it is to win because it shows you have made a commitment to decisive results...the key is to get decisive results to accomplish the mission."

But in the words of this report on Powell, "Most military analysts say that Gen. Powell's approach served U.S. well in invasion of Panama and Persian Gulf War, where overwhelming military force was used to achieve a quick victory w/minimal American casualties.  But Pentagon critics say Pentagon's doctrine seems designed to fight the last war, a no-holds-barred air and land war, rather than the next war, where force might be used selectively, not to vanquish an enemy, but to slow aggression stemming from ethnic conflicts and bolster diplomacy to end the fighting.  Powell complained angrily about the impetuousness of civilians, who he said had been too quick to place American forces in jeopardy unwisely for ill-defined missions.  He cites Lebanon as classic example, where 241 died as a result."  *Ibid.*

93.  On August 17, *Time* magazine featured a front-page cover story of Muslim prisoners in a Serbian detention camp.  Headlines stated: "Atrocity and Outrage: Specters of barbarism in Bosnia compel the US and Europe to wonder: is it time to intervene?"  "So far the responses have been confused and tentative.  As often happens, political considerations are at odds with military realities.  What can outsiders do? ... Western analysts point out that the fathers and grandfathers of today's fighters tied down 30 Axis divisions for four years during WWII."

94.  See Thomas L. Friedman, "Bosnia Reconsidered," April 8, 1993, p. A1.

95.  The point about the Balkan conflicts constituting an "internal civil war" is food for thought.  By such a definition, outside powers automatically limit the argument for intervention, following the centuries-old international legal code of non-intervention by external parties in the affairs of sovereign independent states, whose territorial integrity is sacred.  Certainly such perceptions have hindered collective diplomacy in stopping fighting in the Balkans.  *The Economist*, July 18, 1992, noted the limits of collective diplomacy in post-communist Europe.  The international bodies—the EC, the UN, the WEU; NATO and the CSCE have been weak or slow.  "Resisting local bullies needs single minded leadership...the new Balkan statelets thrown up by the collapse of communism are like those that emerged after the end of the Hapsburg and Ottoman empires; they expect big powers to boss them about, and as Mr. Milosevic has shown, the Serbs are quick to misbehave when nurse looks the other way."

The *Christian Science Monitor*, July 23, reported that Defense Secretary Richard Cheney is widely quoted as stating that the Balkan conflict is "an internal civil war." Cvijeto Job, a Washington columnist for VREME, an independent magazine in Belgrade, stated, however, that this is untrue.  Job argues that Serbia's aggression is a "cross border operation."  Job pointed out that the Pentagon calls Yugoslavia a potential "quagmire."

96.   President Bush said on October 3, 1992, that he was ready to use U.S. military forces to impose a ban on combat flights in Bosnia–Herzegovina, a step that could introduce American air power into the Balkan War for the first time.   In a written statement, he announced that he was seeking a UN resolution banning all flights in Bosnia airspace except those authorized by the world body. He said Serbian bombing attacks showed a "flagrant disregard for human life." This announcement, representing a significant widening of American willingness to become involved, *was the first time that the Administration said that it was willing to use American military power to protect the Bosnian Muslims from attack.*  His statement also moved American policy closer to the more assertive posture recommended by Governor Bill Clinton.  Serbian forces at the time had about 20 combat planes and had been flying as many as 30 missions a day, dropping cluster bombs.

Bush stated that: "1.  Having resumed U.S. relief flights into Sarajevo, I am prepared to increase the U.S. share of the airlift.  2.  We will make available air and sea lift to speed the deployment of the new 6,000 UN force needed immediately in Bosnia to protect relief convoys.  We will also provide a hospital and other critical support for this force.  3. The U.S. will furnish $12 million in urgently needed cash to the UN High Commissioner for Refugees for the purpose of helping preparations for the winter. That's in addition to the $55 million we have already committed.  4.  We will offer to the UN and Red Cross help in transporting and caring for those being freed from detention camps.  5.  We will seek a new UNSC Resolution with a provision for enforcement, banning all flights in Bosnian airspace except for those authorized by the UN." See *The New York Times*, October 3, 1992.

97.   See *Newsweek*, November 30, 1992.

98.   See *The New York Times*, December 17, 1992.

99.   See *The New York Times*, December 29, 1992, p. A10.

100.   See *Newsweek*, December 28, 1992, pp. 36–37.

101.   *The Washington Post*, January 5, 1993, p. A10.  The plan consisted of three sections: (1) the reorganization of Bosnia into 10 provinces, these proposals being embodied in a map; (2) constitutional principles for the republic, allowing a large measure of autonomy for the provinces within a decentralized state; and (3) cease–fire and demilitarization arrangements to end the current conflict.  See *Keesings Record of World Events*, January 1993, pp. 39277– 39278.

102.   *The New York Times*, February 11, 1993.

103.   Ibid.  On the same day Secretary of State made this announcement, Chairman of the JCS, Colin Powell, said that he might retire "a month or so" ahead of schedule. *The Washington Post*, February 11, 1993.

104.   *The Washington Post*, February 14, 1993, p. A39.

105.   *The Christian Science Monitor*, February 22, 1993, p. 1.

106.   *The New York Times*, March 11, 1993, p. 11.

107.   The relief drops began on March 1, 1993.  See *The Washington Post*, March 2, 1993, p. A1.

108.   See *The New York Times*, April 1, 1993.

109.   Air strikes against Serbian forces and installations, however, were under consideration—along with arming Bosnian forces.  See *The New York Times*, April 17, 1993.

110.   Russia abstained from voting, but did not veto the measure.

111.   *The New York Times*, April 23, 1993, p. A1.

112.   Ibid.

113.   Ibid.

114.   *The Washington Post*, May 26, 1993, p. A1.

115.   Ibid.

116.   Ibid.

117.   *The Washington Post*, May 27, 1993, p. A1.

118.   *The New York Times*, June 4, 1993, p. A1.

119.   See Peter Grier, "U.S. Quietly Concedes Bosnia, Focuses on Limiting Conflict," *The Christian Science Monitor*, June 23, 1993, p. 1.

120.   Elaine Sciolino, "U.S. Ends Bosnia Effort; Blames Europe for Crisis," *The New York Times*, July 22, 1993, p. A8.

121.   *The New York Times*, May 23, 1993, p. A1.

122.   France, Britain, Canada, and Spain already had contributed troops; Russia was planning to do so by this time. *The New York Times*, May 23, 1993, p. 1.

123.   *The New York Times*, June 6, 1993, p. 13.

124.   See Alberto R. Coll, "Power, Principles, and Prospects for a Cooperative International Order, *The Washington Quarterly* (Winter 1993), pp. 5–14.

125.   The Balkans in many respects is like Lebanon, where U.S. policy went awry during 1982–1984.  The Balkans, as in Lebanon during 1982–1984, in the words of Thomas L. Friedman, is "haunted with ambiguity."  Right and wrong depend upon whose history book one is reading, what ethnic/religious group one belongs to, and which tribal leader one listens to in these ambiguous wars.  Navigating the Balkans' perilous shoals of diplomatic complexity is extraordinarily complicated as President Reagan discovered in Lebanon and as the Clinton Administration realized in Yugoslavia once it assumed power.

126.   William C. Adams, "Opinion and Foreign Policy," *Foreign Service Journal*, Vol. 61, No. 5 (May 1984), pp. 30–31.

127.   Ibid., p. 10.

128.   Numerous factors come into play here, such as use of the UN in a non-neutral manner to protect one country against another's aggression, as in Korea in 1950 and the Persian Gulf in 1991.  In so many of the emerging conflicts—as in former Yugoslavia—the conflict is not only between two states, as in Serbia versus Croatia, or Serbia versus Bosnia—but also of an intra-state nature as in Croatia's Serbs versus Croatians or Bosnian Serbs versus Bosnian Muslims.  America and Western Europe need to think creatively on how to more effectively utilize the UN, when the new conflicts are more intra-state than inter-state in character.

129.   See Maynes, *Op. Cit.*, p. 5

130.   See Maynes, *Op. Cit.*, pp. 14–15.

# 2

# World Turned Upside Down: Ethnic Conflict in the Former Soviet Union

*Wayne P. Limberg*

With the dissolution of the USSR, little-known corners of the old Soviet empire have been catapulted into the news, and along with former Yugoslavia, have come to symbolize what threatens to be the scourge of the post-Cold War era: ethnic conflict. Tens of thousands died in ethnic-related warfare in the former USSR since 1991. Hundreds of thousands are refugees. Nor is an end in sight. Sixty million people live outside their national homelands in the former Soviet Union, including twenty-five million Russians. Each of the fifteen successor states has one or more significant ethnic minorities within its borders, and in a majority, ethnic-related problems have complicated and retarded reform and threatened regional stability.

## Ethnic/Nationalist Reawakening

Even before the coup attempt of August 1991 and the subsequent demise of the USSR, there had been a pattern of increasing ethnic tensions and violence in many of the Soviet republics. The advent of *glasnost* (openness) under Gorbachev emboldened various individuals and groups and, perhaps more importantly, made it easier for them to organize and publicize their arguments.

The views expressed in this chapter are those of the author and do not necessarily reflect the views or policies of the U.S. government, the Department of State, or any other agency of the U.S. government.

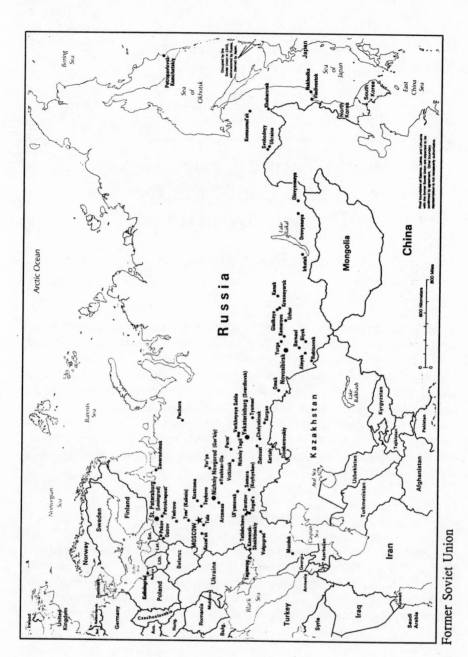

Former Soviet Union

A good deal of the pent-up anger was directed at the central authorities, and since the Russians had historically been the dominant group, opposition took on an anti-Russian coloring. As early as the fall of 1986, a campaign was launched to preserve the Byelorussian language; eventually similar anti-Russification movements were seen in the Ukraine, Baltics, Kazakhstan and Moldavia.[1] In December 1986, there were riots in Alma-Ata, Kazakhstan over Gorbachev's replacement of party chief, Kunayev (a Kazakh), with Gennadii Kolbin (a Russian). The riots left at least 20 dead.[2]

Throughout 1988, ethnic and nationalist demands became louder, joining with the growing "green" movement and leading to calls for greater economic and political autonomy. This was especially true in the Baltic republics. The Balts began to press for a revisiting of World War II and their loss of independence. Smaller groups, most notably the Crimean Tatars, demonstrated for the right to return to their homeland. Even the Russians themselves were not immune to the "nationalist epidemic": the right-wing, Great Russian nationalist group Pamiat, though still small, received increased attention and press. The fiercest and bloodiest example of rising ethnic consciousness, however, occurred in the Caucasus. As early as 1985, the Armenians had demanded the return of the Nagorno-Karabakh region, which had been ceded to Azerbaijan in the 1920s by Stalin. In early 1988, they redoubled their efforts, leading to demonstrations in Yerevan, bloody riots in Sumgait, Azerbaijan, and, finally, open warfare between the two republics.[3]

In each instance, Moscow tried to respond: the Armenian and Azerbaijani parties were disciplined; Kolbin would eventually be replaced by Nursultan Nazarbayev, an ethnic Kazakh; the Balts would be repeatedly brought to heel. However, none of the measures proved entirely successful; nationalist movements grew, and their demands increased.[4] By the time of the August 1991 coup attempt, nationalist movements were up and running in the majority of the republics. Indeed, in many, they controlled the republic governments. This was especially true in the smaller "historic" nations of the Baltics and Caucasus. Central Asia lagged behind as did the larger, more industrialized and cosmopolitan republics with large Russian or Slavic populations like the Ukraine, Moldavia and Byelorussia.[5]

## Independence and Violence

Independence by no means meant the end of ethnic tensions and violence. If anything, these intensified. From February, 1988 to January 1992, approximately 1500 people were killed in Nagorno-Karabakh on both sides; by mid-1993, that number had probably tripled as Armenian Karabakh forces overran Azeri villages, drove the Azerbaijan forces out of Nagorno-Karabakh, opened a land corridor connecting the region to Armenia and crossed into

Azerbaijan proper. By mid–1993 Karabakh Armenian forces controlled ten to twenty percent of Azerbaijani territory, and the Armenian government controlled three Azerbaijani villages. The fall of 1993 saw further Karabakh Armenian gains. At least 300,000 refugees exist on both sides, with some estimates running as high as a million.[6]

In the new republic of Moldova in the first half of 1991 as many as 1000 were killed in fighting between government police and Russian separatists—joined by Cossack volunteers and soldiers of the 14th Army—who were attempting to establish an independent Trans–Dnestr state. Eventually Romania, Russia and Ukraine mediated a ceasefire. The ceasefire has more or less held, but the separatists have established their own "republican" government and armed forces. There has also been sporadic fighting between the government police and the Gagauz Turks in the south of Moldova who have declared their independence.[7] The Gagauz and Trans–Dnestr separatists have established contacts independent of Chisinau.

Georgia has faced two ethnic challenges. In August 1990, the Abkhaz in the western part of the country declared themselves an autonomous republic and rejected central Georgian control; the South Ossetians in the northeast followed suit a month later, demanding reunification with North Ossetia in the Russian republic. Tbilisi refused to accept either move. Fighting began between Georgian and Ossetian irregulars and continued into 1992, intensifying in April. At least 500 died and 85,000 South Ossetians became refugees in Russian–controlled North Ossetia. Moscow, in the name of the Commonwealth of Independent States (CIS) mediated a ceasefire in the summer of 1992. The ceasefire was to be policed by a Russian–Georgian–Ossetian force, but resulted in a Russian controlled South Ossetia.

No sooner was the Ossetian problem under control than the Abkhaz increased their activities. Georgian forces were reluctant to use force and Shevardnadze attempted to negotiate a settlement. His ability to compromise, however, was limited by Georgian nationalist sentiment; Georgian forces attacked Abkhazia in August 1992. Over the next year, an estimated 4000 combatants and civilians were killed in Abkhazia, and over 100,000 became refugees.

Russia's response was at best ambiguous. The Russians had important naval holdings in Abkhazia, and the Russian military had little love for Shevardnadze, whom they held responsible for the fall of the USSR. Moscow recognized, however, that Shevardnadze was the best hope for stability in Georgia and did not want to see the troubles in Georgia spread to the ethnically diverse and volatile North Caucacus. By mid–1993, the Abkhaz were being aided by Chechen, Russian and Cossack "volunteers." Local Russian military commanders allegedly turned over arms and ammunition to the Abkhaz rebels and on several occasions Russian aircraft reportedly attacked Georgian positions. The Georgians were reportedly being aided by Ukrainian "volunteers." Both

Moldova

Ukraine and Moldova condemned the rebels and left little doubt they thought Moscow was behind Tbilisi's troubles.

In late July, 1993, Moscow mediated a ceasefire and began disarming both sides. In mid–September, 1993, however, the Abkhaz broke the ceasefire, and despite Russian condemnations and sanctions, by month's end had defeated the Georgians and declared their independence. The United Nations organized a meeting in Geneva in December between the Abkahz and Georgians. More importantly, armed supporters of ousted Georgian President Zviad Gamsakhurdia seized the moment to go on an anti-government offensive in western Georgia, cutting the strategic railway from the Black Sea port of Poti to Tbilisi.   The Shevardnadze government with Russian help successfully counterattacked and reopened the railroad, but at the cost of Georgia joining the CIS.[8]

Finally, the civil war in Tajikistan has claimed at least 20,000 lives, according to officials in Dushanbe, and left at least 350,000 homeless.  The conflict has pitted Muslim against Muslim, Tajik against Tajik, region against region, as local families, clans and political dynasties rushed to fill the vacuum left by the fall of the communist regime.  Over 60,000 refugees fled south to Afghanistan.  Russia provided the embattled regime in Dushanbe military aid. Under a January 1993 collective security agreement, Russia, Kazakhstan, Kyrgyzstan and Uzbekistan have sent troops forces to defend the Tajik–Afghan border.  Afghanistan has supplied sanctuary, arms and training to some of the rebel groups.  In July 1993, rebel forces crossed the border and killed 25 Russian soldiers guarding the border.  Over the next month fighting along the Afghan/Tajik border escalated.  Cross border shelling and raids became an almost daily event.  The Russian 201st division stationed in Tajikistan was reinforced and began operations against rebel forces in Tajikistan, supported by Russian aircraft.  Cross–border raids and skirmishes continued into the fall and winter.  The country remained divided along both north/south and east/west axes.[9]

Smaller incidents of violence and ethnic tensions were seen in the other former Soviet republics.  Russia itself was no exception.  Some estimates put the number of ethnic fault lines in the Russian federation as high as 200, and ethnic based violence has been on the rise, especially in the North Caucasus region.  Chechenya declared its independence early on, and 1992–93 saw open warfare between North Ossetia and Ingushia.  Elsewhere, Russian–Estonian relations neared the boiling point in the summer of 1993 over Tallinn's treatment of the Russian minority in Estonia.  Ukrainian internal politics increasingly divided along East–West, Russian–Ukrainian lines.

Several things explain the increase in the intensity and number of armed conflicts since the USSR's dissolution.  In many areas, especially the Caucasus, Soviet forces had acted as a buffer and helped preserve the peace between groups and republics.  On withdrawing from the various republics, CIS forces have either turned their weapons over to the locals or had them seized; in any event, the firepower of all sides has increased.  Armenia and Azerbaijan may have as many as 220 tanks, 220 combat vehicles, 285 artillery pieces, 100 combat aircraft and 50 attack helicopters apiece—their share of the former Soviet arsenal allotted them, ironically, under the 1992 Conventional Forces in Europe agreement.[10]  While some of the republics may be receiving outside help and training, most are fairly undisciplined; rules of engagement and war are virtually unheard of.  Moreover, there is little medical aid for combatants or civilians.

## History's Dead, Long Live History

Although ethnic tensions and strife were familiar parts of the political landscape in the Third World and elsewhere, the intensity of the ethnic/nationalist movements in the Soviet Union caught all but a few specialists off guard, and even they were divided over what impact these movements would have. As late as 1979, a distinguished western scholar told an international congress of political scientists meeting in Moscow that the USSR had solved the nationality question.[11]

Given the fact that the USSR had 128 recognized nationalities with only 53 having official claim to their administrative units and only 27 living in their national homelands, this may seem surprising. All the more so given western liberal thought. Since the Enlightenment, the nation–state has been held up as the apex of historical development. Even avowed internationalists were forced to acknowledge the power of national and ethnic ties.[12] Drawing from Western European history, where states had arisen around dominant national groups, the nation–state based on an ethnic and linguistic group was posited as the ideal. By the turn of the 19th century, this was captured in the theory of national sovereignty: each group was entitled to its own territorial nation–state.[13]

There were exceptions—polyethnic states like the U.S., for example—but these were just that, exceptions that made the rule. Where minorities existed within state borders, their rights would be protected by legal and democratic institutions. Over time, they would be politically accommodated if not culturally assimilated. The disappearance of ethnic and national distinctions were natural byproducts of economic progress, of modernization. Both the nationalist and internationalist schools put their faith in economic development as the key to ethnicity and nationalism, whether they were Wilsonian democrats or Marxist–Leninists.[14]

The obvious problem is that the multinational empires of Eastern Europe never fit this mold. In neither tsarist nor Soviet Russia nor in the Ottoman and Austro–Hungarian empires was there an adequate "fit" between the ethnic communities and the "ethnic model" of the nation–state. Many minority groups were too small to be viable independent entities. Others were dispersed over large geographic areas.[15] This has led some to question the territorial/genetic basis for national and ethnic consciousness, and to denigrate the importance of things like common language, shared culture and history, association with, though not necessarily control of, a certain territory, and a sense of belonging to an identifiable if not definable group.[16]

Ultimately, however, ethnic or group identity is a device of self–definition, both for the individual and for his or her society, and a means of transferring meaning and values across generational lines. To the degree it is both the result of an individual's and group's history and a means of interpreting and understanding that experience, it is very real, even definitive. In the extreme, it can be the last [and best] line of defense against chaos, and it should come as no surprise that ethnicity often comes into play during periods of social and political upheaval.[17]

## Nation Building, Soviet Style

During 70 years of communist rule, official policy actually contributed to the development of ethnic and national self-consciousness and cultural awareness, the establishment of large ethnic demographic bases in old geographical homelands, and the creation of republic-based economies.[18] There is a certain irony in this since Marxist-Leninist theory argued that ethnic consciousness and modern nationalism were the natural result of capitalism and would disappear with the triumph of socialist internationalism. As early as 1913, Lenin posited the right of self-determination and even secession but insisted that the rights of the workers as represented by the Party take precedence. The Party was to be internationalist and centralized; there was no room for nationalist organizations or sentiments.[19]

Nationalism would prove to be a stronger force than anticipated, and the Bolsheviks had to bow to it if the revolution were to survive. They thus made concessions to the various nationalities, many of whom had already tasted independence and self-rule during the civil war. The idea of a unified state was abandoned in favor of a federation. The Party remained the centralizing force, but Stalin at least would argue for encouraging greater participation by members of the various ethnic and national groups.

Nationalism remained a means, not an end, however; actual self-determination and statehood were not accepted characteristics of a nation; and while the 1923 constitution establishing the USSR provided for secession, it included a "Catch-22" that rendered that right all but meaningless.[20] Nation-building in non-Russian areas was to take place only as part of the effort of building and maintaining party rule. In any case, the long-term objective was the consolidation and merging, not differentiation of nations.[21]

Through the 1920s and well into the 1930s, a policy of *korenizatsiia* or nativization was vigorously pursued. By 1933, 69 percent of the Uzbek, 59 percent of the Kirghiz and 53 percent of the Tajik party leaders were from the indigenous population.[22] The aim was to develop a native communist leadership and proletariat to win support for the revolution and party and diminish the perception of Russian domination and chauvinism.

Yet, at the same time, Stalin moved against the native leaderships in the non-Russian areas. Well before the show trials and purges in Russia, nationalist leaders and intelligentsia were being removed, imprisoned or killed, and replaced by more compliant and trustworthy types. Much of the old intelligentsia and leadership had been nationalist or even anti-Bolshevik, but even loyal communists if they had become too strong or independent in their republics were removed as the purges gathered steam.[23] The thousands of republican leadership positions in the 1930s and through the war years were increasingly filled by Russians. By 1939, 66 percent of the Central Committee of the Communist Party of the Soviet Union was Russian, by 1952, 71 percent. This reflected an increase of Russians in leadership positions in the republics.[24] The crackdown on the national leaderships was, of course, in addition to more drastic attempts at national engineering, namely, the forced relocation of whole populations and arbitrary redrawing of borders to divide and rule, pitting one ethnic group against another.

While the various nationalities were not allowed full sovereignty, *korenizatsiia* with its emphasis on the establishment of ethnic units in a federal system did lead to the creation of "solid demographic bases...national cultural institutions...and...Communist and intellectual cadres...from the dominant nationality."[25] This was especially true in Ukraine and the Caucasus. Even after nativization fell by the wayside, Georgians and Armenians continued to receive preferential treatment and have higher representation in their own republic governments and party structures. Similarly, as early as the 1930s, both groups could count considerable numbers of their kinsmen among the industrial proletariat.[26]

The result was an increasingly indigenous albeit loyal leadership and population. The price Moscow would pay for this, however, was a keener national and ethnic consciousness and a revival of traditional social structures that competed with official ideology and organizations for popular allegiance. Khrushchev grasped this change and established what amounted to an affirmative action program for national minorities throughout the USSR. Increasingly, the center had to work through the indigenous elites. What legitimacy these elites had, however, depended more on their ability to appear as defenders of the majority ethnic group than on their links to Moscow.

During this period of "indirect rule," the local elites in many areas, especially the Caucasus and Central Asia, were able to extend their power bases through favoritism, creation of complex networks of clients and patrons and "family circles," the creation of and exploitation of a "second economy" or "black market," and finally, simple corruption.[27]

Demographic changes also tended to support the trend toward nativization and continued well after *korenizatsiia* itself disappeared. The Caucasian and Central Asian republics' populations grew at rates well above the overall Soviet level; from 1959 to 1989, for example, the Azerbaijani population increased by 131%, the Georgians by 48%, and the Armenians by 66%. More importantly, the dominant ethnic groups in many of the republics became ever more dominant, garnering a disproportionate number of party, government, professional and white-collar jobs.[28] The exceptions were Latvia, Estonia and Kazakhstan, where Russian immigration was encouraged and the Russian percentage of the populations grew to around 40 percent; even in these republics, however, Moscow was careful to keep the top party jobs in local hands.

These trends continued under Brezhnev. Changes took place only when absolutely necessary. Declining economic conditions in the Caucasus, under-ground economic activity, and corruption, for example, eventually forced Moscow to take action. By the mid-1970s, the Armenian, Azerbaijani and Georgian parties had new chiefs. Petro Shelest was replaced in the Ukraine, allegedly for nationalist sentiments. In each case, however, Moscow felt compelled to appoint nationals as replacements.[29]

Regardless of Brezhnev's efforts to keep the lid on, nationalist dissent appeared in nearly every republic. In many instances, it surfaced in the form of a cultural or linguistic revival. The Georgians, Armenians and Ukrainians all successfully opposed further russification and preserved their native tongues. Then Georgian party chief Eduard Shevardnadze faced open rebellion in 1978 when Brezhnev attempted to remove Georgian as the official language of the republic. Similar efforts in Armenia and Azerbaijan were also abandoned. Though not as pronounced, similar developments would be seen in Central Asia. In the Baltics, as subsequent events would show, cultural preservation was a cover for nationalist movements in general. Georgia and Armenia saw the birth of dissident nationalist groups in the 1970s; in the case of Armenia, there were several instances of anti-regime and anti-Russian violence. The republics also saw the formation of civil and human rights movements by the majority ethnic groups and many of the minority ones.[30]

Gorbachev's reforms fanned the embers of nationalist and ethnic dissent. Criticism and removal of local leaders for failure to get on the Gorbachev bandwagon undermined the pro-center, indigenous elite, but bought no new loyalty for Gorbachev and Moscow. Gaidar Aliyev, for example, removed as head of the Azerbaijani party in 1987 for his stalling on economic reform, remained popular in Azerbaijan as, ironically, a symbol of Azeri independence; in 1991, he would be elected head of Nakhichevan (legally a province of Azerbaijan, but separated from it by Armenian territory). Aliyev's successor as the head of the Armenian party would be replaced in 1988 for failure to deal with the outbreak of ethnic violence in Nagorno-Karabakh. That dispute, like others, was stoked, though not caused, by the growing economic pinch brought on by Gorbachev's reforms. As the economic pie shrank, competition among various ethnic groups for a bigger piece grew in each of the three republics. As noted, by mid-1991, national independence movements like Rukh in Ukraine, Sajudis in Lithuania, the Armenian National Movement, the Azerbaijan Popular Front, and the Chavchavadze Society in Georgia were prospering, even controlling their respective republics. As a harbinger of future problems, national independence groups were also active among various minority peoples, including the Abkhaz and South Ossetians in Georgia; Kurds, Meskhetian Turks and Nagorno-Karabakh Armenians in Azerbaijan; Tatars, Germans, Chechen and Ingush in Russia; Gagauz Turks and Slavs in Moldova.[31]   With the dissolution of the USSR, these groups became ever more vocal and, in some instances, violent.

## A Range of Motives

Yet if ethnic and national groups became more vocal and active, they hardly spoke with one voice or from one agenda.  The size, diversity and history of the former Soviet Union and its various peoples mean a considerable range of views and goals.  Moreover, many of the ethnic and national groups and movements themselves are unclear or divided over objectives.  At risk of oversimplification, probably the best that can be done at this point is a rough classification of general types of ethnic conflict with the caveat that none are mutually exclusive; there is considerable overlap.  One type of conflict can transmute into another, and several of the ongoing and potential conflicts can fall under more than one category.  Nor is the list exhaustive.

*Minority/Majority Rights.*  By far the most common, this type of conflict is also the most diverse.  Examples are found in all fifteen successor states. Demands can range from increased civil rights—the Tatars in Russia—to full independence—the Abkhaz in Georgia and Trans-Dnestr Russians and Gagauz Turks in Moldova.  There is usually something of an escalation of activity, self-consciousness, and demands.  Older, "historic" minorities, however, may *begin* with declarations of independence.  Frequently, though demands for greater cultural freedom and autonomy appear first, accompanied by complaints of economic inequalities and second-class citizenship.  A twist on this is where the dominant group feels exploited by minorities under its control.  Before the dissolution of the USSR, Russians complained that they were being asked to subsidize the rest of the empire.

It is also difficult at times to sort out who the minority and majority are. Russians account for over 30 percent of the populations of Latvia and Estonia and hold clear majorities in several Baltic cities.  Ethnic Russians are also the majority group in eastern Ukraine and account for nearly 40 percent of the population of Kazakhstan with large, almost entirely Russian pockets in the north.  See Table 2.1 for a breakdown of Russian and Russian-speaking populations in the former republics of the USSR.  An added complication is when an ethnic group is divided across republic borders as in Nagorno-Karabakh.  The Karabakh Armenians are a minority in Azerbaijan but can look to Yerevan and a diaspora for support.  Similarly, Tajiks have looked to Afghanistan for refuge, arms and training.

*Irredentist.*   All of the republics have outstanding border disputes and territorial claims against their neighbors.  Some are the result of earlier attempts to divide and rule, and involve ethnic minorities, as in the case of

Nagorno–Karabakh and Ossetia. Others are due to Soviet expansion, war and international agreement, as in the case of the Baltic borders and Moldova and Belarus. Still others seem almost whimsical—Khrushchev's decision to cede the Crimea to Ukraine. In more than one case, claims to territory have been lodged by ethnic groups who no longer live in the contested area; for example, the Crimean Tatars and Meskhetian Turks, who were forcibly relocated under Stalin. With the exception of Ukrainian–Russian tensions over the Crimea, none of these claims have been pressed. One reason for this is that all of the new states are vulnerable to irredentist claims from their neighbors, and thus, all have an interest in not stirring the pot. The potential for trouble over borders is there, however, especially when combined with trans–border ethnic divisions and economic concerns—such as, water rights in Central Asia.

*Religious.* Religion is one of the most common and enduring aspects of ethnicity. With the notable exception of the Armenian–Azerbaijani dispute, however, ethnic conflict in the former USSR has not to date been associated with confessional differences. The largest loss of life—Tajikistan—has been Muslim against Muslim, and Sunni at that. Similarly, in Georgia, the two most troublesome groups, the Abkhaz and Ossetians, are predominantly Christian. But once again, the potential for conflict is there.

Although religious differences may not be the immediate cause of strife, they can feed and justify it. Territorial, political and economic disputes can take on religious colorings. The Islamic Renaissance Party (IRP) was one of the main antagonists of the Tajik civil war. The IRP was hardly an advocate of Islamic fundamentalism, and as with other Muslim movements in Central Asia, it invoked Islam more as a cultural than religious phenomenon. Nevertheless, its pronouncements took on a decidedly more religious tone as the war progressed. Religious differences also reinforce the Ismaili Pamiris' sense of isolation from the rest of Tajik society. The Caucasus is a patchwork of Christian and Muslim communities, with religion often being the one factor separating otherwise ethnically homogeneous groups. The east/west linguistic, ethnic and economic divisions in Ukraine are paralleled by a Uniate–Catholic/Orthodox division. Even in the relatively tolerant Baltic states, there is a risk of growing tensions between Protestant or Catholic majorities and Orthodox minorities.

Nor are confessional differences the only source of tension. Conflict can also arise along religious/secular lines. During the Tajik civil war, the more russified and secular Leninabad region made it clear that it would secede if an Islamic government came to power.

Finally, religious differences can invite outside interference, especially—but not only—in Central Asia and the Caucasus. Turkey, Iran, and Saudi Arabia have already championed Muslim rights, and the Vatican has become involved in Ukrainian church politics.

*Center/Periphery.* In many ways disputes between the center and periphery may be a variant of minority/majority conflict. In a great number of cases, the

## TABLE 2.1

### The Russian and Russian-Speaking Populations in the Former Republics of the USSR, 1989

| Republic | Including | Russians | | People Who Called Russian Their Native Language | |
|---|---|---|---|---|---|
| | | Thousands of People | In Percentage of Population | Thousands of People | In Percentage of Population |
| **USSR Overall** | 285,742 | 145,155 | 50.8 | 163,758 | 57.2 |
| Russia | 147,021 | 119,865 | 81.5 | 127,306 | 86.6 |
| Other Republics | 138,720 | 25,289 | 18.2 | 36,721 | 26.1 |
| **Including:** | | | | | |
| Ukraine | 51,452 | 11,355 | 22.1 | 16,898 | 32.8 |
| Belarus | 10,151 | 1,342 | 13.2 | 3,243 | 31.9 |
| Uzbekistan | 19,810 | 1,653 | 8.3 | 2,151 | 10.9 |
| Kazakhstan | 16,464 | 6,227 | 37.8 | 7,797 | 47.4 |
| Georgia | 5,400 | 341 | 6.3 | 479 | 8.9 |
| Azerbaijan | 7,021 | 391 | 5.6 | 528 | 7.5 |
| Lithuania | 3,674 | 344 | 9.4 | 429 | 11.7 |
| Moldova | 4,335 | 562 | 13.0 | 1,003 | 23.1 |
| Latvia | 2,666 | 905 | 34.0 | 1,122 | 42.1 |
| Kyrgyzstan | 4,257 | 916 | 21.5 | 1,090 | 25.6 |
| Tajikistan | 5,092 | 388 | 7.6 | 495 | 9.7 |
| Armenia | 3,304 | 51 | 1.6 | 66 | 2.0 |
| Turkmenistan | 3,522 | 333 | 9.5 | 421 | 12.0 |
| Estonia | 1,565 | 474 | 30.3 | 544 | 34.8 |

Source: "Naseleniye Rossii. Yezhegodnyy demograficheskiy doklad" [The Population of Russia. Annual Demographic Report], Center of Demography and Human Ecology, Moscow, 1993, p 15.

dissenting minority hails from a border region or is removed from the capital; as noted, complaints of economic discrimination are common. Examples are the Polish minority in Lithuania and the Ukrainians pre-independence. Center/periphery disputes are worth consideration on their own, however, for two reasons. First, they can cut across ethnic lines. Before the dissolution of the USSR, both ethnic Russians and Ukrainians in Ukraine complained of Moscow's economic exploitation of their republic; since independence, both groups in eastern Ukraine have criticized Kiev's efforts at economic reform. Second, center/periphery disputes can give birth to regional independence or autonomy movements that resemble ethnic or national movements. The civil war in Tajikistan was an example of this, and the potential exists in the east/west divisions in Ukraine.

Regionalism is probably a greater threat to Russian unity than traditional ethnic divisions given that minorities account for less than twenty percent of the population of the Russian federation. Twenty-one of the twenty-two republics in the federation are named after an ethnic group, but in all but four of the twenty-one, Russians outnumber the titular ethnic group. Even before the dissolution of the USSR, there were signs of growing regional self-consciousness. By the end of 1990, most of the republics in the federation had declared their sovereignty, and some regions were threatening secession in protest over Moscow's politics. With the breakup of the union, regional and republican demands for autonomy and, in some cases, independence increased.[32]

Center/periphery relations have been one of the main engines of recent Russian politics and constitutional development. At times they have been overshadowed by the executive/legislative power struggle in Moscow, but at other points they have been entwined in it. One of the things frustrating reform has been former communists trying to maintain their power at the regional level. Nor has Yeltsin shied away from using the republics and regions in his battles with conservatives in parliament and the provinces. One example was his appointment of presidential envoys to the various regions; another was his readiness to compromise on the 1992 Federation Treaty.[33] Through the late summer of 1993, Yeltsin would again play on regional and republican sentiment, holding out the possibility of a territorially determined upper house in parliament under a new constitution. Ultimately, the regions would play an important role in determining the outcome of the October 1993 crisis in Yeltsin's favor. Before the month was up, however, Yeltsin moved to replace provincial leaders and limit regional powers. In part, this was a crackdown on individuals and local soviets that had supported his opponents in parliament. At the same time, measures such as the removal of any mention of the Federation Treaty or republican sovereignty from the draft constitution were intended to bolster the center's powers at the expense of the regions and republics.[34]

The political content of any of these conflicts can and does vary. Some are conservative/traditionalist, even reactionary, in that the goal is to preserve the status quo or restore a golden past. The Trans-Dnestr separatists in Moldova, for example, are attempting to preserve the special status and rights they enjoyed under communism. The Baltic states look back to the inter-war period for models. The goals can also be revolutionary, seeking to overturn the existing order—including borders—and to institute a new social and economic system, as seen in Nagorno-Karibakh and Tajikistan. Whether out of conviction or convenience, most groups involved in the various ethnic disputes subscribe to basic human rights and democratic institutions. Indeed, most claim that their actions are in defense of these rights and institutions, even if it means, paradoxically, denying access to these same institution and rights to others.

## Ethnic Conflict and the New States

Whatever the origins or goals of the ethnic movements they confront, the Soviet successor states share some basic attributes and problems. All are new entities and are in the process of building political and economic systems. As part of this, each of these states is grappling with its national identity, with what it means to be a Moldovan, Georgian or Ukrainian. In some cases such as Armenia, ethnicity plays a large role. In others—Ukraine, for example—there is an effort to define the state as a political entity, not a national homeland. This process is complicated in nearly all the new states by differences between official policy and popular sentiment and by the existence of official and unofficial elements of society eager to exploit nationalist and ethnic sentiments.

Contributing to the problem is the weakness of most of the new governments' claims to legitimacy. None of these societies have a strong tradition of democratic rule or parliamentary government. Although elections have been held in most of the new states, none can claim a clear mandate in terms of economic or social programs. In each of the former Soviet republics, the people knew what—or whom—they were against, but they had only the vaguest notion of what they wanted or how to get it. In all too many of the new states, the government's strongest claim to legitimacy is based on ethnicity.

Although all the new states have gained international recognition, many see genuine independence as eluding them and resent being perceived by the rest of the world as second-class citizens or younger siblings of Russia. They remain economically dependent on Russia, especially for energy. All except the Baltic states have accepted the need for greater cooperation and signed the CIS economic pact in September 1993.[35]

All of the new states also perceive internal and external security threats. The internal threat is often associated with the presence of ethnic minorities. It can also be a result of competing domestic elites or factions as in Tajikistan or

Georgia.    The problem is that in these multiethnic societies essentially non-ethnic disputes can quickly take on ethnic overtones.    Moreover, one conflict can trigger another, ethnic or not.    The Abkhaz revolt, for example, was provoked in the summer of 1992 by Georgian government efforts to crackdown on the activities of the Zviadists, the supporters of ousted President Zviad Gamsakhurdia.    The Zviadist anti-government offensive in western Georgia in the fall of 1993 was, in turn, triggered by Tbilisi's loss of Abkhazia.[36]

A majority of the new states view Russia as the external threat.    It is probably no accident that these states have Russian military facilities or troops on their soil.    While Moscow still figures large in the thinking of the other states, the immediate perceived threat is more likely to be a neighbor.    In those Central Asian states controlled by former communist elites, Islamic fundamentalism has been forwarded as the greatest external danger.    Once again, these threats can assume ethnic dimensions.    The Baltic states' desires to see Russians leave included more than just the troops stationed within their borders.    Domestic challenges can reduce perceptions of the immediacy or danger of the external threat.    Georgia welcomed Russian help against the Zviadists.[37]

The greatest single challenge facing all the new states is the need to show economic progress.    This means reform, but in the popular mind reform means prosperity, not dislocation and downturn.    Popular frustration and displeasure with the lack of economic progress contributed to the return to power of the former communists in Lithuania in 1993.    Parliamentary unhappiness with the slow pace of reform cost Ukrainian Prime Minister Fokin his job in the fall of 1992.    Competition for a bigger piece of the shrinking economic pie also lies behind much of the ethnic and center/periphery tension in the new states.[38]

These goals and problems are interrelated; one supports the other. Unfortunately, they can also be contradictory, even mutually exclusive.    For example, the stronger a government's popular legitimacy, the more able it is to conduct major economic reform.    Economic reform, however, can undermine social and political stability and thus legitimacy.    Similarly, a strong sense of national identity can increase social cohesion and thus legitimacy.    But it can also be a destabilizing factor if it pits one group against another, creates scapegoats, or invites outside interference.

## Security Implications

It would be bad enough if the problem of ethnic conflict in the former Soviet Union were only a matter of loss of life and property and infringements of human rights.    Regrettably, the dangers ethnic conflict in the former USSR pose extend well beyond humanitarian and human rights issues.    The democratic and economic reforms the West has encouraged and supported are unlikely to survive or prosper in the face of widespread ethnic strife in any of the new states. No less than three governments were toppled in Azerbaijan because of their inability to deal successfully with Nagorno-Karabakh. The potential of regional and ethnic problems generated by economic dislocation has retarded Ukrainian reform efforts. Moldova, Armenia, Azerbaijan and Georgia have seen their economic reform efforts stall. In the face of the Abkhaz revolt, Shevardnadze instituted presidential rule, which included proroguing of parliament, a crackdown on the political opposition, stricter control of the media, and summary execution of looters.[39]

Nor have the centrifugal forces that tore apart the USSR necessarily stopped. Russia, Georgia, Moldova, Azerbaijan, Ukraine, Kyrgyzstan and Tajikistan face secessionist movements. The security risk is the creation of ever smaller, less politically and economically viable entities, in a word, balkanization.

Another danger of ethnic conflict is the potential for it to transmute into interstate tensions and crossborder violence. Many of the various ethnic minorities are divided by state borders; this, plus the nature of interethnic conflict, makes spillover and, in turn, escalation a very real possibility in a number of cases. Ethnic tensions have yet to spark an actual war or major confrontation between any of the former Soviet republics. However, Azerbaijan and Armenia have come to blows over Nagorno-Karabakh, and in the summer of 1993, Russian objections to Estonian draft legislation on citizenship, which Moscow saw as discriminating against ethnic Russians, strained relations and prompted CSCE mediation. In Tajikistan, the civil war quickly involved the Russians, Uzbeks and eventually the Kazakh and Kirgiz. As seen, the Ukrainian, Russian and Romanian governments became involved in the Trans-Dnestr and the Russians in South Ossetia.[40]

Continued ethnic and interstate strife also invites outside interference from other states of the region. Afghanistan was drawn into the Tajik civil war early. Turkey and Iran are already vying for influence in Central Asia, and the Chinese have increased their presence in the region. Under the 1921 Treaty of Kars, Turkey has claimed the right to intervene in the Nakhichevan region of Azerbaijan to protect ethnic Turks. The Iranians and Turks expressed concern over Karabakh Armenian offensives in the spring and summer of 1992, and Ankara provided military advisors to Baku. The Turkish press in October 1993 also accused the Armenians of providing sanctuary and support for Kurdish terrorists.[41]

Following offensives in October, 1993 which put the Karabakh Armenians in control of large tracts of Azeribaijani territory bordering Iran and saw thousands of Azeri refugees flee to Iran, Iranian President Rafsanjani visited Baku and brokered a ceasefire. While in Baku, Rafsanjani pledged continued support for Azerbaijan's efforts to resist Armenian "aggression," warning that Iran would not tolerate instability on its northern border. The Iranians repeated these warnings when the ceasefire they brokered collapsed shortly after Rafsanjani's return to Tehran. In early November 1993, Iran called on the United Nations Security Council to take "immediate steps to confront the crisis" in Azerbaijan.[42]

More troubling is the attitude of Russia itself and its policy toward the so-called "near abroad." As early as August 1992, Russian Foreign Minister Kozyrev listed protection of Russians abroad as a Russian foreign policy priority. Yeltsin took a similar tack in an October 8, 1992 interview. Over the next year, Yeltsin and Kozyrev returned to this theme on a number of occasions. Protection of Russian minority rights would, for example, be a major issue in Moscow's dealings with the Baltics.[43]

Moreover, Moscow's definition of who was Russian and thus deserving of Moscow's protection tended to expand. At first, it was only Russian *citizens* living in the other new states; later it became *ethnic* Russians, and then Russian *speakers*. This redefinition of who was Russian has little practical meaning in places like Latvia or Estonia where ethnic Russians and Russian speakers tended to be the same. In areas like the eastern Ukraine, however, where large numbers of ethnic Ukrainians were Russian speakers, it has more ominous overtones, especially when relations are already strained and when accompanied by signs of a more assertive Russian policy toward the "near abroad" in general as in the Caucasus and in Kozyrev's speech to the United Nations General Assembly in September 1993.[44] Announcement of the new Russian military doctrine with its sanctioning of stationing Russian troops abroad and call for more mobile, quick response forces with domestic and international peace-keeping capabilities only heightened concerns.[45]

The importance of this rhetorical shift in terms of actual Russian policy is open to debate. The Yeltsin leadership, particularly Kozyrev, through most of 1992-93 were under attack from the right and left in parliament for its alleged desertion of Russians abroad in areas like the Trans-Dnestr and Baltics. Kozyrev, however, did not abandon his tougher tone after the storming of the Russian parliament in October 1993. On the contrary, in mid-October, he would warn that no one should "think that abolition of this pinkish or red-brown Supreme Soviet will lead to the situation when we shall refuse to defend Russia's position even...when it is linked with contradictions with the west or our partners within the CIS."[46] Through the fall of 1993, Moscow continued to link withdrawal of Russian forces from Latvia and Estonia to Riga's and Tallnin's willingness to guarantee the rights of Russian minorities in each country, even though it risked loss of U.S. economic aid under the Byrd Amendment.[47]

Russia has interests in the "near abroad," however, that go far beyond protection of Russian minorities, and it would not be first state to justify the pursuit of such interests to domestic and international audiences by invoking minority rights. Nor, as seen in Georgia in the fall of 1993, has the absence of a significant Russian minority, however defined, stopped Moscow from intervening; it simply found other justification. In the case of Georgia, it was humanitarian, that is, refugee relief and keeping open the transport lines serving eastern Georgia, Azerbaijan and Armenia.[48]

Using protection of minority rights to justify policy has its own dangers, however. Popular passions are hard to turn off, and Moscow could find itself pursuing policies that did not serve its larger interests, just as tsarist Russia did when it championed romantic Pan-Slavism in the 19th century.[49] Ironically, this is all the more likely as—and if—Russia moves toward a more democratic, mass-participatory society. Even if Moscow has no intention of actively defending Russian minorities abroad, its statements can fuel suspicions in official circles in the other Soviet successor states and raise false expectations in the Russian diaspora itself.

## Challenge for the West

The end of the Cold War brought with it the unexpected dissolution of the world's last multiethnic empire, the USSR. Ethnic conflict is but one of the consequences—and causes—of the USSR's dissolution, but it is key in that it influences, even determines many of the others. Each of the states is groping for a way to deal with the problem, recognizing that ethnic strife will not disappear and can be its undoing. The United States and its allies, however, have yet to come to terms with the problem, let along develop a solution. Central is the West's reluctance, even failure to decide whether the break-up of the USSR was a positive development. Clearly, the answer to this question will go a long way in determining western approaches toward ethnic conflict and successor states of the Soviet Union.

The western stake in ethnic conflict in the former USSR ranges from the humanitarian to strategic and varies in intensity from region to region, conflict to conflict. A differentiated, even case-by-case approach is all but inevitable. This does not rule out, however, development of a consistent, broad-gauged policy based on respect for human rights and a commitment to the building of democratic institutions. Standards for dealing with ethnic differences must be articulated, evenly applied, and enforced. As part of this, the United States and its allies must be prepared to offer extensive economic and technical aid to all the successor states and ensure that it is effectively used. The international community must also re-examine its approach to peace-keeping and conflict resolution. New devices—and forces—must be developed. Specifically in the case of the former USSR, the United Nations and CSCE needs to come to terms with what role Russia will play in the "near abroad." There will be great temptation to let Moscow take the lead in peace-keeping operations in the territory of the former USSR. But while Russian sensitivities, interests and capabilities must be taken into consideration, they should not be the sole determining factors.

Clearly, none of this will be easy or cheap. Nor will it solve the problem of ethnic conflict in the former Soviet Union. It can, however, help alleviate some of the worst manifestations and possibly prevent others. In any case, the United States and allies have little choice. Ethnic conflict and its associated problems are not likely to disappear soon, and could get worse. The West can rightfully take pride that it stayed the course and won the Cold War. To the victor go the spoils. But so does the responsibility for a just and lasting peace.

## Notes

1. Movements for the preservation of national languages had been seen before; the Ukrainians and Georgians both won battles in the 1970s to make their native tongues the official languages of their republics.

2. For a detailed overview of the burgeoning ethnic/nationalist problem under Gorbachev, see Bohdan Nahaylo and Victor Swoboda, *Soviet Disunion: A History of the Nationalities Problem in the USSR* (New York: Free Press, 1990.)

3. Ibid.

4. Ibid.  For an overview of the Baltic movements during this period, see Jan Arveds Trapans, *Impatient for Freedom?  The Baltic Struggle for Independence* (London: Institute for European Defense & Strategic Studies, 1990).

5. In one of the odder examples of ethnic differences during this period, the ethnic Poles in western Lithuania actually supported the August 1991 coup attempt against Gorbachev, fearing that he would eventually grant Lithuania independence and thus worsen their lot.

6. Carol Migdalovitz, *CRS Issue Brief: Armenia–Azerbaijan Conflict*, Order Code IB92109 (Washington, D.C.: Library of Congress, January 25, 1993). *Time*, April 19, 1993, p. 32. Estimates of dead have run as high as 15,000. Margaret Shapiro, "Russian Mediation Urged in Caucasus," *Washington Post*, 9 September 1993; and ITAR-TASS, September 4, 1993. In October, 1993, the Red Cross put the refugee figure at 800,000.

7. Sergiu Verona, *CRS Report for Congress: Moldova Conflict: An Update*, No. 92–495 F (Washington, D.C.: Library of Congress, June 8, 1992). (*Literaturnaya Gazeta* December 23, 1992). The Trans–Dnestr rebels are mainly ethnic Russian and come from families who have been living in the region for generations. 50% of the officers and 90% of the NCOs have local roots. (FBIS–SOV–93–044, March 9, 1993, p. 45). They fear that Moldova will eventually reunify with Romania. Even in tsarist times the region was heavily Russian and extremely nationalistic. Trans–Dnestr volunteers reportedly fought on the conservative side during the October 1993 crisis in Moscow. The Trans–Dnestr rebels clearly have some sympathy in the 9000 strong 14th Army and even in Moscow, which assumed responsibility for the 14th; elements of the 14th presumably on their own initiative and authority helped the rebels. When Rutskoi visited the troops in the spring of 1992, he told them to enforce the peace and respect Moldovan sovereignty. Defense Minister Grachev, however, in mid-1992 warned the Moldovans not to attack the Trans–Dnestr and has accused Romania of interference. In

September 1993, the commander of the 14th was elected to the Trans–Dnestr separatist legislature, but later resigned when the separatists supported the anti–Yeltsin forces in Moscow in October. RFF/RL Daily Report #198, October 14, 1993, p. 6.

8. Bernard Gold, *CRS Report for Congress: Georgia: Basic Facts*, No. 92–159 F (Washington, D.C.: Library of Congress, June 10, 1992; National Public Radio interview with Shevardnadze, broadcast March 9, 1992; Michael Dobbs, "Russian Jets Downed in Georgia," *Washington Post*, March 20, 1993, pp. A17–18; Jim Nichol, *CRS Report for Congress: Georgia in Transition*, No. 93–794 F (Washington, D.C.: Library of Congress, August 24, 1993), p. 5; Serge Schmemann, "Georgia Truce Collapses In Secessionist Attack on Black Sea Port," *New York Times*, September 19, 1993, p. 13; John Lloyd, "Embattled Georgia Facing Collapse," *Financial Times*, September 22, 1993, p. 5; Daniel Sneider, "Key Georgian City Falls to Abkhazian Rebels," *Christian Science Monitor*, September 28, 1993, p. 6; and Wendy Sloane, "Desperate Georgians Flee the War in Abkhazia," *Christian Science Monitor*, October 12, 1993, pp. 1, 2. Russian action in Abkhazia may have been as much a matter of internal affairs as external policy. Russian commanders on the scene may have aided the Abkhaz at first without Moscow's knowledge, and eventually, even in defiance of the Yeltsin government. Up to the Abkhaz breaking the July 1993 ceasefire, Shevardnadze held Moscow responsible for what was going on but never blamed Yeltsin personally. Yeltsin, however, apparently came under increasing nationalist pressure through the crisis and took a harder line as time went on, even calling on the United Nations to grant Russian special protective powers over former Soviet territory, including Georgia. After the loss of Abkhazia, Shevardnadze would blast Yeltsin and others for not doing anything to stop the Abkhaz. cf. Catherine Dale, "Turmoil in Abkhazia: Russian Responses," *RFE/RL Research Report*, (Vol. 2, #34, 27 August 1993), pp. 48–57.

9. Serge Schmemann, "War Bleeds Ex–Soviet Land at Central Asia's Heart," *New York Times*, February 21, 1993, pp. 1, 12; Keith Martin, "Tajikistan: Civil War Without End?," *RFE/RL Research Report* (Vol. 2, #3, 20 August 1993), pp. 18–29; ITAR–TASS, October 26, 1993; Bess Brown, "Tajikistan: The Conservatives Triumph," *RFE/RL Research Report* (Vol. 2, #7: 12 February 1993), pp. 9–13.

10. Migdalovitz, op. cit.

11. M. Crawford Young, "The National and Colonial Question and Marxism: A View from the South," in Alexander Motyl, ed., *Thinking Theoretically About Soviet Nationalities* (New York: Columbia U. Press, 1992), p. 67.

12. One of the young Marx's feuds was with the Young Hegelians over the primacy of the nation–state as an expression of history; yet even Marx would admit ethnic and national differences and the need to take them into consideration; see for example his early essay *On the Jewish Question*. For a summary and analysis of early Soviet effort to reconcile nationalism and internationalism, see Crawford, op. cit.

13. Anthony D. Smith, "Ethnic Identity and Territorial Nationalism in Comparative Perspective," in Motyl, ed., *Thinking Theoretically About Soviet Nationalities*, p. 49.

14. Ibid., pp. 46–49, and Crawford, op. cit., p. 71.

15. Smith, op. cit., pp. 48–49.

16. Ibid., pp. 47–50, and Armstrong, op. cit., pp. 25–26.

17. Ibid., pp. 25–26.

18. Crawford, op. cit., p. 73.

19. Ibid., p. 38–42.

20. Gerhard Simon, *Nationalism and Policy Toward the Nationalities in the Soviet Union* (Boulder: Westview Press, 1991), pp. 20–22, and Crawford, op. cit.

21. Ibid., p. 23, and Bohdan Nahaylo and Victor Swoboda, *Soviet Disunion*, pp. 47–59. The constitution allowed a republic to secede if its action was in the best interest of the proletariat and revolution and did not threaten the integrity of existing socialist states, i.e., the USSR; since any secession would threaten the USSR's integrity and by definition, the welfare of the proletariat, the right was moot. On any of this it is dangerous to generalize; there was considerable disagreement in the party. Lenin and even more Bukharin leaned toward a gradual transition and were comfortable with a federal system. Stalin, however, favored a centralized structure though he was accepted the need for tactical compromises.

22. Simon, *op. cit.*, p. 23.

23. Ibid., p. 165.

24. Ibid., pp. 25–27, 164–65.

25. Ibid., pp. 164–65.

26. Ibid.

27. Ibid., pp. 25, 34.

28. Suny, op. cit., p. 229.

29. Ibid., pp. 234–5, 238–9, and Simon, loc. cit.

30. Ibid., pp. 231–2.

31. Ibid., pp. 243–4.

32. Jim Nichol, *CRS Report For Congress: The Russian Federation: Will It Hold Together?* (Washington, D.C.: Library of Congress, October 6, 1992), pp. 9–10, 35–43. As early as January 1992, there were calls for the creation of a North–Asian United States comprised of the Urals, Siberia and the Far East and separated from what remained of Russia by the independent republics of Bashkortostan and Tatarstan. Three months later, a Congress of Siberian Deputies met to explore formation of a Siberian republic. In June 1992, leaders of Krasnoyarsk Territory threatened to form a Yenisey republic if the federal economy continued to deteriorate. A Confederation of Mountain Peoples of the Caucasus was formed early on, and while not an ethnic group, various Cossack groups have demanded self–rule. New calls for a Urals republic appeared in Sverdlovsk in late summer 1993.

33. Paul Henze, *The Transcaucasus in Transition*, Rand Note N–3212–USDP (Santa Monica: RAND Corp., 1991.), pp. 13, 17–19; Vera Tolz, "Power Struggle in Russia: The Role of the Republics and Regions," *RFE/RL Report* (Vol. 2, #15, April 9, 1993), pp. 8–13; Daniel Sneider, "Yeltsin's New Deal Reneges on Promises to Republics," *Christian Science Monitor* (November 5, 1993), pp.1, 4.

34. *RFE/RL Daily Report*, No. 183, September 23, 1993, p. 2; *RFE/RL Daily Report*, No. 205, October 25, 1993, p. 1; John Lloyd and Dmitri Volkov, "Yeltsin Seeds Unfettered Powers for Presidency," *Financial Times* (October 29, 1993), p. 1; Wendy Sloane, "Russia's Baskhir Republic Pushes for Its Autonomy," *Christian Science Monitor* (October 26, 1993), p. 2.

35. Justin Burke, "Amid Political Tumult in Moscow, Yeltsin Forges CIS Economic Union," *The Christian Science Monitor* (September 27, 1993), p. 2. Ukraine and Turkmenistan signed on as "observers," however.

36. Claudia Rosett, "Shevardnadze Finds Fine–Honed Diplomatic Arts Can't Feed His Crumbling and War–Torn Georgia," *Wall Street Journal* (November 2, 1993).

37. Ibid.; Steve LeVine, "Shevardnadze's Comeback Credited to Russia," *Washington Post* (October 27, 1993), p. A27; Steve LeVine and Dorinda Elliott, "Big Guns, But No Idea Where to Shoot," *Newsweek* (November 1, 1993), p. 37; "Threat Declines Among Latvians But Ethnic Differences Persist," *USIA Opinion Research Memorandum* (October 1, 1993) and "Ethnic Estonians Continue to Fear Outside Attack," *USIA Opinion Research Memorandum* (October 4, 1993).

38. Saulius Girnius, "Lithuania: Former Communists Return to Power," *RFE/RL Research Report* (Vol. 2, No. 1: January 1, 1993), pp. 99–101.

39. Vladimir Socor, "Moldova's 'Dniester' Ulcer," *RFE/RL Research Report* (Vol. 2, No. 1: January 1, 1993), p. 12; Elizabeth Fuller, "Transcaucasia: Ethnic Strife Threatens Democratization, " *RFE/RL Research Report* (Vol. 2, No. 1: January 1, 1993), pp. 17–24; Claudia Rosett, "Shevardnadze Finds Fine-Honed Diplomatic Arts Can't Feed His Crumbling and War-Torn Georgia, "*Wall Street Journal* (November 2, 1993); Natasha Alova, "Police Use Expulsions in Moscow Crackdown," *Washington Times*, (November 2, 1993); *RFE/RL Daily Report* (#211: November 3, 1993), p. 2; Daniel Snieder, "Georgia on the Brink as Shevardnadze Turns to Russia," *Christian Science Monitor* (November 1, 1993), p. 3; Elizabeth Fuller, "Geidar Aliev's Political Comeback," *RFE/RL Research Report* (Vol. 2, No. 5: January 29, 1993), pp. 6–11.

40. B. Brown, "Tajik Civil War Prompts Crackdown in Uzbekistan," *RFE/RL Research Report* (Vol. 2, No. 11: March 12, 1993), pp. 1–6; Lee Hockstader, "War on Russia's Edge Turns Into Rout," *Washington Post* (September 12, 1993), pp. A1, A36; Steve LeVine and Dorinda Elliott, "Big Guns, But No Idea Where to Shoot," *Newsweek* (November 1, 1993), p. 37. The Confederation of Caucasian Peoples which claims to represent Caucasian ethnic groups in Russia, met in Sukhumi, Abkhazia in late October 1993 and pledged support for the new Abkhaz republic; the federation had "recognized" Abkhaz independence and sovereignty earlier. ITAR-TASS, 0906 GMT, October 26, 1993.

41. Elizabeth Fuller, "Nagorno-Karabakh: Internal Conflict Becomes Internationalized," *RFE/RL Research Report* (Vol. 1, No. 11: March 13, 1993), pp. 1–6; Elizabeth Fuller, "Nagorno-Karabakh: Can Turkey Remain Neutral?" *RFE/RL Research Report* (Vol. 1, No. 14: April 3, 1993), pp. 36–39; *RFE/RL Weekly Review* (Vol. 1, No. 23: June 5, 1993), p. 69; *RFE/RL Daily Report* (#209: October 29, 1993), p. 2; Colin Barraclough, "Azeri-Armenian Clashes Force Thousands Into Iran," *Christian Science Monitor* (November 1, 1993), p. 3; *Aktuel* (October 27, 1993).

42. *FBIS-SOV-93-207* (October 28, 1993), p. 69.; *FBIS-SOV-93-208* (October 29, 1993), pp. 75–80; *FBIS-SOV-93-207* (November 30, 1993), pp. 61–62; *FBIS-SOV-93-211* (November 3, 1993), p. 75; and *FBIS-SOV-93-214* (November 7, 1993), pp. 74–75; *RFE/RL Daily Report* (#209: October 29, 1993), p. 2.

43. John Lough, "The Place of the 'Near Abroad' in Russian Foreign Policy," *RFE/RL Research Report* (Vol. 2, No. 11: March 12, 1993), p. 22; *RFE/RL Daily Report* (No. 194: October 8, 1993), p. 2; *RFE/RL Daily Report* (No. 202: October 20, 1993), p. 2; and *Rossiyskaya Gazeta* (October 30, 1993), pp. 1, 7.

44. John Lough, "The Place of the 'Near Abroad' in Russian Foreign Policy," *RFE/RL Research Report* (Vol. 2, No. 11: March 12, 1993), p. 22–23; *Russian Federation Press Release: Address by H.E.Mr. Andrei Kozyrev, Minister for Foreign Affairs of the Russian Federation Before the 48th Session of the United Nations General Assembly* (New York: September 28, 1993); *Washington Post* (September 29, 1993), p.

1; *New York Times* (September 29, 1993), p. 1. According to USIA polls conducted in the summer of 1993, the majority of ethnic Estonians and Latvians in Estonia and Latvia still considered the presence of Russian troops on their soil a threat; ethnic Russians in both countries did not. "Threat Declines Among Latvians But Ethnic Differences Persist," *USIA Opinion Research Memorandum* (October 1, 1993) and "Ethnic Estonians Continue to Fear Outside Attack," *USIA Opinion Research Memorandum* (October 4, 1993).

45. Fred Hiatt, "Russia Shifts Doctrine on Military Use," *Washington Post* (November 4, 1993), pp. A1, A33; Daniel Sneider, "Russia Drops No–First–Use Pledge on Its Nuclear Weapons," *Christian Science Monitor* (November 4, 1993), pp. 1, 20. One of the more interesting reactions came from Ukrainian President Kravchuk. It had earlier been rumored that the new Russian military doctrine would contain some language on protecting Russian abroad; with this apparently in mind, Kravchuk attacked the doctrine, claiming that Kiev could defend all its citizens, Russians or otherwise, before he had even had a chance to read the document. (Moscow Interfax, 1739 GMT, November 5, 1993). In mid–October 1993, Ukrainian Foreign Minister Zlenko called Kozyrev's position on peace–keeping and the 'near aborad' "unacceptable to Ukraine." (Kiev) *Unian* (October 15, 1993).

46. Moscow Interfax, 1143 GMT, October 14, 1993.

47. The Byrd Agreement to the 1993 U.S. aid bill for Russia and the CIS demanded that funds not be distributed to Russia unless Russian troops were out of the Baltics by October 6, 1993, negotiations were underway, or the U.S. President certified significant progress toward this goal had been made.

48. John Lough, "The Place of the 'New Abroad' in Russian Foreign Policy," *RFE/RL Research Report* (Vol. 2, No. 11: March 12, 1993), pp. 22–29; *RFE/RL Daily Report* (#211: November 3, 1993), p. 2; *RFE/RL Daily Report* (#212: November 4, 1993), p. 3; *RFE/RL Daily Report* (#213: November 5, 1993), p. 2; *Izvestiya* (October 9, 1993), p. 1; "Russian Troops Kill Anti–Shevardnadze Rebels," *Washington Times* (November 2, 1993), p. 8.

49. Hugh Seton-Watson, *The Russian Empire, 1801–1917* (London: Oxford University Press, 1967), pp. 447–459.

# 3

## Russo–Ukrainian Relations:
## The Containment Legacy

*G. Paul Holman, Jr.*

### Introduction

The relationship between Russia and Ukraine resembles a fairy tale about two quarrelsome brothers, whose abusive and domineering father has just died. No last will and testament can be found. The brothers disagree sharply about how to divide their father's many assets as well as how to pay off his gambling debts. The younger one seizes this opportunity to declare his adulthood and independence, while the older refuses to admit that his brother has really come of age. Just when it seems that fratricide is imminent, an old *babushka* knocks at their door. She warns them that an ancient curse lies upon their legacy. If they cooperate and divide it peacefully, both can live in wealth and comfort. But if they quarrel and fight over their patrimony, both will end up far sadder than they were.

In reality, Russians and Ukrainians have less historical reason for animosity toward each other than do Serbs and Croats or Armenians and Azeris. They resemble each other so closely that the Ukrainians' very right to nationhood, let alone sovereignty, has often been challenged. As Richard Pipes remarks,

> Throughout its existence, the Ukrainian movement had to develop in an atmosphere of skepticism in which not only the validity of its demands but the very existence of the nationality it claimed to represent was seriously questioned by persons unconnected with the movement. This accounts, at least in part, for the great vehemence with which Ukrainian nationalists tended to assert their claims.[1]

Even so, many rivalries now fuel their nationalist fires. Among the causes of current or potential disagreement are their borders, languages, religions, minorities, and industries, as well combat ships and aircraft. They are the two giants of the post–communist countries, and the presence of over 1,600 nuclear weapons on Ukrainian soil makes their nationalist rivalry uniquely dangerous for global peace and stability. Yet there is a paradox here: this contaminated legacy from the old Soviet Union may have a positive impact on thoughtful people in both countries—above all, on the professional military officers who once served side by side.

From the perspective of American national security decision making, the sudden end of the Cold War has destabilized a large and populous region of the globe. Political scientists have no clear model of post–communist society, while economists have little experience with helping countries survive this unprecedented transition.[2]

The result is a host of thorny questions about the Western response to the collapse of communism. What kind and level of humanitarian aid is appropriate? How can we foster investment, trade, and progress toward the market system, under conditions of endemic corruption and political uncertainty? What are the best ways to foster democracy and pro–Western foreign policies? How can we assure the implementation of such breakthroughs in arms control and disarmament as the Strategic Arms Reduction Talks (START), the Non–Proliferation Treaty (NPT), the Conference on Security and Cooperation in Europe (CSCE), and the treaty on Conventional Forces in Europe (CFE)?

Such questions deserve prompt and pragmatic answers, as a basis for Western policy toward the formerly communist countries. Yet even high levels of outside aid and investment may prove quite pointless if conflict erupts between Russia and Ukraine. Indeed, the United States and its allies may find it increasingly difficult to serve as objective, honest brokers between these two natural rivals. As a result, their nationalist perceptions and agendas deserve careful attention from Western planners, not simply to clarify current crises but also to chart the possible course of events in Eurasia over the coming decade.

The goal of this chapter is to clarify the Russo–Ukrainian relationship by examining its historical development. Western observers and many Russians, too, must understand that Ukrainian nationalism is deeply rooted, drawing its strength not simply from centuries of ethnic, religious, cultural, and linguistic development, but also from decades of human suffering in the Soviet period. The chapter then speculates about why the collapse of communism came as a surprise to virtually all observers and examines the major causes of post–Soviet acrimony. Finally, we explore the dispute over Ukraine's nuclear weapons, arguing that Russo–Ukrainian tensions directly threaten global order and international security.

## The Rise of Ukrainian Nationalism

### *Princes, Tsars, and Emperors*

The oldest irony of Slavic history is that Kiev was the cradle of civilization for both the Russians and the Ukrainians. The Russian chronicles declare that a kingdom was founded here in 882 A.D. which adopted the Christian faith in 988, thus making ancient Kiev the direct ancestor of modern Russia.[3] Helene Carrere-d'Encausse, a French historian, stresses the decisive importance of Russia's exposed geographical position:

> It cannot be emphasized too often that Russia was first and foremost an open space, without frontiers. The country was itself a frontier between an emerging Europe and Asia. From the start, the princes of Kiev had to defend every inch of their territory against the invaders who threatened on every side. The flowering of Kiev, under such circumstances is little short of miraculous.[4]

It prospered for several centuries but then fell victim to invaders from the east. For some two and one-half centuries, Russia was dominated by the Mongols. Kiev was sacked in 1240, and the territory of modern Ukraine did not regain its original importance until the post-Soviet period. When Russia finally emerged as a full player in world politics, the much younger city of Moscow had become its capital. Moreover, the new Russia had a set of cultural and strategic imperatives that differed sharply from those of its western neighbors:

> It was necessary to create a 'nation,' define its territory, decide on its frontier—in Europe or facing Europe?—and set up a state that could administer and defend such a vast area, the protection of which required that the frontier be constantly pushed back. Other countries knew the glories of the Renaissance; Russia struggled with the nascent nation. Russia was never in line with the rest of Europe: lagging back until 1917; rushing ahead in the following utopia.
>
> It is this tormented history that has made the Russians an unhappy people, constantly in search of consoling myths.[5]

By the fourteenth century (if not earlier), the Kievan Russians had begun to divide into three distinctly different ethnic and linguistic groups: the Great Russians, usually called simply Russians; the Belorussians, or White Russians; and the Ukrainians (meaning the people who lived near the *krai*, or frontier). Religion, culture, and politics often sharpened the differences among them. The Ukrainians (and to a lesser extent the Belorussians) experienced a high degree of Westernization, thanks to the proximity, the influence, and sometimes the direct rule of Catholic Poland and Lithuania. The Great Russians, however, were largely out of reach for such European powers and developed a special sense of global mission on behalf of Orthodox Christianity.

Ukraine and Russia Border

By the early 1500s, the princes of Moscow were claiming direct descent from the Byzantine and even the Roman emperors. Their defenders proclaimed the doctrine of Moscow the Third Rome: The first Rome had fallen because it had betrayed true Christianity; Constantinople, the Second Rome, suffered a similar fate for a similar reason; Moscow, the Third Rome and the capital of the only truly Christian sovereign, was to continue forever.[6]

One effect of this claim—perhaps its real motive—was to strengthen the rulers of Moscow in their own realm by preaching the divine origin of their secular power. Some Western authors have gone further, looking for consistency in Russian expansionism over the centuries and thus citing it repeatedly "as evidence of a secular Russian imperialism and aggression."[7] But to Ukrainians, such claims had immediate and practical importance. For good or for ill—for protecting Ukraine against western aggression or for subjugating it to a new despotism—the Muscovite tsars had declared their intention of "gathering the Russian land" and recovering the inheritance of the Kievan princes.[8]

By the sixteenth century, religion had also begun to divide the Ukrainians from the Russians. Under heavy pressure from Poland, the Council of Brest established the so-called Uniate Church in 1596. Although subordinate to Rome, rather than Moscow, this church was Eastern in ritual and Slavonic in language (as well as retaining such Eastern practices as allowing its priests to marry). The Orthodox community split bitterly over this action; most Orthodox bishops in the Polish state seem to have supported the union, while most of the laity rejected it. Anathemas thundered from both sides, with the Polish government and the Holy See forcibly suppressing the non-Uniate Orthodox believers as rebels and heretics.[9] Thus the Ukrainian people were simultaneously divided among themselves and separated still further from the Russians.

The final ingredient in shaping the Ukrainian national tradition was the phenomenon of the "Cossacks" (from the Turkish word for freebooter). These anarchic societies of frontiersmen were first mentioned by the Russian Chronicles in 1444 and rapidly acquired a formidable military reputation. Ethnically diverse, they included runaway serfs and adventurers as well as vagabonds and criminals. More politically assertive than mere explorers or settlers along the borders of a growing empire, they worked for centuries to rule themselves and conduct independent foreign relations. Even so, Moscow valued them highly for their role as self-motivated, often unpaid irregular forces in the long struggle against the Turks and other enemies. Many cossack hordes arose on the territory of modern Ukraine, where they sought political autonomy through a complex web of intrigue, war, and alliance. They usually supported their Russian neighbors, but on several key occasions they rebelled against Muscovite authority and even allied themselves with the Turks and the Poles.

> It was in the southern steppes that the free and unruly communities of the Cossacks came into being. To the Russian state as an organized political body, and to the bulk of its population—landlords, artisans, merchants, and farmers—the steppes remained for centuries a deadly menace. But to those who were driven to despair by domestic oppression, and to those adventurous souls who cherished the dream of a perhaps somewhat anarchistic freedom—a dream that has never been realized in the course of Russia's history—the steppes were a hope and a promise.[10]

The Cossacks were quite distinct by 1714, when a Russian decree stressed the importance of mixing Russians with Ukrainians and sending more Russian officials to assure government control over the region.[11] Although most were legendary for their loyalty to the Romanov dynasty, the Cossacks also contributed heavily to Ukrainian culture and folklore. Indeed, Richard Pipes declares that "with their ideal of unlimited external and internal freedom—[they]

developed a new socio–economic type of great importance for the future Ukrainian national consciousness."[12]

Finally suppressed by Catherine the Great, the Cossacks lost their *Sech* (or democratic assembly) on the Dnieper River in 1775, as well as most real autonomy for their Don and Ural "hosts." What was worse, Catherine also gave legal status to the hated system of serfdom in Ukraine, adding social injustice to the many Ukrainian grievances against the Russians. General Petro Grigorenko, perhaps the single most influential Ukrainian dissident of the Soviet period, has provided a powerful portrait of his people's division and oppression under the Russian Empire.

> The Austrians set out to Germanicize the Ukrainians and the Russians to Russify them. ... Mass terror campaigns were carried out against the Ukrainian population together with a cruel system of serf exploitation. ... During the centuries they spent in the Russian imperial state, the Ukrainians began to forget their national name and became accustomed to the name their colonizers had bestowed upon them—the Malorosi, or Little Russians; or the khokhkly, or 'Topknots.' ... And for the most part the Russian intelligentsia even came to believe that there was no such language as Ukrainian, that it was only a dialect of Russian.[13]

Grigorenko contends that the Ukrainians' "extremely low level of national self-consciousness" was one basic reason for their failure to secure their independence. The other reason was another Russian intervention in Ukrainian affairs.

## Marx and the Soviets

The founding fathers of Marxism did not hesitate to condemn Russian mistreatment of the Ukrainians, seeing their liberation as one of many ways to weaken Russia and thus to hasten the working people's revolution. Karl Marx referred to Russia as the "prison house of nations," while Friedrich Engels specifically rejected Russian claims to Ukrainian territory on the grounds that, "at least the Ukrainians did not really speak a Russian dialect but an entirely separate language."[14]

The creator of the Soviet state, Vladimir I. Lenin, claimed to follow in the footsteps of Marx and Engels. During his many years as a political dissident, he harshly condemned Moscow's suppression of the Ukrainians and other minorities and promised them the right of "national self-determination." Yet at the same time, Lenin also advocated complete assimilation of all peoples, after the revolution, and bitterly resisted any attempt to divide the workers' movement along ethnic lines. Indeed, he declared in 1905 that, "We shall always stand for a single provisional government of all-Russia, and a Russian one at that."[15]

In 1914, the outbreak of World War I forced Lenin to rethink his entire position on nationalism. Realizing that patriotism had proven stronger than socialism, destroying working class solidarity from one end of Europe to the other, he asserted that there were two kinds of national pride—one reactionary and the other revolutionary. In a memorable article entitled "On the National Pride of the Great Russians," Lenin cited a famous aphorism from Marx and Engels: "'No nation can be free if it oppresses other nations.'" Claiming that he was "very full of a sense of national pride," Lenin condemned the war because it aimed "to throttle" Poland, the Ukraine, and other democratic movements. He assured all the non-Russians that their "*socialist* interests" entirely coincided with the "interests of the Great Russians' national pride."[16] Thus Lenin attempted to fuse socialism with nationalism, in an amalgam that lasted for decades but ultimately proved too weak to hold the Soviet state together.

After the abdication of Emperor Nicholas II in the February Revolution of 1917, Lenin specifically endorsed the Ukrainian right of secession. Prophetically, he warned that force could not check Ukrainian aspirations for freedom but would only embitter them. Even so, he did not abandon his ultimate goal of unifying the Ukrainians and the Russians under one revolutionary government. "Only unqualified recognition of this right [to secede] makes it possible to advocate a free union of the Ukrainians and the Great Russians, a *voluntary* association of the two peoples in one state. ... We do not favor the existence of small states."[17]

After seizing full power just a few months later in his own October Revolution, Lenin violated the letter but fulfilled the spirit of his promises. The Ukrainian Rada (or central council) proclaimed a republic after the overthrow of the democratic Provisional Government, which Lenin briefly recognized. Its representatives even took part in the first peace talks with the Germans, without Russian challenge, but within weeks everything had changed. Lenin deposed the Rada with his Red Army in February of 1918 and claimed the right to negotiate for Ukraine, only to see the Rada restored by the advancing German Army. A bewildering array of foreign puppets and legitimate politicians then struggled to dominate Ukraine over the three-year course of the Russian Civil War. Germans, Poles, White Russian forces, and even anarchists presented rival agendas, endlessly dividing the Ukrainian people and precluding a unified fight for independence. Soviet authority was restored by the autumn of 1919, and Ukrainian nationalism was extinguished until the next German invasion.

The true extent of Ukrainian suffering under Lenin and Stalin is beyond reckoning. Two to four million died in the great famine of 1932–1933 alone, not just because of disastrous agrarian policies but also because of Stalin's determination to stamp out the hardy peasants (*kulaks*) who survived in Ukraine.[18] Hosts of others died in Stalin's many purges of the 1930's, often for the alleged crime of being Ukrainian nationalists. Nikita S. Khrushchev minced no words in May 1938, when he was building a new Ukrainian party apparatus: "I pledge myself to spare no effort in seizing and annihilating all agents of fascism, Trotskyites, Bukharinites, and all those despicable bourgeois nationalists on Ukrainian soil."[19]

Little wonder, then, that Ukrainian nationalists took up arms again in 1941 when the Germans returned. Predictably, however, the Ukrainians divided once more among themselves. Many welcomed the Nazis in the hope of regaining Ukrainian independence.[20] Some even joined German military units, but still others fought loyally in the Red Army or behind German lines as pro–Soviet partisans.

Stalin's victory over Germany again suppressed Ukrainian aspirations for independence, although the Communists attempted to accentuate the positive. As Nikita Khrushchev later remarked, "Our borders had been pushed west, and history's injustice to the Ukrainian people was being set right. Never before had the Ukrainian people been united in a single Ukrainian state. Only now, in the Soviet era, was this dream at last coming true."[21] However, the war did not end for Ukraine (nor for Lithuania) in 1945. Stepan Bandera's Ukrainian Nationalist Movement continued to conduct guerrilla operations against the Soviets until at least the late 1940s.[22]

Although defeated militarily and suffering again from intense division within their own ranks, Ukrainian resentment of Russian authority continued to smolder. Even within the Communist Party of the Soviet Union (CPSU), the Ukrainian apparatus was a cohesive and powerful bloc which functioned almost as a personal fiefdom. Khrushchev, like several later Soviet leaders, used it as the regional base of his fight for national power in Moscow.[23] This may be why he decided in 1954 to detach the Crimea from Russia and give it to Ukraine, as a sort of political payoff.[24] Two years later, Khrushchev informed the 20th CPSU Congress that the Ukrainians might have suffered much worse than they did under Stalin. Guardedly admitting at least some of Stalin's crimes in his famous "Secret Speech," he stressed that only the huge size of the Ukrainian population had prevented their deportation *en masse*: "The Ukrainians avoided meeting this fate because there were too many of them, and there was no place to which to deport them."[25]

Throughout the decades that Khrushchev and Leonid I. Brezhnev ruled, Ukrainian nationalism was at its lowest ebb. The Soviet press printed periodic attacks on Ukrainian emigre organizations, but the major focus of Ukrainian sentiment seemed to be within the safe and politically acceptable channels of the CPSU. Vladimir Shcherbitsky, as party boss for Ukraine, was renowned for ruling a gray, conformist republic as something approaching a communist fiefdom.

Under the shadowy cover of the *samizdat'* (self–publishing) movement, however, an entirely different form of Ukrainian nationalism was still alive (although its members were often safer in Moscow and Leningrad than in Kiev).

Poets, novelists, historians, investigative journalists, and other cultural figures risked their freedom and sometimes their lives to present uncensored views of Soviet reality.[26] Perhaps the most important in political terms was General Major Petro Grigorenko. Broken in rank and then institutionalized, he was the only Soviet general ever exiled for his political views. Not only did he take a prominent part in the Ukrainian human rights movement, he also brought international attention to the plight of the Crimean Tatars.[27]

The official CPSU position, however, was that the multi-national Soviet population lived in peace and harmony, compared to the ethnic strife experienced in capitalist countries. The Ukrainians and all the others supposedly did not resent the special Russian role as their "elder brothers." Thanks to ever increasing levels of economic development, social mobility, and education, the spread of the Russian language was inexorably unifying all nationalities. Yuri Andropov spoke for the entire gerontocracy that ruled the Soviet Union in the early 1980s, seeing no serious threat to its survival from the Ukrainians or other nationalists:

> The peoples of our country offer special words of gratitude to the Russian people. Without their unselfish, brotherly help, present-day achievements in any of the republics would have been impossible to attain. The one factor of exceptional importance in the economic, political and cultural life of our country, in the rapprochement of all its nations and nationalities, in their introduction to the wealth of world civilization, has been the Russian language which has entered into the lives of millions of people of all nationalities in a natural way.[28]

## American Misperceptions of Communism
## and Nationalism

Why did virtually no one, on either side of the Iron Curtain, predict the triumph of nationalism over communism? It seems clear in retrospect that the politicians were usually befuddled, the scholars were mostly wrong, and the intelligence agencies were hilariously inaccurate in their long range predictions about the future of the Soviet Union and its communist neighbors.

One possible explanation for such erroneous predictions is that Western observers fundamentally misperceived the relationship between communism and nationalism. Only one theoretical model—totalitarianism—dominated Western assessments of the communist countries.[29] It sank into disrepute—perhaps unjustly—during the Vietnam War, when many Western scholars, journalists, and politicians blamed the totalitarian model for demonizing communism and thus leading the United States into a needless conflict. New concepts proliferated, drawing heavily on anthropological, economic, and sociological models reflecting Western experience, but none shaped the minds of an entire generation of scholars, as totalitarianism once did.

By the late 1980's, two highly politicized factions had emerged. Believers in totalitarianism still dominated the Department of Defense—and most especially the Defense Intelligence Agency—where they tended to portray communism as socially stagnant, illegitimate, and inherently hostile toward the West. Doubters dominated Academia, and some components of the Central Intelligence Agency. In general, these post-totalitarian models were less complimentary to the West and more prone to view the communist systems as pluralist, legitimate, and at least potentially benign.[30]

These two rival views of communist reality differed sharply about many things, yet they agreed upon at least one: both saw ethnic nationalism as a negligible factor in the communist future.[31] Conservatives usually argued that Stalin had drowned ethnic nationalists in blood and that his heirs ruled a politically passive population. Liberals leaned to the view that economic development, modernization, linguistic tolerance, upward mobility, and social services had created new loyalties transcending ethnic nationalism. Among the only major exceptions—who resolutely contended that nationalism still survived and might ultimately threaten communist control—were scholars of East European origin.[32]

Both views could be found in national security circles, and they combined to shape Secretary of Defense Dick Cheney's *Soviet Military Power: Prospects for Change 1989*. At least by Department of Defense standards, it was an extraordinarily balanced document. Unlike some previous editions of this assessment, it discussed Western as well as Soviet military capabilities and took quite seriously the reforms of then General Secretary Mikhail Gorbachev. The tone was guardedly optimistic:

> It is, therefore, clear that despite the dramatic changes occurring in the Soviet Union and the Soviet leadership's declaration of benign *intentions* toward the Western democracies, Soviet military *capabilities* continue to constitute a major threat to our security. We should encourage Moscow to continue pursuing those policies that promote pluralism at home and international stability abroad.[33]

Although admitting that much had changed in the USSR, Cheney concluded with the traditional thinking of the national security community.

> Our experience in this century has shown again and again that, especially with *totalitarian states*, seemingly friendly relations can change very quickly at the decision of a few powerful individuals. Military capabilities, by comparison, change much more slowly. Until we are able to see clearly what new security environment we are entering, maintaining our military strength and political resolve seem a small price to pay to preserve our security and freedoms.[34]

Cheney's assumption that "a few powerful individuals" could rapidly reverse the course of "totalitarian states" reflected a conservative view, but most of those who rejected the totalitarian model had reached the same conclusion. Perhaps the best known holder of the anti–totalitarian view was Jerry Hough. In early 1991 he engaged in a major debate with the intelligence community, which had warned that the Soviet Union was on the verge of major upheaval. Hough did not agree:

> Now when it is 99.5 percent certain that the radicals in both Russia and the republics are in major decline and that there will be no revolution or disintegration in the next two–three years at a minimum, the intelligence community seems to have become even more united in the view that this is 1917, that the situation in the Soviet Union is deteriorating further instead of stabilizing, and that reform is over and revolution is the only hope. ... [T]hat is a profound misreading of the situation.[35]

Neither believers in totalitarianism nor anti–totalitarians foresaw that nationalist movements would soon tear apart the Soviet Union itself. Even those observers who saw the power of separatist nationalism warned against the greater threat of a Russian backlash. This is, of course, precisely the opposite of what actually happened over the next two years, as the Soviet Union crumbled and Ukraine was reborn.

## Nationalism After Communism

### *The Legacy of Chernobyl*

The birthplace of modern Ukrainian nationalism was neither in Kyyiv (the preferred post–Soviet spelling) nor Moscow, but rather Chernobyl. And what exploded on April 26, 1986 was not just an atomic reactor, but rather the entire Soviet mentality of censorship, propaganda, and the conspiracy of silence about virtually all unpleasant events.[36] Mikhail S. Gorbachev had just begun his second year in power when the disaster occurred. In spite of all his rhetoric about *perestroika* (reconstruction) and *glasnost* (openness), his government denied for four days that anything untoward had happened. When Gorbachev himself finally discussed the event in public, he minimized the damage and accused Western journalists of exaggerating its importance.[37]

The reality of Chernobyl soon made Gorbachev seem callous and mendacious to the tens of millions of Ukrainians and Belorussians who fretted in its shadow. A new generation of investigative journalists castigated bureaucrats for "The Big Lie," ironically revelling in his relaxation of censorship at the same time as destroying Ukrainian respect for his honesty. In this, as in many other incidents involving Armenians, Azerbaijanis, Balts, and Central Asians, Gorbachev demonstrated his utter inability to comprehend the non–Russians. As he remarked in 1990, "one has to admit that we underestimated the forces of nationalism and separatism that were hidden deep within our system...creating a socially explosive mixture."[38]

Since the collapse of Soviet power, there have been endless claims that the former Soviet Union suffers from the world's worst case of environmental destruction by radiation.[39]  Indeed, considering the half-lives of the isotopes involved, they may be the most durable legacy of the communist system.  They guarantee a dreary agenda of nasty disputes between Russia and Ukraine, as the two impoverished countries confront the costly imperative of environmental cleanup.  Yet Chernobyl also caused social and political changes which have helped to revolutionize them both.  In modern Ukraine, as well as Russia, there is now an assertive environmental movement.  It testifies loudly and publicly to the need for ending governmental secrecy, reducing the power of the military, and establishing the rule of law.[40]  Although far from pacifistic, many members of this movement lean toward interdependence and understanding between their two countries, rather than chauvinist extremism.

## Elite Behavior

Gorbachev destroyed the communist system by allowing his *glasnost* to expose its weaknesses long before his *perestroika* could revive its economy.  Yet he went quietly after losing the political battle.  He did not whip up the forces of Russian nationalism to keep himself in power—unlike Lenin and Stalin before him—although many communists and nationalists would have rallied to his side if he had used their slogans.  Whatever his faults and his mistakes, Gorbachev deserves primary credit for allowing the Soviet empire to collapse peacefully rather than violently, as in Yugoslavia.  Russia did not behave like Serbia, thanks to Gorbachev, and his moderation has set a vital precedent for later Russian leaders.

Boris Yeltsin deserves similar and perhaps greater credit.  He has exhibited more trust in the Russian people than any of their previous modern leaders and relied far less on coercion.[41]  He periodically invokes Russian nationalism to justify his policies, but without the xenophobic themes of his major rivals, Ruslan Khasbulatov (the former parliamentary leader) and Aleksandr Rutskoi (the former vice president).  Yeltsin's original group of young intellectual advisers were remarkably pro–Western in their views, but he has steadily moved away from them.  Many public figures now urge him to rely more pointedly on patriotic themes, not simply to arouse the  masses but also to build political alliances, as the economy continues to collapse.  The future course of Russo–Ukrainian relations will rest heavily on his shoulders.

President Leonid Kravchuk of Ukraine is a far more difficult figure to assess.  He did not come to power through any kind of anti–communist revolution, for he was the Communist Party Chairman of Ukraine when the August 1991 coup took place in Moscow. Artfully ambiguous about his politics as Gorbachev fell, Yeltsin staked his post-communist future on nationalism by declaring his independence from Moscow. Vyacheslav Chornovil, a former leader of the Ukrainian dissidents, noted the irony of the Ukrainian situation in early 1992: If you look at a map of Ukraine to see how democratic it is, then three-quarters of the territory should be painted red or pink because, even today, it is under control of our sovereign Ukrainian communists.[42]

Not only has Kravchuk treated his domestic enemies with scant regard for the rule of law, he has often indulged in stridently anti-Russian tirades. He and his subordinates are fond of identifying Yeltsin's Russia with the old Soviet empire, accusing Moscow of still failing to treat Ukraine as an independent, sovereign state.[43]

Perhaps even worse than Kravchuk's insults against Russia have been his many errors in reforming the Ukrainian economy. As a British analyst observed,

> Ukraine's economy is collapsing because nationalists secured their country's independence by co-opting, not overthrowing, the local communist elite. Many of the same party bureaucrats who earned Soviet Ukraine a reputation as the most zealously obedient of all the Soviet Union's republics are still in power today, struggling to relearn the Ukrainian vocabulary they once deliberately forgot.[44]

## Nuclear Dilemmas

Kravchuk's greatest offense, in the eyes of both Russian and U.S. observers, has been to drag his heels on making Ukraine a non-nuclear state. No other issue in Russo-Ukrainian relations affects Ukraine's future in the post-Soviet world quite so powerfully as the more than 1,600 long-range weapons still on Ukrainian soil. Russia has declared that it will not put into force the START-1 and START-2 treaties until Ukraine ratifies START-1 and enters the 1968 Non-Proliferation Treaty as a non-nuclear state. The United States, during the Bush administration, objected to Ukrainian retention of the nuclear weapons so vigorously as to produce precisely the wrong result. Kravchuk and his colleagues clearly decided that the weapons were central to Ukrainian sovereignty, giving Kyyiv a means of diplomatic leverage that it would not otherwise possess.[45]

Shortly after President Clinton's inauguration, Secretary of State Warren Christopher repeated the Bush administration's view that Ukrainian failure to move ahead on the nuclear issue would adversely affect the future of the relationship."[46] Ukrainian Foreign Minister Anatoli Zienko replied on March 24, 1993, that the United States ought not to press Ukraine at the present time. He did reaffirm his government's commitment to its 1992 pledge to rid itself of nuclear weapons, ratify START-1, and sign the 1968 Non-Proliferation Treaty.

For now, however, he claimed there was opposition in Kyyiv's parliament to giving up the nuclear weapons on its soil at a time of great uncertainty in Russia. Yeltsin's unending political instability had allegedly "dimmed political support in Ukraine for eliminating nuclear weapons left on its soil by the former Soviet Union."[47]

Zienko also identified three other unresolved problems which would affect the pace of Ukrainian disarmament. His government was unhappy with international responses to the security guarantees which it had requested from the declared nuclear weapon states (United States, Russia, Britain, France, and China). Moreover, it needed financial assistance for dismantling and destroying weapons on Ukrainian soil, as well as cleaning up the environment. The United States had offered $175 million, but Zienko claimed the true cost would be more like $3 billion. Zienko also asserted that Ukraine should be reimbursed for the sale of highly enriched uranium from warheads on Ukrainian soil.[48]

Western analysts have disagreed sharply about Kravchuk's intentions. Some accused him of simple blackmail aimed at massive transfusions of economic aid, while others worried that he really meant to keep the weapons. A few, rather more cynical authorities have expressed some sympathy for the Ukrainian strategic situation, warning that the country's survival may impose a difficult choice on the West: either tolerate Ukrainian possession of nuclear weapons or give it the strong security guarantees which Kravchuk has requested.[49]

## The Black Sea Fleet

Dividing the ex–Soviet Navy will be another difficult challenge for Russia and Ukraine. The Black Sea Fleet was smaller than the Northern and Pacific Fleets, but still larger than any Western Navy other than the U.S. Navy. Its last commander lost his job for supporting the disastrous coup d'etat of August 1991, but political tensions since then have been resolved with surprisingly little violence.

There has been a long "war of the flags," as different ships supported one country or the other, culminating in occasional mutinies. The most photogenic was surely the maiden voyage of the *Admiral Kuznetsov*. Designed to be the largest aircraft carrier in the Soviet Navy, it had been built in Ukraine's Mykolaiv yard (formerly Nikolayev), with commissioning trials in early 1992. Instead, however, it sailed straight for Russia's Northern Fleet. Muscovites cheered, while Kyyivans protested this so-called hijacking from their infant Ukrainian Navy.

The Ukrainians cited both geography and nationality in laying their claim to some fraction of the Black Sea Fleet. Although it had small bases in Moldova and Georgia, as well as two large ones in Russia (Novorossiisk and Tuapse), the fleet was based primarily in Ukraine (Balaklava, Fedosiya, Izmail, Kerch,

Ochakov, Odessa, Oktyabirskoye, Saki, and Sevastopol). The Ukrainians also stressed its ethnic composition: 19% of the officers and 30% of the enlisted were ethnic Ukrainians.

The industrial base of the ex–Soviet Navy has also exacerbated nationalist tensions. Three of the six yards which once produced capital ships for the Soviet Navy are located in Ukraine. Most important is Mykolaiv—the only one in the former Soviet Union capable of producing what the Soviets called "aviation capable cruisers" and the West called aircraft carriers.

Kravchuk and Yeltsin met five times in 1992–1993 to resolve their many differences, with nuclear and naval matters figuring most prominently. They initially agreed to divide the Black Sea Fleet in half by 1995, but its predominantly Russian officer corps vigorously opposed such a solution. Thus the two presidents tried again in September of 1993, reaching a novel compromise: Russia would buy Ukraine's share of the fleet and dismantle the nuclear weapons on Ukrainian soil, in exchange for the uranium extracted from their warheads. Yeltsin declared that, "Russian payment for its share of the fleet will be counted against Ukrainian debts to Russia. If the balance is in Ukraine's favor, then Russia will pay."[50]

Members of the fractious and often demagogic Ukrainian Parliament promptly condemned this agreement, which may fail the test of democratic process like its predecessor. Even so, it testifies to the good sense of both presidents. Perhaps more importantly, it may also indicate the success of the Clinton administration in first reassuring the Ukrainians of Western support and then altering their position on the crucial nuclear dispute.

## Regional Conflicts

Ethnic rivalries throughout the CIS have weakened all the post–Soviet regimes, exacerbating social instability and frustrating hopes for economic revival. Most observers believe that such tensions help no one, although a few contend that Moscow benefits from these troubles and may be trying to manipulate them. Indeed, Mark Galeotti finds some evidence to argue that "Moscow has a forward policy in the old empire."[51]

The Crimea could roil Russo–Ukrainian waters for many years to come. It belongs to Ukraine because of Khrushchev's bizarre behavior in 1954, although the majority of its citizens are Russian. It is also the major port of the Black Sea Fleet, serving as home for a large and highly politicized body of Russian officers. The Ukrainians have already granted it special status within their country, promising full respect for the civil rights of all citizens. Some Russian extremists would prefer to detach it from Ukrainian control, favoring a plebiscite which would only exacerbate current tensions and weaken the presidents of both countries. The situation is further complicated by the determination of the original residents—the Crimean Tatars—to return home, which they have done in growing numbers.

Another potentially troubling conflict lies on Ukraine's western border, in the neighboring ex-republic of Moldova. Ethnic Russians and Ukrainians constitute a majority along the left bank of the Dniester River and have declared the independence of their break-away Dniester Republic. General Aleksandr Lebed, the commander of Russia's 14th Army in Moldova, has supported the secessionists and appealed for help from Moscow. Sporadic violence has convinced the United Nations to provide international observers, and the region's future is in doubt.

Some Russian parliamentarians have advocated incorporating the Dniester Republic into the Russian Federation, even at the risk of annoying Ukraine. The area was once part of Ukraine, but by no stretch of the imagination could it be called Russian. Kravchuk has not yet tried to stir up trouble for Russia in this region, and he has made some efforts to prevent outside weapons from entering it. He has suggested that the Dniester Republic should become an autonomous republic within Moldova, but it is unclear to what extent Kravchuk and Yeltsin may be following a coordinated policy toward this trouble spot.[52]

The crises in both Crimea and Moldova reflect a broader and more intractable problem: the presence of some 25 million Russians outside Russia's present borders. At least 11 million Russian-speakers reside in modern Ukraine, and they are concentrated in especially large numbers along its border with Russia. Many are worried about the risk of revenge for the centuries of Tsarist and Communist exploitation, although there have been remarkably few Ukrainian threats as yet.

Many experts in both Ukraine and the West have found evidence of aggressive intentions in Russia's 1992 draft military program.[53] More reactionary than Gorbachev's 1990 version, it expresses concern about the possible mistreatment of ethnic Russians—and even those who sympathize with them—in other states. Whether or not it actually reflects the serious plans of responsible military officials, the 1992 draft military program does constitute a warning to Mother Russia's neighbors not to mistreat her scattered children.

There is no doubt that Russian military personnel have been deeply involved in the bewildering array of armed upheavals in Moldova, Georgia, and Tadzhikistan—as well as Moldova and perhaps Crimea—but Yeltsin and his Foreign Minister Kozyrev are not necessarily to blame. Indeed, Moscow's ability to control the Russian Armed Forces is very much open to question. Indiscipline, mercenary behavior, corruption, and covert agendas of many kinds may be increasingly troublesome for both Russia and Ukraine.

## The Future of Russo–Ukrainian Relations

The rise of an independent Ukraine from the wreckage of the Soviet Union will have a major but contradictory impact on international relations. So long as the new state survives, it will tend to stabilize Eurasia—and perhaps the entire world—in at least two ways: weakening Russia by the denial of economic and military assets it once controlled and blocking potential Russian expansionism through the creation of a buffer state. However, Ukrainian independence may also exacerbate regional tensions in eastern and central Europe by altering the local balance of power, reviving territorial disputes, delaying economic recovery, intensifying ethnic hostilities, and inciting local arms races.

President Kravchuk, like President Yeltsin, realizes that both countries would profit from cooperation. Each needs trade with the other, as they attempt to cut inflation, reduce unemployment, adopt market-oriented reforms, and reverse their economic declines. Likewise in ethnic politics, neither Kravchuk nor Yeltsin would profit from exacerbating tensions between Russians and Ukrainians. On the contrary, both leaders would prefer to minimize social unrest as they confront the same domestic agendas: arranging a stable separation of power between the executive and legislative branches of government, as well as between their respective capitals and their rambunctious outlying regions. Both must contend with fractious and sometimes chauvinist parliamentarians, who ill understand democracy and often frustrate attempts at moderation or tolerance.

However, Russo-Ukrainian relations seem likely to deteriorate over the long term as both countries experience rising unemployment, inflation, crime, corruption, and environmental destruction. To satisfy public opinion (as well as the private agendas of the ex-communist elites still deeply rooted in the infrastructures of the two countries), both states will periodically engage in economic protectionism, even at the cost of their economic growth and stability. Ukraine would suffer more than Russia in the event of a trade war, and moderate reforms will not solve the country's economic woes. Falling standards of living are likely to exacerbate ethnic hostility, undercutting reformist leaders in both countries and favoring the rise of political extremists.

## The Conventional Military Context

Both Russia and Ukraine are presently reducing their military budgets, cutting manpower, slashing perquisites, training less intensively, and thus experiencing a steady decline in combat readiness. Ethnic unrest will likely impose a growing burden on the political reliability of military and security forces in both countries (especially if Moscow continues to involve its troops in protracted wars beyond current Russian borders).

The Ukrainian National Guard (some 15,000 troops directly subordinate to Kravchuk) consists primarily of ethnic Ukrainians and is reported to be reliable. The military officer corps, however, does not enjoy Kravchuk's complete confidence. About half of the officers (and a large majority of the generals) are ethnic Russians. Their loyalty to Kyyiv would be questionable in the event of domestic upheaval, rioting, or a serious conflict between Russia and Ukraine.

Ukraine and Russia are both restructuring their ground forces as they adjust to the military implications of the Soviet collapse. Kyyiv must consider potential invasion corridors from the north through Belarus and from the east. An amphibious attack from the south is another possibility, aimed at seizing Crimea in the event that Moscow and Kyyiv are unable to settle the future of the disputed peninsula by peaceful means.

The Ukrainian leadership can anticipate lower levels of trouble from most of its neighbors. The region abounds in territorial disputes and ethnic rivalries, which will complicate national security planning for each country. In the event of prolonged rivalry between Russia and Ukraine, the other states of eastern and central Europe would face a difficult choice. Some might try to bolster Ukraine as a useful buffer against Russian expansionism, while others might join with Russia in an attempt to take disputed territories away from Ukraine. In the worst case, such a scenario could culminate in the complete dismemberment of Ukraine (much as Poland was dismembered among Russia, Prussia, and Austria in the 18th century).

## Conclusions

There is a real possibility that Ukraine may not survive all these economic, political, and military threats. In the absence of some ambitious new system of collective security for the region, Ukrainians will divide sharply over the wisdom of surrendering the nuclear weapons currently on their soil.

Some Ukrainians—including both regular officers and parliamentarians— aspire seriously and openly to making Ukraine a nuclear state. A number of Americans have tried without success to convince these officials that their nuclear weapons would have no military utility and thus no deterrent value. Such Ukrainians respond by citing various models for their putative nuclear strategy. They know that both France and China overcame strong international opposition to their nuclear programs, and both of them were continental powers who sought to deter Russian attack by threatening nuclear retaliation against conventional aggression.

Russian officials privately expressed their belief in mid–1993 that Kyyiv had the technical ability to take control of some nuclear weapons by the end of the year and was attempting to do so. Ukrainians responded with similarly dour predictions of their own, fearing secret or open attempts to remove the weapons from Kyyiv's control.  Such nuclear nightmares could exacerbate the other tensions between Russia and Ukraine and create fertile soil for future crises.

If democracy survives in Ukraine, the large and vocal anti-nuclear movement may make an increasingly effective case for giving up the nuclear weapons.  To the extent that Ukrainian leaders worry less about the many threats to their national existence, they are more likely to ratify START and eventually to join the NPT as a non-nuclear state.  The chances for this most desirable outcome would be enhanced by high levels of financial assistance from the West (both governmental and private), firm guarantees of Ukrainian security, and the continuation of democracy in Russia.

But if democracy collapses in Ukraine, as it well may, Kyyiv could behave quite unpredictably, either for good or for ill.  Ruling as a dictator, Kravchuk might well order the removal of nuclear weapons from Ukrainian territory, especially if he felt secure in Western and Russian assurances of Ukraine's continued sovereignty.  However, a dictatorship after Kravchuk—perhaps comprised of extreme nationalists—might be unwilling to trust either Russia or the West.

In the extreme event that they perceive an imminent threat to their national existence, Ukrainians could decide to defy the West as well as Russia and to find allies wherever they can.  India, Saudi Arabia, and moderate Arab states would be early candidates for economic as well as political ties.  China, Iran, Iraq, Libya, North Korea, and other "rogue states" would also be attracted by the lure of Kyyiv's strategic weaponry and its technological expertise.  Such relationships could be quite harmful to global stability and might cause further proliferation of weapons of mass destruction.  The chances of this most undesirable outcome would be maximized by low levels of financial assistance from the outside world, flimsy guarantees of Ukrainian security, and the collapse of democracy in Russia.

Ukraine has been dismembered several times in its long history, and some Ukrainian politicians view nuclear weapons as their best assurance of survival. Diplomatic pressure and threats of economic retaliation are unlikely to resolve the nuclear dispute, especially if Kyyiv concludes that it has been abandoned by the West.  The country confronts a number of other contentious issues—most notably the disputes over Crimea and the Black Sea Fleet—which could incite ethnic violence and terminate its experiment with democracy.  In the face of all these threats, Ukraine's survival is by no means certain.

The ultimate challenge to Ukrainian sovereignty, however, may be neither military, nor political, nor economic.  Rather, it seems likely to be cultural, spiritual, and psychological.  Precisely how strong is Ukrainian nationalism? Are the Ukrainians prepared to suffer the economic upheaval that their president has thus far deferred?  Does their contaminated legacy truly divide them from the Russians, or will they decide that national sovereignty is not worth the cost?

Aleksandr Solzhenitsyn—perhaps the greatest Russian dissident of the Soviet era—advocates reunion between the Russians, Ukrainians, and Belorussians. He rejects the use of force, speaking to Ukrainians *"as one of their own"* because he is half Ukrainian by birth. Even the most tenacious Ukrainian nationalists may have difficulty rejecting his plea for unity between these two great and long–suffering peoples:

> To separate off the Ukraine today would mean to cut across the lives of millions of individuals and families; the two populations are thoroughly intermingled; there are entire regions where Russians predominate. ... There is not even a hint of intolerance between Russians and Ukrainians on the level of the ordinary people.
>
> Brothers! We have no need of this cruel partition. The very idea comes from the darkening of minds brought on by the communist years. Together we have borne the suffering of the Soviet period, together we have tumbled into this pit, and together, too, we shall find our way out.[54]

## Notes

1. Richard Pipes, *The Formation of the Soviet Union. Communism and Nationalism, 1917–1923*, rev. ed. (New York: Atheneum, 1968), pp. 9–10.

2. The appropriate scholarly materials for charting such progress have only begun to appear. For example, see *Post–Soviet Affairs* (formerly *Soviet Economy*), which is published in association with The Joint Committee on Soviet Studies of the American Council of Learned Societies and the Social Science Research Council. A fine collection of essays appears in Shafiqul Islam and Michael Mandelbaum, eds., *Making Markets: Economic Transformation in Eastern Europe and the Post–Soviet States* (New York: Council on Foreign Relations Press, 1993).

3. See, for example, the Soviet regime's official treatment of the millennium of Russian Christianity: "Kievan Rus entered the circle of European Christian states in 988—a crucial event in history. 'Russian cultural history began when Russia embraced Christianity. This is also true of Ukrainian and Belorussian cultural history,' says Academician Dmitri Likhachev." "1,000 Years of Russia's Christianity," *Soviet Life*, July 1988, No. 6 (382), p. 42.

4. Helene Carrere d'Encausse, *The Russian Syndrome: One Thousand Years of Political Murder*, trans. Catherine Higgitt (New York: Holmes & Meier, 1992), p. 399.

5. Ibid., pp. 400–401.

6. Michael T. Florinsky, *Russia: A History and an Interpretation*, 2 vols., 2nd ed., (New York: Macmillan, 1953), I, 165.

7. Nicholas V. Riasanovsky, *A History of Russia*, 2nd ed. (New York: Oxford University Press, 1969), p. 138.

8. Ibid., pp. 69 and 138.

9. Florinsky, I, pp. 258–259.

10. Florinsky, I, p. 4.

11. Interestingly, this same decree defended its policy by citing English success in dominating the Scots, Welsh, and Irish. Riasanovsky, p. 257.

12. Pipes, *The Formation of the Soviet Union*, p. 9.

13. Petro Grigorenko, *Memoirs,* trans. Thomas P. Whitney (New York: W.W. Norton and Co., 1982), pp. 344–345.

14. For a useful anthology of Marxian thoughts about Russia, see Paul W. Blackstock and Bert F. Hoselitz, eds., *Karl Marx and Friedrich Engels, The Russian Menace to Europe* (Glencoe, IL: The Free Press, 1952), especially pp. 29–30.

15. V.I. Lenin [Vladimir I. Ulianov], "Speech on the Amendments to the Resolution on the Provisional Revolutionary Government," *Collected Works*, translation of Russian 4th edition, 45 vols. (Moscow: Foreign Languages Publishing House and Progress Publishers, 1963–1970), VIII, 399. Richard Pipes suggests that Lenin's pre–revolutionary propaganda assumed that a capitalist government would unite the nationalities into an indissoluble state. Thus he promised self–determination to the non–Russians precisely because he never expected to implement such a program. "Solving the Nationality Problem," *Problems of Communism*, XVI, No. 5, (September–October, 1967), 127.

16. Lenin, "On the National Pride of the Great Russians," *Works*, XXI, 104–106.

17. Lenin, "The Ukraine and the Defeat of the Ruling Parties of Russia," *Works*, XXV, 101 and 84–90. When militarily pressed during the Civil War, Lenin explicitly appealed to Great Russian love of their homeland: "Until the proletariat of Germany rises and triumphs, it is the sacred duty of the workers and peasants of Russia devotedly to defend the Republic of Soviets... *Long live the socialist fatherland!*" "The Socialist Fatherland is in Danger," *Works*, XXVIII, 30–31.

18. Carrere d'Encausse, *Russian Syndrome*, p. 348: "While the rural population of the Ukraine was literally dying of hunger and children killed and ate old people in order to survive, the grain silos were full and the country was exporting cereals."

19. This quotation was inserted by Edward Crankshaw in his notes to Nikita S. Khrushchev, *Khrushchev Remembers*, trans. and ed. by Strobe Talbott, (Boston, MA: Little, Brown and Company, 1970), p. 90.

20. For a graphic account of suffering under the Soviet regime and Ukrainian nationalist responses, see Nikolai Tolstoy, *Stalin's Secret War* (New York: Holt, Rinehart and Winston, 1981), especially pp. 154 and 242–255.

21. Khrushchev, *Khrushchev Remembers*, p. 147.

22. Tolstoy, *Stalin's Secret War*, p. 265.

23. For a classic treatment of Khrushchev's use of the Ukrainian party machine, see Carl A. Linden, *Khrushchev and the Soviet Leadership, 1957–1964* (Baltimore, MD: Johns Hopkins Press, 1966), esp. p. 96.

24. This peninsula had been a Russian territory for centuries, although the majority of its people were Tatars until World War II. The Crimean Tatars were one of the seven peoples deported in their entirety after the war for their alleged collaboration with the Germans. Their civil rights were restored in 1967, but they were not permitted to return to the now Slavic–populated peninsula. Frederick C. Barghoorn, *Politics in the USSR*, 2nd ed. (Boston: Little, Brown and Co., 1972), p. 77, views the transfer of jurisdiction over the Crimea in terms of both "concessions to national sentiment" and "a continuation of the Stalinist policy of assimilation."

25. "Secret Speech of Khrushchev Concerning the Cult of the Individual," delivered at the 20th Congress of the CPSU, Feb. 25, 1956, in *The Anti–Stalin Campaign and International Communism* (New York: Columbia University Press, 1956), p. 64.

26. For a first-hand account of Ukrainian perspectives on these difficult years, Grigorenko, *Memoirs*, pp. 315–390.

27. Grigorenko, *Memoirs*, pp. 343–344.

28. Speech celebrating the 60th anniversary of the Soviet Federation. Cited by Rasma Karklins, *Ethnic Relations in the USSR: The Perspective From Below* (Boston: Allen & Unwin, 1986), p. 32.

29. For the classic presentation of the totalitarian model, see Merle Fainsod, *How Russia is Ruled* (Cambridge, Mass., 1963).

30. Jerry Hough, a former student and co-author of Merle Fainsod, was perhaps the most influential political scientist who explicitly abandoned the totalitarian model. See, among his prolific works, *Russia and the West: Gorbachev and the Politics of Reform* (New York: Simon and Schuster, 1988). 31.Alexander J. Motyl remarks that Sovietologists fixated upon Russia and marginalized studies of the non–Russians. He blames this tendency upon domination of the field by Government intelligence agencies—which wanted only "'the facts'" as opposed to theoretical complexities—and upon "'totalitarian bashing'" by those who disliked the totalitarian model and all it implied. "Building Bridges and Changing Landmarks," in Alexander J. Motyl, ed., *Thinking Theoretically About Soviet Nationalities*, pp. 261–263.

32. For example, see the many works of Zbigniew K. Brzezinski (who served as President Carter's Adviser on National Security Affairs) and Lev E. Dobriansky (who became President Nixon's Ambassador to the Bahamas).

33. Richard B. Cheney, *Soviet Military Power: Prospects for Change 1989*, (Washington, DC: U.S. Government Printing Office, 1989), p. 5.

34. Ibid., p. 143.

35. Testimony before the Senate Foreign Relations Committee, March 1991, cited by Adrian Karatnycky, "Getting it All Wrong: The Fall of Sovietology," *Freedom Review*, Vol. 23, No. 2, March–April 1992, p. 33.

36. Even as late as 1989, official Soviet spokesmen stressed the international implications of Chernobyl, in terms of favoring progress toward arms control and disarmament, but still minimized its domestic impact. See Abel G. Aganbegyan, ed., *Perestroika Annual*, Vol. II (Washington, DC: Brassey's ((U.S.)), Inc., 1989), pp. 62, 85, and 257.

37. For Chernobyl's political impact, see Hedrick Smith, *The New Russians* (New York: Random House, 1990), pp. 98–99, 370 and 440.

38. Gorbachev, speech to Russian Communist Party Congress, June 19, 1990, cited by *Foreign Broadcast Information Service. Daily Report*, June 20, 1990, p. 90.

39. For example, see Leonid Skoptsov, "Our People Have More Nuclear (sic) Exposure than Anyone in the World," *Nezavisimaya gazeta* (Moscow), Vol. III, Issue 4–5, June 1992, p. 9. He contends that "since 1949 the country has been living in a situation of nuclear lawlessness."

40. David R. Marples, "The Greening of Ukraine: Ecology and the Emergence of Zelenyi svit, 1986–1990", pp. 133–144, in Judith B. Sedaitis and Jim Butterfield, eds., *Perestroika From Below: Social Movements in the Soviet Union*, (Boulder, CO: Westview Press, 1991).

41. See Fainsod, *How Russia is Ruled*.

42. Cited by Laurie Hays, "As He Builds a National Ukraine, Chief Becomes Thorn in Yeltsin's Side," *Wall Street Journal*, March 17, 1992, p. 1.

43. Taras Kuzio, *Ukraine—The Unfinished Revolution* (London: Institute for European Defense and Strategic Studies, 1992), pp. 9–10.

44. "Ukraine Over the Brink," *Economist*, Sep. 4, 1993, pp. 45–46.

45. Steven J. Blank, *Russia, Ukraine and European Security* (Carlisle Barracks, PA: Strategic Studies Institute, U.S. Army War College, 1993), p. 8, detects "a vocal and growing trend to keep the nuclear card in response to Russian imperialist leanings."

46. Don Oberdorfer, "Ukraine is Loath to Yield Nuclear Arms," *Washington Post*, March 25, 1993, p. 29.

47. Ibid.

48. Ibid.

49. See the strong exchange of views between John Mearsheimer, "The Case for a Ukrainian Nuclear Deterrent," and Steven E. Miller, "The Case Against a Ukrainian Nuclear Deterrent," *Foreign Affairs*, Vol. 72, No. 3 (Summer 1993), pp. 50–80.

50. Celestine Bohlen, "Ukraine Agrees to Allow Russians to Buy Fleet and Destroy Arsenal," *New York Times*, Sep. 4, 1993, pp. 1 and 5.

51. Mark Galeotti, "Decline and Fall—Russia's Long Arm," *Jane's Intelligence Review*, Vol. IV, No. 11, November 1992, p. 482.

52. Radio Free Europe/Radio Liberty Daily Report, No. 139, 23 July 1992.

53. Galeotti, "Decline and Fall," p. 482.

54. Aleksandr Solzhenitsn, *Rebuilding Russia: Reflections and Tentative Proposals*, New York: Farrar, Straus and Giroux, 1991, pp. 14–18.

# 4

## *O Patria Mia*:
## National Conflict in
## Mountainous Karabagh

*Audrey L. Altstadt*

National identity in modern times is intertwined with the possession of territory regarded as the historic land of one's people, the nation. Love for the homeland, the *patrie*, is expressed in the literature and music of national movements and is thus linked to other defining elements of the nation—language, culture, history and consciousness.[1]

When a nation achieves statehood or political autonomy, control over territory becomes a political as well as historical or emotional issue. Historical or pseudo-historical arguments are often employed in the political realm to defend territorial claims, complicating or blurring the issues, but sharpening emotional reactions. Definition of "historic" patrimony is always problematical, and depends on the period of history national leaders choose as a precedent. The choice invariably reflects the peak, not the nadir, of a civilization, a glorified and mythologized era. It dictates maximum territorial demands, including lands held at other times by other peoples.

The national movements in Caucasia* during the late nineteenth and early twentieth centuries linked national identity to territory as the German and Italian national movements had done in Europe. The major nationalities of Caucasia—Armenians, Azerbaijani Turks[2] and Georgians—sometimes advanced claims to the same land. When they achieved independent statehood in 1918,

---

*Caucasia refers to both the greater Caucasus Mountains and the region to the south where Georgia, Armenia, and Azerbaijan are located. The term "Transcaucasia" reflects the northern, or Russian, perspective that is inappropriate in this context.

Georgia

their arguments produced armed clashes.   Bolshevik conquest in 1920–21 "settled" the territorial disputes in a way that facilitated Moscow's control over the restive peoples.

Subsequently Soviet policy institutionalized the nation–territory linkage, and pegged a range of cultural and political rights to the status of a territory. Boundaries of republics or regions (*oblast*) were drawn in such a way as to divide ethnic populations, defy historical precedent, and ensure competition over land and other resources.   The borders of all Central Asian republics represent all these calculations[3].   Union republics (Soviet Socialist Republics, SSRs) were guaranteed cultural autonomy, inviolability of borders, and the right to secede from the USSR; autonomous regions had cultural autonomy without the right to secede.   Such attention to national issues may seem incongruous for Marxists who did not recognize nationalism as more than an epiphenomenon.   It was, however, in keeping with the recognition by the pragmatic Lenin of the strength of nationalism,  and with the  disposition of Commissar for Nationalities' Affairs

Armenia

J. V. Stalin, whose criteria for defining a nation[4] constituted a major basis of Soviet nationality policy.

Despite official rhetoric about the "flowering" (*rastsvet*) of cultures in the USSR, symbols of national identity and the substance of identity itself were unceasingly manipulated. National pride could safely be expressed in folk dancing, but not in accurate writing of history. The titular language of republics was lauded and often made the "official" language. From the 1920s, however, native languages were confined to the cultural realm as the Russian language

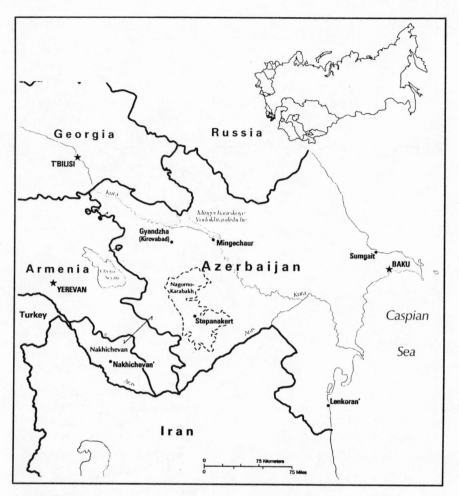

Azerbaijan

monopolized technical literature, education and politics. Upwardly mobile
young people were forced into the Russian-speaking educational track which
included not only physics and chemistry, but the study of Peter the Great and
Pushkin. "Modernization" became inseparable from russification. The native
languages were down-graded, and alphabets of Turkic and Iranian languages
were replaced first with the Latin, then with the Cyrillic alphabet.[5] In the
post-Stalin period, some republics fought these policies, but all remained
discontent.

As the USSR weakened under Gorbachev, elites of each nation began to
demand genuine cultural freedom. The various national territorial units soon
demanded political autonomy, then independence. In the case of Georgia, the

minority Abkhazians and Ossetians who had been given, respectively, autonomous republic and autonomous region status within the small Georgian SSR, advanced their cultural demands against Georgian cultural dominance just as the Georgians began to raise their voices against Russian cultural oppression, economic mismanagement, ecological devastation, and political control. When Georgians began to speak of secession from the USSR, the Abkhaz and then the Ossetians threatened to secede from Georgia, a move which would cripple Georgia and block its efforts to establish itself as a viable independent state. The Soviet national–territorial system thus worked as it was meant to, and made any attempt to exercise the constitutionally guaranteed "right" to secession a form of political suicide. At the same time, Moscow took active advantage of its opportunities and lent verbal support to "oppressed minorities"—meaning minorities, including Russians, in non–Russian republics, but never non–Russian minorities in the Russian federation—and later armed the Ossetians and Abkhaz who fought the Georgians, the latter into the autumn of 1993.[6]

Similar Russian rhetoric and tactics were applied in the longest–lived national conflict in the former USSR, which was the bloody war between Armenians and Azerbaijani Turks over Mountainous (Nagorno-) Karabagh. The case constitutes an important example of national conflict and Russian rule.

## Historical Roots of Conflict

The current round of this dispute began with an Armenian initiative in 1986–87 to accomplish the transfer of the Nagorno–Karabagh Autonomous Region (NKAR) from the jurisdiction of the Azerbaijan SSR to the Armenian SSR. The NKAR had been created by Bolshevik party authorities in western Azerbaijan during 1923 as a politically autonomous, predominantly Armenian enclave in the Azerbaijan SSR. By early 1988, fighting had started, with each side accusing the other of drawing the first blood.

At the most fundamental level, this clash concerns a piece of land which both peoples regard as historic patrimony, and the present conflict is, therefore, bound up with historical claims: (1) beliefs and loyalties forged in the national movements of both peoples starting in the nineteenth century and continuing to the present moment; (2) conflicting territorial claims of the period of independence of the two republics after World War I and the Bolshevik decisions about territory when Russia reconquered the Caucasus; (3) pre–modern historical claims put forward in connection with the national movements.

### National Movements in the Nineteenth Century

National movements of the Armenians and Azerbaijani Turks began, like their European counterparts, in the cultural arena with efforts to discover and write the nation's history, to codify and record grammar, to write down oral literature.

In Armenian identity, the Armenian Orthodox Church, the Armenian language, beliefs about early Armenian history and territorial irredentism are intimately connected. Christian since the fourth century, Armenian national identity is virtually synonymous with membership in the Armenian Gregorian Church, an autocephalous orthodox church. The Armenian Church has retained its independence, its Patriarchate at Echmiadzin, and, with the exception of a few years at the turn of this century, its lands. The Armenian national movement entered a political phase with the creation of nationalist political parties. Armenians in Tbilisi (then Tiflis), center of the Armenian national movement in the Russian Empire, founded the most important Armenian political party, the Armenian Revolutionary Federation (Dashnaktsutiun), in 1890. Like the Russian Socialist Revolutionaries, the Dashnaktsutiun regarded terrorism as a legitimate weapon in the political struggle. It was influenced by socialist thought. The party has survived continuously since that time outside Armenia and today leads a faction in the Armenian parliament. Initially aimed at the Ottoman Empire, it focused increasingly on the Russian Empire after confiscation of Armenian Church lands by the Viceroy of Transcaucasia at the turn of the century (their attacks led the Viceroy to return the lands) and the so-called "Armeno-Tatar war" (with Azerbaijanis) in 1905.[7]

The Azerbaijani Turks launched their cultural movement on the heels of the Russian conquest, and it was directed against Russian dominance in all spheres.[8] Scholars wrote local history, codified language, and strove to reform education and some social practices (such as arranged marriage). The Azerbaijani Turks began to call themselves by this name only in the late nineteenth century; it appears in newspapers and in the 1897 imperial census.[9] Until that time, they identified themselves as members of larger communities, as Turks or Muslims, or, if nomads, as members of their tribe or tribal confederation. For the Turks of Azerbaijan, the formation of national consciousness entailed separating themselves from the larger Turkic and Muslim world of which they were a part. Their national identity, bound to the territory they inhabited and local political and economic interests, evolved as a combination of ethnic and religious elements, the latter drawing on the Islamic reformist *jadid* movement[10]. The national movement was shaped by ideas to which their educated elites were exposed in Europe—constitutionalism, socialism, nationalism. As a result, the Azerbaijani national movement was secular and reformist, anti-clerical but not irreligious; it demanded greater autonomy within the Russian Empire, control of local government and education. Primary education reform programs exemplified the effort to merge East and West—students were to study traditional (religious and native language and literature) and Western subjects (accounting, European and Russian history, Russian language).[11] The leaders of this movement led Azerbaijan to independence in 1918 but were forced to flee or were killed by the Bolsheviks in 1920.

Armenians and Azerbaijani Turks had very different relations with the Russian regime and the Russians. Armenians had actively supported Russian annexation of Caucasia since the late 18th century[12] and were favored under Russian rule. They occupied many posts in regional administration, imperial academic and military offices, and their Church retained its separate existence.[13] Azerbaijani Turks, although given citizenship status (Central Asians were classified only as *inorodtsy* or "aliens"), were at a severe disadvantage. Legally classified as Muslims, their ability to enter various professions was curtailed, and they could not take advantage of all legal reforms of the late nineteenth century. The enfranchised electors for the Baku City Council were about 80% Azerbaijani Turks, but law prevented the Council from having more than half non-Christian members.[14] Thus Azerbaijani national awareness was directed against Russians; whereas the Armenian national movement regarded Turks—Ottoman and Azerbaijani—as their main foe.[15]

The Azerbaijani Turks' national movement entered a political phase during 1905 as the revolutionary movement that year forced the tsar to accept petitions from his subjects. The petition movement led to political meetings and organization. Clashes with militant Armenians during the year gave further impetus to political organization in Baku and Ganje (then Elizavetpol). Caucasia was the scene of class and national violence, but class solidarity was short-lived.[16]

Both Armenians and Azerbaijani Turks were subjects of neighboring empires as well as the Russian—Armenians, of the Ottoman Empire and Armenians and Azerbaijani Turks, of Iran. As in Russia, each group had dissimilar positions in the neighboring empires. A great deal might be said of the Armenian position in the Ottoman Empire, but for present purposes it is sufficient to note that they remained an entirely separate ethno-religious community (*millet* in the Ottoman system, which for centuries enjoyed self-government) that did not share culture, language or religion with the ruling Ottoman Turks. The Armenians' position in Iran was similar in these respects. In both empires they filled a valuable niche as merchants and translators. It was in the Ottoman Empire that Armenian revolutionary activity began.

The Turks of Iranian Azerbaijan, on the other hand, were integrated into empire. Numerous ruling dynasties of Iran, including the Safavid (1501–1735) and the Qajar (1797–1925), were ethnic Turks originating in Azerbaijan. Shah Ismail (1501–25) wrote poetry in "Türki" and later shahs continued to use it as the court language.[17] In the 16th century, the Azerbaijani Turks like Persians in Iran were converted to Shi'ism, making them the only Turks to be predominantly Shi'a and thus driving a wedge between them and Turks in the Ottoman Empire and Central Asia. After the Russian conquest of Caucasia (sealed by Treaties of Gulistan in 1813 and Turkmanchai in 1828), those on the Iranian side of the border remained in Tehran's political orbit.

Therefore, unlike the Armenian movement which appealed to Armenians living in both Russian and Ottoman Empires, the Azerbaijani Turks' national movement was directed almost exclusively toward those living in the Russian Empire. By 1907, the Dashnaks had turned their attention to conditions in the Viceroyalty of Transcaucasia and advocated a federal structure with an autonomous Armenia in both Russian and Ottoman Empires.[18] Were this to be accomplished, the ground would be laid for the creation of an independent Armenian state, the original aim of the Dashnaktsutiun. Even autonomy in a federal empire would require territorial delimitation. The lands which the Armenians regarded as "historic Armenian lands" to be included in an autonomous province or independent state encompassed eastern Asia Minor and several areas in Caucasia in which Armenians were a minority (demography below) and which Azerbaijanis never doubted was their own ancestral land.

Azerbaijani Turks did not consider forming their own state before the fall of the tsar. Secession was not part of any party program before 1917. In the spring of 1918, as the Bolsheviks struggled to negotiate a peace with the Germans, the Ottoman authorities demanded that the Caucasian republics negotiate with them as an independent body. Reluctantly, the Transcaucasian Federation was born in April 1918. Within six weeks it broke up into the Georgian, Armenian and Azerbaijani republics.[19]

## Territorial Disputes, 1918–1920

The period of republican independence was characterized by political unrest, a struggle for economic stability, and territorial dispute. Dashnaks ran Armenia, and the nationalist Musavat Party (founded 1911) ruled Azerbaijan. The two republics laid claim to several territories of which Karabagh was only one. Both governments included all claimed areas on their respective official maps which were then——and subsequently—used as "proof" of possession. Both republics sent delegations to the Paris Peace Conference to plead for recognition of their legitimacy and their territorial claims. But the decisions of the western leaders and their emissaries in the field were shaped by their own goals—Britain's determination to protect India, France's desire to retain a foothold in the Middle East, widespread fear of Bolshevism, and the intention to carve up the Ottoman Empire, then being delayed, and ultimately thwarted, by the Turks' republican movement under Mustafa Kemal (Ataturk).

British General Thomson, occupying Baku from November 1918 until August 1919, appointed an Azerbaijani governor over Karabagh and another disputed area to the southwest, Zangezur. Armenian leaders protested vehemently. Karabagh Armenians later accepted a resolution to remain within Azerbaijan until its final status was resolved by the Peace Conference. A third disputed territory, Nakhichevan, lay further southwest. Both parties' claims were ignored by Britain, and Nakhichevan became part of a "neutral zone" to keep the Turks out of Caucasia.[20]

When the Red Army conquered Azerbaijan during the summer of 1920, all Azerbaijan's territorial claims were recognized by Moscow. Once Armenia was occupied the following winter, the struggle for territorial control became Moscow's to exploit. The Azerbaijan Revolutionary Committee (Azrevkom)[21] was persuaded to offer in November 1920 to cede Zangezur to Armenia as a "symbol of friendship," but really to sweeten Soviet rule. The December 1920 treaty between Erevan and Moscow recognized the transfer of Zangezur, which has since then formed the strip of Armenia between Nakhichevan and the rest of Azerbaijan.[22] Whether Baku offered to give up Karabagh is disputed. The disagreement over documentation highlights the intractability of this conflict.

According to Armenian sources, the November Azrevkom declaration, published in the Baku newspaper *Kommunist* of 2 December 1920, was a short telegram that proclaimed that all three territories, Zangezur, Karabagh and Nakhichevan were henceforth to be part of Armenia.[23] The fact that the transfers were "never given effect,"[24] has subsequently been called an "historical injustice." This apparent promise is partly the basis for the call for "reunification" of Karabagh with Armenia.

A book of documents published in Baku[25] reprinted a long statement by the Azrevkom, apparently the same one, from the newspaper *Kommunist* of 2 December 1920. In that text, the three territories are named only as places of conflict. Zangezur is surrendered; Nagorno-Karabagh is offered "self determination." Recovery of the newspaper would resolve this point, but both sides are acting on their interpretations of many promises.

After the Russian-Armenian treaty of December 1920, Zangezur went to Armenia, Karabagh remained in Azerbaijan, and Nakhichevan was physically isolated from Azerbaijan, but confirmed to have a "close relationship" with it.[26] The settlement served Russian strategic needs more than any local claims or "historical justice." Domestically, it suited Bolshevik attempts to divide and rule by fostering discontent with a neighboring republic rather than Moscow. In foreign policy, confirmation of Nakhichevan's link to Azerbaijan fulfilled the demands of the Turkish national movement just at a time that its leaders and the Bolsheviks were signing a cooperation treaty. Despite the Bolshevik-Kemalist rapprochement of the time, Russia has long been wary of expanded Turkish influence across the Caucasus into Turkic Central Asia. In such an expansion by whatever government ruled Turkey, Azerbaijan would have been a necessary land bridge and Nakhichevan, a key link in the chain. The separation of Nakhichevan from Azerbaijan by placing Zangezur in Armenia addressed this Russian strategic concern. Thus separated from the rest of Azerbaijan, Nakhichevan could not constitute a link between Azerbaijan and Turkey.[27]

Efforts to expand Armenian control over Karabagh continued. From December 1922, the Central Committee of the Azerbaijan Communist Party, an organization dominated by Armenian and Russian rather than native communists, began administrative procedures to establish an autonomous region for the Armenian population in mountainous Karabagh. The Party simultaneously pursued a "balancing" policy to ensure Nakhichevan's status as part of Azerbaijan, culminating in March 1924 when Nakhichevan was formally made an Autonomous Soviet Socialist Republic of Azerbaijan. After disputes with the Azerbaijan government which, unlike the party was dominated by Azerbaijani Turks, the Transcaucasian Regional Committee, headed by Stalin's man Sergo Ordzhonikidze, ordered the Azerbaijan party's Central Committee in 1923 to create an Autonomous Region for Nagorno-Karabagh (NKAR). For that purpose Sergei Kirov, a Stalin crony and close associate of Ordzhonikidze, was appointed first secretary of the Azerbaijan communist party organization. Unlike neighboring republics where natives held top party posts, a Russian headed Azerbaijan's Communist Party. In the NKAR, Armenian was to be the language of administration and education, and the party organization sent there was overwhelmingly Armenian. No corresponding provision was made for larger numbers of Azerbaijani Turks living in Armenian Zangezur or in Georgia. The "resolution" of the dispute caused lasting resentment among Azerbaijanis for diminishing the government's rule over the NKAR, a part of its territory, and among Armenians that their claims were not fully honored by transferring jurisdiction to Erevan.

## Political Uses of History

In the recent dispute as at the turn of the century, Armenians and Azerbaijani Turks have advanced their claims to land primarily in historical, rather than economic or strategic, terms. In both cultures, even seemingly remote historical issues have an immediate and compelling meaning. As the present crisis sharpened, publicists and partisans made grander and simpler claims, obscuring the work of many careful scholars. Edmund M. Hertzig, wrote, "Occasionally parts of Armenia have achieved a temporary and partial independence between powerful neighbors, but such interludes have been rare as well as brief."[28] Nicholas Adontz's scholarly *Armenia in the Period of Justinian* describes the shifting conditions and borders:

> Armenia was set in the midst of a group of small countries to which she was culturally and ethnically related to some degree: Iberia, Albania, Atropatene, Syria and Cappadocia, and her fate was similar to theirs. The territorial extent of the countries did not remain unchanged; boundaries often shifted, and they were set in any given period by the interaction of the contemporary powers.[29]

Such precise treatment has been overshadowed by romanticized images. Concerning Karabagh, the popularized Armenian position—not painted in such simple colors by Armenian scholars—is that the historic kingdom of Armenia included Karabagh as well as Nakhichevan and other lands now in Azerbaijan, Georgia, Iran, and Turkey. Azerbaijani Turks have argued, drawing on the work of some nineteenth century Russian scholars, that the ancient kingdom of Caucasian Albania was the predecessor to modern Azerbaijan and neighbor to Armenia, and that it included Karabagh and Nakhichevan. Each side has produced a large body of academic and literary material, drawing on pre-Islamic, even pre-Christian sources, specifically to bolster these claims and refute those of the other. Since the mid-1980s various materials have proliferated; some are mainly polemics, others present documented arguments.

One of the first works in the current campaign appears to be writer Zori Balayan's 1984 book surveying the whole sweep of Armenian history, *Ochag*. Gorbachev described a Greater Armenia of the past, stretching "from sea to sea." A member of the editorial board of the prestigious *Literaturnaia Gazeta* (Moscow), Balayan became one of the most vocal proponents of the transfer of Karabagh. *Ochag* was criticized in a lengthy article by a young researcher at the Azerbaijan Academy of Sciences Oriental Institute as "large-scale and multifaceted falsification of history."[30] The critic was Isa Gambar(ov),[31] later co-founder of the Azerbaijan Popular Front. In 1987, when the political side of this struggle was beginning, a Erevan journal attacked an Azerbaijani doctoral dissertation on Caucasian Albania, saying it "falsified Armenian history." Andrei Sakharov, Nobel-prize winning physicist, entered this historical debate on the Armenian side. The rebuff came from the Director of Oriental Studies of the Azerbaijan Academy of Sciences, Ziya Buniatov.[32]

Thus historical claims underlay the political movement, and many historical and pseudo-historical "duels" preceded the political campaign that began in 1986 when Armenian economist Igor Muradyan launched a petition drive to "demand *return* of Karabagh to Armenia."[33] The same intellectuals would lead the political movement as well as the cultural.

Early historical claims are difficult to verify, but those concerning nineteenth century administration and demographic shifts can be substantially clarified. At the time of the Russian conquest early in the nineteenth century, the semi-independent khanates (princely states) of Karabagh, Ganje, Nakhichevan and others outside Georgia were ruled by Muslim Turks (some may have been Persians). They accepted the Iranian shah as their suzerain.[34] The earliest Russian military population surveys showed the population of the region was overwhelmingly "Muslim." As a result of two Russo-Iranian and one Russo-Ottoman war, thousands of "Muslim" families (ethnic designations were not made) fled and Christian Armenians immigrated to the area.[35] Based on the earliest Russian statistics on western Caucasia, the composition of the population in the Nakhichevan and Erevan khanates in 1826 was about 80%

Muslim and 20% Armenian.  By 1832, with the flight of Muslims and the immigration of "some 57,000 Armenians from Persian and Ottoman territories, the Christian population rose considerably and matched the Muslim."[36]

The trend continued.  By the end of the century when the first Russian imperial census was taken, large Armenian minorities were found throughout Caucasia, and Armenian majorities in several areas including the mountainous part of Karabagh.  In those *uezdy* ("counties" Jebrail, Shusha and Jevanshir in the Elizavetpol province) from which Nagorno-Karabagh was later carved, Armenians constituted a majority only in the Shusha *uezd*, but substantial minorities in the others:

TABLE 4.1
Population of Part of the Elizavetpol province in 1897

| Uezd | Population | Azerbaijanis | Armenians |
| --- | --- | --- | --- |
| Jebrail | 66,360 | 49,189 | 15,746 |
| Jevanshir | 72,719 | 52,041 | 19,551 |
| Shusha | 138,771 | 62,868 | 73,953 |

Similarly, the population of the Nakhichevan area, then an *uezd* in the Erevan province, was 100,711, of which 64,151 (about 64%) were Azerbaijani Turks and 34,672 (about 34%) were Armenians.[37]

After the national conflicts of the early twentieth century and population shifts during World War I, cities, neighborhoods and whole regions became more ethically homogeneous.  Armenians moved from Nakhichevan to Zangezur, and Muslims, from Zangezur to the Shusha area of Karabagh.[38]

Neither the demographic nor the administrative history of the Caucasus region are so simple as the partisans in the struggle over Karabagh suggest. Throughout the traceable history of the region, borders and populations have shifted; independence was won and lost.  Parties involved in this, or any dispute, may act on their beliefs or interpretations of history, and analysts must be mindful of those beliefs.  But the analysts must make use also of verifiable history and beware the pitfalls inherent in the political applications of history.

## Nationalist Identity and Political Expression

Continued and renewed national consciousness provides the context of the Nagorno-Karabagh war.  Political grievances that have been revealed since the 1980s are articulated in Armenia and Azerbaijan, as in all non-Russian republics, in national terms. Environmental protection is the guarding of the homeland and its historic monuments; economic injustice robs the nation to the benefit of another. Issues that affect the transmission of identity—language and history—are especially sensitive.

National sentiment among Armenians has exhibited great continuity since the nineteenth century. It has been kept alive in Armenia and, perhaps more successfully, by Armenians living in Europe and the United States. One cornerstone of identity, the Armenian language, is almost exclusively used in Armenia. The 1979 census (the last taken before the unrest began in 1988) shows that Armenia was the most homogenous of all Soviet republics, with nearly 90% of its population belonging to the titular nationality. Russian street signs were rare in Erevan; student identification cards in the university were only in Armenian, as were most publications of the University and the Armenian Academy of Sciences. Yet approximately one-third of the Armenians in the USSR lived outside the Armenian republic, with a significant number in Russia. The supportive relationship with the Russians is reflected in data on language use. About one-third of the Armenians in Armenia speak Russian as a second language. Among Armenians in the USSR as a whole, nearly 50% spoke Russian (including 8.4% who regarded it as their native language). Armenians are not only well placed in the Russian political and academic establishment, but their proficiency in Russian enables them to disseminate their views in Russian and to reach a wide audience in Russia and among Western analysts who know Russian.

Armenians in the United States, France, the Middle East and other parts of the world have maintained large, well-funded cultural and political organizations. They have been able to produce works of history and culture that the Soviet establishment could not block. In the Karabagh conflict, these communities have provided financial and political support and disseminated the Armenian perspective in Western languages.

Azerbaijani Turks' relationship to the Russians continues to be problematical. As was true at the turn of this century, Azerbaijan's national assertiveness has been directed primarily against the Russians. With the resurgent national movement in Azerbaijan since the 1970s, historians and writers have tried to rewrite Azerbaijan's history which was long distorted by Soviet dicta that demanded documentation of the "great friendship"[39] between Russia and Azerbaijan. As part of that effort, they have revived memories of the turn of the century cultural and political leaders and their national programs. Finally, these elites have worked not merely to confirm the official use of the Azerbaijani Turkish language, as opposed to Russian, but to ensure its actual use. Though "Azerbaijani" (called "Turkish" until 1937) had been the official language of the republic since the 1950s, Russian was more often used in communist party documents and speeches and in government transactions.[40]

Compared to Armenia, Azerbaijan is far more heterogeneous, with about 80% of the republic's population belonging to the titular nationality in 1979. Only about 29% of the Azerbaijanis know Russian, and those live mostly in Baku, a city with large Russian and Armenian minorities, where Russian is commonly used. Pressure to increase Russian-language education was regarded by the Communist Party as an important aspect of "drawing nearer" of the nationalities, a key theme of the Brezhnev era. It was urged energetically by First Secretary Heidar Aliyev (1969-83).[41]

Because Azerbaijani Turks rarely leave their homeland, Azerbaijanis outside Azerbaijan are either the offspring of those national leaders who fled the Bolsheviks or of prisoners of war from World War II who escaped forced repatriation. They are concentrated mainly in Turkey, Germany, and France. The emigres themselves had been leaders of anti-Bolshevik movements in Europe, but unlike their Armenian counterparts, they lacked an enduring political organization and are on the whole less wealthy. Their children have often blended in with their new surroundings, and except in Turkey, may not even know Turkish or feel any connection to Azerbaijan.

Armenians generally regard Russia as a "protector" of Armenia from its neighbors. Since the present conflict reemerged, some Armenian critics of Russia have noted that Moscow has not always acted as a "protector." Indeed, Gorbachev was accused of being "pro-Azerbaijani" (to the Azerbaijanis' amazement) for refusing to support Armenian demands for the transfer of the NKAR to Erevan's jurisdiction. Nonetheless, numerous Russians have actively supported the Armenian side.[42]

Azerbaijani Turks regarded Russia as a colonial power to which they and their land have been subject. Such verbiage was long suppressed but was heard again in 1986, perhaps stimulated in part by Gorbachev's own presentation of himself as a Russian and a baptized Christian. Yet there are differences among Azerbaijanis. Many were educated in schools in which the language of instruction was Russian. They know Russian language and culture, and have Russian friends. Russian is widely used in Azerbaijan, even in government offices (the administration of President Abulfez Elchibey did not favor this, but it reemerged after his overthrow). As a multinational city, Baku has had a large Russian community since the oil boom of the 1870s. Many Azerbaijanis are deeply offended that Russians born in Azerbaijan never learn the language of the republic, thus displaying their colonial mentality. Others seem indifferent to the issue and view the use of Russian as a practical necessity.

## Nationalist Views in the Karabagh Conflict

The Karabagh conflict has been articulated in terms of national identity, national goals and historical ideas. Since the late 1940s, Armenians have put forward their demands for the transfer of the NKAR to Armenia, calling for "our lands" to be "returned."[43] Early reports on the latest renewal of the movement noted that the demands for the transfer of the NKAR were now associated with other issues such as environmental protection and restoration of a famous monastery near Shusha. Protesters complained that Armenians in the NKAR could not receive Erevan television. One observer suggested that demographic trends made it imperative for the Armenians to act before their majority was further diminished: the Armenian population of the NKAR had fallen from 84% in 1959 to 76% in 1989.[44]

Gorbachev met with leaders of the movement, Zori Balayan, poet Sylvia Kaputiyan and others, and offered partial fulfillment of their demands. Gorbachev reportedly promised that schools in the NKAR would be subordinated to the Armenian rather than Azerbaijani SSR, a move that would undermine Azerbaijan's sovereignty over a portion of its own territory. Gorbachev also approved a change of party leadership in the NKAR, part of the Azerbaijan Communist Party, again without consulting Baku. He replaced a Russian with an Armenian who repeated Moscow's refusal to change the status of the territory.[45] In pragmatic terms, Gorbachev could not afford to open the Pandora's Box of redrawing boundaries.[46] His decision had a sound legal basis—statutes of the Soviet and republican constitutions stated that no republican borders could be changed unless all concerned republics agreed.

Azerbaijan did not agree. The first response to Armenian demands did not come from the government or Party, which were later criticized for failing to defend national interests so leaders could protect their careers, but from the intelligentsia. People's Poet Bahtiyar Vahabzade and historian Suleiman Aliyarov wrote the first rebuff, in the journal of the Writers' Union *Azerbaijan* in Azerbaijani Turkish (thus it remained unknown in the West until a translation was published four months later).[47] Addressing a speech made in Paris by Gorbachev's economic adviser Abel Aganbegian,[48] Vahabzade and Aliyarov drew on history and literature to refute Armenian claims that Karabagh was historically Armenian. They criticized Armenians for claiming it as their own land to which they had immigrated in the last century. Other historians and writers, who soon became leaders of the national movement, argued that Armenians discriminated against Azerbaijanis both inside Armenia and within the NKAR, where the government and party bureaucracies were predominantly Armenian. Azerbaijanis were distressed that close advisors to Gorbachev advocated the Armenian position.

To answer the few who included "socio-economic development" complaints in their demand for the transfer of the NKAR, Azerbaijani scholars published data on nine socio-economic indicators, including numbers of hospital beds and doctors per capita, libraries, child care facilities, and living space. According to these indicators, the NKAR was ahead of Armenia on all but two factors, ahead of the Azerbaijan aggregate figures on all but one, and ahead of the USSR averages on five of nine factors measured and nearly even on a sixth.[49] Perceived problems in the NKAR were apparently less a product of Azerbaijani rule than of Soviet conditions of low productivity, neglect of the environment and a wide range of other problems that plague many regions of the USSR including Azerbaijan and Armenia.

The administrative and party apparatus of the NKAR was heavily Armenian and had been since the creation of the NKAR. Language data for 1979 showed that most Armenians living in the NKAR did not know Azerbaijani (only 4% used it as their second language while 31% used Russian),[50] revealing that Armenians could apparently live their lives in the NKAR without knowing the language of the republic where it was located. That suggested a genuine cultural autonomy. A few available budgets of Azerbaijan showed that the NKAR got either more money than the larger and more populous Nakhichevan, or more per capita.[51]

All the development data, however, was beside the point—the central idea behind Armenian demands was righting a perceived "historical injustice." The point was made clearly by G. Aivazian, "party member since 1939 and member of the USSR Union of Journalists," in a letter to the newspaper *Sovetskii Karabagh*: "Karabagh residents know that no reform, no economic or cultural development measures will take the place of the main issue raised by the toilers of Nagorno Karabagh—the reunification of the NKAR to the Armenian SSR. They ask the Central Committee to fulfill this historically just demand."[52] More important than actual conditions in the NKAR, which were apparently no worse than the rest of the USSR, was the nationalist idea that being ruled by some other nationality is by definition "oppression."

Violence associated with this struggle began in late 1987. "Clashes" were reported among villagers in NKAR in the fall of 1987. Various sources mention two Azerbaijanis killed in a demonstration in early 1988 in Erevan,[53] and others in Armenian demonstrations in the NKAR.[54] At least one historian from the Azerbaijan Academy of Sciences reported on systematic deportations of Azerbaijanis from Armenia, in the Zangezur area, in the winter of 1987–88. The information was suppressed by the Azerbaijan authorities, but the report was circulated later.[55] Western reports said the Azerbaijanis "fled."[56]

The first widely publicized bloodshed was the incident in the Azerbaijan industrial town Sumgait, just north of Baku, in February 1988. Official figures put the death toll at 33, of which 26 were Armenian. Soviet sources for the first time used the word "pogrom." Armenians believed the actual numbers were far higher, but were being concealed.[57] Sumgait became a focal point for Armenian anger. Witnesses of both nationalities stated police did nothing to quell or control the violence and some suggested this was a "provocation" by police or KGB, claims recorded later by human rights investigators.[58] Azerbaijanis were tried in Russia for "anti-Armenian" activities. When

Azerbaijani victims were attacked in Erevan the following June,[59] there were no references to "anti-Azerbaijani" actions.

As an "undeclared war" began in the NKAR, the Azerbaijani press was filled with reports of well-armed Armenian units raiding Azerbaijani villages in and outside the NKAR.[60] Such stories did not usually make it to the all-Union press. According to a Russian correspondent for *Ogonek*, that newspaper refused to run his story on Armenian attacks on Azerbaijan trains crossing Zangezur. The Russian-language Baku newspaper *Vyshka* later ran the story.[61]

Fighting was sporadic for several years as villages changed hands, the stream of refugees grew from tens to hundreds of thousands, and stories of atrocities were repeated. It was, wrote a U.S. reporter on the scene, the destruction of the Azerbaijani town of Khojaly in the NKAR in February 1992 that transformed the war from a "feud between neighbors" to a serious regional war. Armenian rival forces attacked, reportedly with the aid of the 366th Brigade of the former Soviet Ministry of Internal Affairs.[62] Western news agencies refused to believe the journalists' initial reports that Armenians were attacking Azerbaijanis, suggesting that he must have it backwards.[63]

The number of refugees and dead grew significantly during 1992 as Armenian forces succeeded in taking all southern Karabagh and Lachin, the city outside the former NKAR (Azerbaijan abolished the city in 1991, and the local Armenian soviet declared independence). The "Lachin corridor" connected Armenia to Nagorno-Karabagh along the region's main southern highway. The parallel northern route was secured in 1993, starting with the successful offensive against Kelbecher, in March 1993. Then Armenian forces, with reports of aid from Russian forces stationed inside Armenia, captured Kelbecher, north of Lachin, also between the former NKAR and the republic of Armenia. Armenian control of Kelbecher region completed the de facto annexation of Nagorno-Karabagh to Armenia. The United Nations High Commissioner for Refugees in Geneva said "tens of thousands of Azerbaijani civilians were fleeing from Kelbecher...many had died of cold, hunger, and exhaustion".[64] Further offensives into the summer consolidated Armenian gains, which by August reached the Iranian border. Azerbaijan's territory was reduced by nearly 20% and the gap between Nakhichevan and the rest of Azerbaijan had doubled. Efforts by the Conference on Security and Cooperation in Europe (CSCE) to mediate began in March 1992,[65] but were constantly frustrated, then rendered moot.

Throughout the conflict, nationalism has continued to supply the language of discourse. In January of 1990, Azerbaijan Communist Party secretary Hasan Hasanov revealed that policies on Karabagh ostensibly made in Baku were made in Moscow. Hasanov castigated his party colleagues as "mankurts," who preferred to save their careers rather than serve their nation.[66] Mankurts were those men in *A Day Lasts Longer than an Age*, a novel by Kirghiz writer Chinghiz Aitmatov, who were captured and tortured to forget their memories;

they became perfect, compliant slaves. One mankurt kills his own mother when she comes to save him. Later criticism of First Secretary, later President, Ayaz Mutalibov was cast also in terms of failure to defend the national interests and territory. He blocked formation of a national army and preferred that Azerbaijan maintain troops within the Soviet, then CIS, armed forces. Critics said this position reflected Mutalibov's continued willingness to accommodate Moscow. He was blamed for the loss of Khojaly and massacre of hundreds of civilians there. It was this event that forced his resignation in March 1992.

Armenian President Levon Ter-Petrossian was one of the leaders of the Karabagh Committee that launched the Armenian campaign to annex Karabagh. Elected President of Armenia in the fall of 1991, he has since attempted to negotiate a cease fire with his Azerbaijani counterpart. Ter-Petrossian's Dashnak opponents in the Armenian parliament regard his posture as "soft," and they several times called for his resignation if he did not defend fellow Armenians in Karabagh.[67]

Ter-Petrossian's government ceased to demand the annexation of Karabagh, and instead began to support "self-determination," i.e. secession from Azerbaijan. Despite denials that Republic of Armenian forces are fighting in Karabagh, in January 1992, Armenian Defense Minister Vazgen Sarkisyan said that "Nagorno-Karabagh is defended by [Armenia's] forces and resources."[68] His successor, Vazgen Manukyan[69] stated more than 18 months later, on the eve of his own removal from his post, that he could not resign "when he is sending men to the front line'—an implicit admission of military involvement by the Republic of Armenia in the fighting in Nagorno-Karabagh."[70] The appointment of the head of Nagorno-Karabagh defense forces (sometimes called the Defense Minister) Sergei Sarkisyan, as Armenia's new Defense Minister in August 1993,[71] confirmed the intimate relationship between Stepanakert and Erevan and may signal the annexation of Nagorno-Karabagh by Armenia.

For its part, Azerbaijan rejected the application of "self-determination" to Armenians in Nagorno-Karabagh since the right has already been exercised in creating the state of Armenia. Azerbaijan relied on the legal principle of "territorial integrity" to defend its retention of Karabagh.[72] Though the argument was persuasive among the United Nations and CSCE, it seems to have been superseded by the Armenian military *faits accompli*.

Neither side has used religious rhetoric, nor attempted to use religion to mobilize the population. They have denied the matter is linked to religion. Nonetheless, the Soviet press, and drawing from it the Western press, have suggested that "Islamic fanaticism" motivated Azerbaijanis. They looked for any sign of this religious foundation, singling out individual portraits of Khomeini in demonstrations full of national flags or reporting "green banners," which one Russian reporter later admitted he had not actually seen.[73] The Iranian press seized on such reports, but local religious leaders in Baku refused to agree that Iran inspired the Azerbaijanis. The reports persuaded various Western scholars who get their information only from the Russian-language sources.[74] Gerard Libaridian, now first deputy foreign minister of Armenia, called simplistic attribution of the problem to religion "an insult to one's intelligence and memory."[75] As the Popular Front grew and, in spring 1992 gained power, it was more successful in clarifying the secular nature of its program. A law on religions guaranteed separation of church and state and legal equality of all religions as long as they do not violate republican law or threaten the existence of the state.[76]

In this and other "national conflicts," violence is fueled not merely by differences between peoples, but by concrete issue to which national identity is tied—a belief that the possession of a piece of land is part of national duty to one's fellow-nationals and to one's ancestors. The issue, not national consciousness, stimulates the clash. If the fact of national identity were the actual cause of violence, as the Russians often argue, then conflict could only be resolved by the obliteration of national identity, in Aitmatov's terms, the "mankurtization" of nations. Attempting such "denationalization" would be a violation of collective and individual rights. It would imply the dominance of the nation that carried it out. And it is, given the Soviet failure to succeed in this despite decades of unrestrained exertion, a goal unlikely to be accomplished.

## Impact of the International Community

### *The Russian Connection*

Despite nominal independence, both republics retain close ties to the Russian economy and polity. Both republics still use the ruble, though Azerbaijan has issued its own currency. CIS, that is Russian, troops remained in Armenia, a CIS member. They left Azerbaijan only in May 1993, but were invited back within months by former communists who had taken power. Road and rail links as well as trade patterns and the use of Russian language all tie these republics to Russia, as they were meant to do.

Russian political aims have included control of Caucasia since the seventeenth century. Russians have justified their control by proclamations of a "civilizing" mission in the nineteenth century and "elder brotherhood" in the twentieth. Though the Russian Empire crumbled in 1918, within five years a new empire was built, and Bolshevik Russia had regained much of the tsarist empire's territory, including Caucasia.[77] Again in the 1990s the Russian-dominated empire crumbled, but was replaced quickly by the so-called Commonwealth of Independent States (CIS). There is no reason to think that the basic geopolitical aims of Russia have changed or will.

Nor are historical patterns the only suggestive indicator. Russian chauvinist Vladimir Zhirinovskii, leader of Russia's Liberal-Democratic Party "wants to reinstall the Russian empire, first within the boundaries of the former USSR, but subsequently along the borders of the former Tsarist empire."[78] Some have dismissed such groups as fringe elements. Galina Starovoitova, then Yeltsin adviser on nationalities affairs, said in September 1992 that Zhirinovskii's group had been "unmasked as a KGB provocation" and had been disbanded.[79] But three months later his party joined a "New Russia" group that included "Officers for Democracy" headed by former KGB general Oleg Kalugin and the People's Party of Russia, headed by Telman Gdlyan, a former prosecutor charged with using brutality in investigations in Central Asia.[80]

Boris Yeltsin himself said in February 1993 that Russia should be "granted special power...to stop ethnic conflicts in the former Soviet Union."[81] He did not indicate who should "grant" Russia such power, but made reference to the world community's understanding of "Russia's special responsibility." In August, a Russian Foreign Ministry official referred, more delicately, to "a Russian campaign in the spring of 1993 to gain international recognition as the regions' official peace keeper" and hoped for support for that role from the United Nations Security Council. He rejected U.S. peace keeping in the former USSR.[82] Russian rhetoric about strengthening the "integration processes" in the CIS was stepped up at that time.[83] These statements showed that, as in tsarist and Soviet times, the mentality of the Russian state and many Russians is imperial rather than nationalist. This stimulates national backlash from the non-Russians in whose eyes Big Brother is trying to make a come-back. The Russian claim that only they can "control" or "resolve" ethnic conflict, which central policies aroused, is a means of getting their boot in the door.

The persistence of the Russian imperial mentality, or perhaps the identification of imperial with national aims, and recent rhetoric from political leaders in and out of power suggest that a new Russian empire, whatever its actual name, is in the making. Russian political behavior can, at least tentatively, be analyzed within the framework of imperial goals which exhibited great continuity in tsarist and soviet times. In Caucasia, Russian-led economic and political integration depended on control over Azerbaijan because of its oil and its strategic location (since the 1930s), as a central link in the Soviet railroad system of the region. Long-term Russian interests as well as short-term economic recovery require the resources of Azerbaijan. An independent Azerbaijan can sell its oil to the West (or to Russia for hard currency at world prices), open its doors to foreign travellers, and threaten to become a springboard of Turkey's influence into Central Asia. This independence Russia can not tolerate.

Instability in the Caucasus region would facilitate Russian control. The situation is not so simple that each event can be attributed to Russian meddling any more than that meddling can be dismissed out of hand. Despite the chaos in Russia, established policy can be carried out. Direct orders are not needed in an organization if major actors share the same spirit, the same goals and have been shaped by years of training. As one Red Army defector noted in an interview on nationality relations in the army, only a few officers needed to know the policy of provoking conflict among nationalities for it to work.[84] Beyond informed circles, self-interest and prejudice can take their course and serve the same end. To rewrite William Butler Yeats, "the center need not hold" if its agents know what to do. Russian behavior is a product of long-established policies of an imperial system encompassing various institutions which, in one form or another, still survive: the army, the communist party, and the Oriental Institute of the Academy of Sciences, where policies on "Muslim republics" originated.[85]

Russia's presence has had direct impact on the Karabagh conflict. Russian (Soviet and CIS) forces have thrown their weight, at different times, to both Armenian and Azerbaijani sides, first criticizing, then supporting some goals and aiding forces. Armenia signed the CIS mutual defense treaty and attempted to invoke that treaty's provisions on common defense against an "aggressor" in order to gain assistance against Azerbaijan. The appeal was ignored since Azerbaijani troops have not entered Armenia. Moscow has contended that Russia is not interfering in the war. Any Russian soldiers in the fight, they say, are mercenaries and reflect the disintegration of the command structure as political authority in the USSR itself broke down. Western analysts have sometimes been persuaded by this. So the case of the five Russian special forces (*spetsnaz*) mercenaries sentenced to death in Azerbaijan in April 1993 aroused interest in many quarters.

When the soldiers were convicted of murders of Azerbaijanis in the Karabagh area, their death sentences evoked appeals for clemency from Yeltsin and his rival Ruslan Khasbulatov. Amnesty International issued an "Urgent Appeal Action" on their behalf. As Thomas Goltz noted, "Beyond the grim details of their activities in the field, the case of the six deserves particular attention because of one curious fact: The self-admitted mercenaries, all Spetsnaz men assigned to the Russian 7th Army in Armenia, were not listed as deserters from their unit until a year after they first went AWOL." Although the men killed, took a vacation on the money thus earned, and went back to Azerbaijan to kill others before being captured, Azerbaijani inquiries at the time of their capture in October 1992 were answered with the claim they were still at their posts. As Azerbaijani prosecutor Rovshan Aliyev noted, "no Russian soldier could take that sort of extended absence from duty...without some sort of collusion much higher up."[86]

The Azerbaijan Popular Front and other non-communists see the Karabagh issue within the framework of Azerbaijan's independence from Russia. After the election of Popular Front leader Abulfez Elchibey to the presidency in June 1992, Azerbaijan's National Assembly rejected CIS membership. Elchibey signed a Treaty of Friendship and Security with Russia,[87] but was plainly moving Azerbaijan away from Russia.

The coup of June 1993 that brought former communist leader Heidar Aliyev back to power signalled a return of Azerbaijan to the Russian orbit. Withdrawing Russian troops armed the rebels who staged the coup. They may have provided GRU (military intelligence), air-assault, or other specialists, and perhaps a tactical plan, as well.[88] In any case, the outcome unquestionably favors Russia, which seems rid of the democratically-elected Elchibey[89] just as he was about to consolidate his own position by leaving the ruble zone, signing a CSCE-sponsored cease-fire agreement, and closing an oil deal with a consortium of eight Western oil companies. The new Prime Minister is coup leader Surat Huseinov, and the new Speaker of the National Assembly and acting president is Aliyev. Yet Moscow is not dependent on Aliyev, for Ayaz Mutalibov, sixteen years his junior and a less forceful individual, is still waiting in a dacha outside Moscow. Russia is assured of access to Azerbaijan's goods and territory and need no longer work within the CSCE, whose efforts it has belittled.[90] Moscow can fulfill its desire to be the sole "peace keeper" in its former colonies.

## Iran and Turkey Vie for Influence

The Islamic Republic of Iran and the Turkish Republic have worked to establish commercial ties and exert cultural influence in the Caucasus, especially Azerbaijan, and in Central Asia. Current Iranian relations touch upon Iran's historic relationship with both Armenians and Azerbaijani Turks. Active in Iranian politics for centuries, Armenians today hold posts in the Iranian government. The relationship of Iranian Azerbaijan ("southern Azerbaijan") to the new Republic of Azerbaijan has stirred questions about possible reunification of the two parts of Azerbaijan, which Tehran fears. Family, cultural and religious bonds between the two Azerbaijans remain despite nearly two centuries of political separation.

As national consciousness has impinged on religious identity a process evident in the nineteenth century, the Azerbaijanis in the north (under Russian rule) grew increasingly critical of Iran and moved closer to their ethnic kin, Russia's great nemesis, Turkey. Elchibey openly criticized the Persianization policies of the government and accused it of repressing Turkish culture. In keeping with its long secular tradition, northern Azerbaijan is extremely wary of Iranian political influence for they believe it threatens their independence and secularism.

In 1992, Iranian deputy Foreign Minister Ali Akbar Veliyati attempted to mediate between Baku and Erevan. As Veliyati tried to negotiate with Ter-Petrossian and Mutalibov, the Armenian attack on Khojaly took place. Negotiations resumed, in Tehran, with Mutalibov's successor Yakub Mamedov. The May attack on Shusha, in which Armenian forces were reportedly aided by the CIS 366th regiment, occurred the day after a cease-fire agreement was signed by them in Tehran.[91]  Iranian mediation was associated with Armenian offensives and Azerbaijani losses.  Iran was rumored to be selling arms to Armenia.  Popular Front leaders in government continued to block Iranian influence, especially religious influence, but the return of Aliyev is already fostering improved relations between Baku and Tehran.[92]

Azerbaijan has a particularly close relationship with Turkey, which both Ankara and Baku have cultivated.  There is no language barrier between the two, and businessmen from Turkey have been active in Azerbaijan since 1992.  Despite their aid to Aliyev when he was in Nakhichevan, the Turkish government affirmed its support of Elchibey after the June coup.  Turkey is, however, moving forward with a planned oil pipeline from Baku to the Turkish coast.[93]

Despite past Armenian–Turkish antagonism, a tentative political rapprochement between the two states permitted a role for the Turkish Republic in mediation efforts.  Many segments of Armenian society were extremely uncomfortable with this.  Turkish public opinion has pressed for more active support by its government for Azerbaijan in the Karabagh conflict, but Ankara has behaved with restraint.  Fighting in summer 1992 between Armenian and Azerbaijani forces in Nakhichevan, closer than Karabagh to the Turkish border and about which Turkey has special concerns,[94] led Ankara to issue verbal warnings about a wider regional war.  With the Armenian offensives of summer 1993, all outside Nagorno–Karabakh, the Turkish Republic's leaders have appealed to the United Nations for intervention.[95]

The latest Armenian gains raise another issue of regional concern.  The territory between the former NKAR and Armenia from Kelbecher to the Iranian border was, at the turn of the century, heavily populated with Kurds.  In the 1920s, Moscow had further subdivided the troublesome Azerbaijan republic by the creation in that region of a short–lived autonomous region for the Kurds adjacent to the NKAR.  Subsequently, Moscow has sporadically presented itself as a champion of the Kurds, supporting Kurdish demands, and perhaps terrorist groups, against neighboring states.[96]  With the seizure of Lachin in 1992, Armenian forces claimed that Kurds fought with them against Azerbaijan.  In August 1993, Armenian leaders stated they did not plan to occupy the Fizuli–Jebrail–Kubatly region in the south "forever," but did desire that areas of Azerbaijan adjoining Armenia be demilitarized.[97]  The possibility that the ground is being laid for a new Kurdish autonomous zone cannot be excluded.

### Position of the United States

Apart from broad support for democracy in the former Soviet Union and peaceful resolution of conflicts, the U.S. does not seem to have a specific policy for the Caucasus.  The U.S. granted diplomatic recognition to the Caucasian republics in the winter of 1991-2, recognizing Azerbaijan several weeks after Armenia. The United States maintains embassies in all three capitals.

As suggested by the lag in recognizing Azerbaijan, U.S. policy toward the republics has not been entirely evenhanded. The conflict between the republics is, because of the large Armenian–American community in the U.S., a constituent issue for many members of Congress and the president. In Congressional investigations, the number of witnesses representing the Armenian side routinely outnumbers those from the Azerbaijani side.[98] Delegations visiting Armenia in the past have not always gone to neighboring Azerbaijan (September 1991).[99] Far more serious was a sanctions amendment directed against Azerbaijan attached to the "Freedom Support Act" that provided aid to Russia. Proposed while Mutalibov was in power, the Act and amendment were passed by both houses of Congress after Elchibey's election.[100] It seemed that Congress was paying no attention to political changes in Azerbaijan, its efforts at reform or its participation in CSCE peace efforts. The sanctions amendment not only denied Azerbaijan humanitarian aid which all the other former Soviet republics received, including those that remain demonstrably authoritarian like Uzbekistan, it essentially blamed Azerbaijan for the "undeclared war" with Armenia. Even stronger action was proposed in early 1993 in the form of a sanctions bill against Azerbaijan.[101] A *Washington Post* editorial called this "A textbook case of congressional mischief making in foreign policy" and argued for "an evenhanded policy".[102]

Azerbaijanis fear Armenian influence in the U.S. and the seemingly intimate link between the U.S. and Erevan. The Republic of Armenia's first Foreign Minister Raffi Hovanissian, was one of several U.S. citizens serving in the Armenian government. The good relations developed by the U.S. Embassy in Baku, opened in March 1992, helped assuage some of these fears. At year's end, however, the State Department announced humanitarian aid for Armenia which, employing rather undiplomatic language, blamed Azerbaijan for Armenia's hardship.[103] Such difficulties undermine the U.S. government as an "honest broker" from Baku's view point.

The U.S. press, at least until spring 1992, reflected the Armenian perspective in its coverage of the war in establishing as standard usage the terminology "return" or "reunification" of the NKAR to Armenia.[104] One UPI story referred to NKAR as "locked inside" Azerbaijan "since 1923."[105] The Western press never failed to identify the parties as "Christian Armenians and Muslim Azerbaijanis," though Azerbaijanis and Armenians both agreed that the dispute is not religious. Azerbaijanis thought the West was trying to identify them with militants in Iran or Libya in order to place blame on them and to justify ignoring Azerbaijani grievances against Russia, which the U.S. aids.

Although the U.S. government may have no clearly defined interests in the Caucasus, U.S. (and other) oil companies do. Azerbaijanis have not entirely overcome their anxieties about foreign businessmen after decades of Soviet rhetoric about capitalist exploitation. Nonetheless, many see oil and foreign cash advances against future production as the key to development and real independence.

## Lessons Learned About Managing
## Regional Conflicts

No state, organization or individual can "manage" a conflict without having the means and the political will to become involved directly in events on the ground. One who "manages" in this way must be prepared to assume responsibility for the outcome. In the Caucasus, neighboring states of Russia, Turkey and Iran have the means, and, to varying degrees, the will to become involved. Only Russia, for whom the area is part of an empire and a key to domestic recovery, has "managed" the conflict enough to affect it significantly. Neither Europe nor the U.S. has had the political will to become sufficiently involved to "manage" the conflict.

U.S. President William Clinton raised the specter of involvement when he suggested in mid-1993 that the U.S. might care to mediate national conflicts in the former Soviet republics. This is a task for which the U.S. is completely unprepared.

One lesson which could be learned from the Caucasian quagmire is that mediators—a more appropriate role than manager—cannot mediate unless they understand the roots and driving force of a conflict. That, in turn, requires both detailed knowledge of the issue's evolution and each disputant's perception of that evolution and of what is at stake. At a time when the U.S. needs more information, funding for many sources of information has been cut. The U.S. intelligence community that knew every detail of Kremlin life was not well prepared to process information on the republics. Rather than devote resources to full retraining of experienced Soviet specialists or bringing in analysts with crucial knowledge of the history and language of the republics, funding was cut because "the Cold War is over." The very important Radio Liberty organization, which engages in extensive information gathering and research on the former Soviet Union and disseminates that information widely in the U.S., has lost funding and may be dismantled because many mistake it solely for a "U.S. propaganda arm" and are unaware of its functions other than broadcasting.

Information gathering organizations need specialists who can read indigenous sources and understand them in their own cultural and historical context. Such specialists are few. Some of those available do not know the language of the republic of their "expertise" and rely solely on Russian sources. Nor is the situation likely to change in the near future—few real specialists are being trained because greater support goes to "technical" education rather than study of the peoples, cultures and languages of the world.

The Nagorno-Karabagh crisis illustrated these weaknesses in the U.S.'s ability to gather and analyze information from the former Soviet Union. Until journalists and diplomats went regularly to Baku in early 1992, little information came to U.S. or other Western institutions from Azerbaijan. Posted to Moscow, western journalists and academic and government analysts often knew Russian and drew information from Soviet sources (English-speaking journalists in Moscow waited for the translations) or the effective Armenian organizations there. Moscow, as the datelines of newspaper reports show, reported less often from Baku than from Erevan or Stepanakert.[106] The Russian intelligentsia, as evident from Supreme Soviet debates and the position of prominent Russian dissidents like Sakharov, generally defended Armenian views. The impact on European and U.S. media and government was great and led to the uneven treatment described.

One example of how little the U.S. understood the fundamental issues in the Karabagh dispute, specifically the importance of land, was a proposal for "territorial swap," discussed in Washington during 1992. In this plan, Azerbaijan was to surrender the NKAR and a connecting corridor to Armenia in exchange for Zangezur which would join Nakhichevan to the rest of Azerbaijan. Both sides promptly rejected the notion because it meant relinquishing "historic patrimony."[107] The Armenian response was especially revealing of the strategic regional perspective it conveyed, and the coincidence of Russian and Armenian interests. The swap, wrote Armenian journalist Armen Khanbabaian, would give Turkey direct rail links to Baku, and thus access to the Caspian Sea and Central Asia. Armenia's transportation networks would then be dependent on Turkey and Azerbaijan, and deprived of "a window to the world with the help of Tehran." Khanbabaian argued that the "Azerbaijanization" of Zangezur could lead not only to regional but to global [sic] destabilization, for Tehran feared Turkey's impact on Azerbaijani Turks in Iran, and Moscow would not accept a plan that drew Central Asia away from Russia and blocked *its key path* [emphasis added] to the Persian Gulf.[108]

This example illustrates that so-called "national conflicts" cannot be explained by national identity alone. Although political interests may reinforce bonds between nations, the process may more often work in the other direction—common interests create the bond and nationalist rhetoric justifies it. One "lesson" to be learned from the Karabagh issue is the need to know and assess the interplay of national aims with other political goals, strategic visions, assessments of capabilities and other factors. Nationalism is a fact of twentieth-century life, and the resolution of conflicts cannot be tied to obliteration of national consciousness.

Many lessons of the Karabagh war are not unique to national conflicts or to this one in particular. Events on the ground can quickly outpace negotiations, so that offensives on the heels of agreements may render long negotiations and documents moot. To quote Mao, "Power comes from the barrel of a gun." Despite negotiations, Armenian gains on the battlefield have altered the de facto borders. Despite Western protests, even "condemnation" of offensives outside Nagorno–Karabagh (Kelbecher in February 1993, Aghdam in July, Fizuli and Jebrail in August), there is no sign of Armenian withdrawal. If outside parties want to contain or stop changes of borders by the force of arms, they must act before the changes are accomplished.

Concerned states might cooperate under such auspices as the UN or CSCE. The response to uses of violence in resolving disputes would have to be prompt and certain. In practice, many problems are connected to such a policy: how would the "aggressor" be determined and by whom; when would a confrontation be serious enough to require sanctions; how would the sovereignty of individual states be protected against wrongful interference; if initial warnings and sanctions failed, would troops be deployed and, if so, by whom? Unless one or more states are willing to enforce policy, then policy statements are of little use.

## Policy and Strategy Alternatives

Before strategies or policies of any sort are considered, fundamental national interests must be defined—a process that will sooner or later require public debate—and their relative importance determined. Interests can then form the basis for integrated and consistent policies in each world area, within parameters determined by capabilities and political will. In connection with these decisions, it will be necessary to decide how much interest groups inside the U.S. will shape foreign policy and, therefore, to what extent foreign affairs may shape relations among those groups inside the U.S. The risk of social fragmentation of the diverse U.S. population, if driven by conflicts elsewhere in the world, is a legitimate national security concern.

Second, policy-makers need to understand fully the self-defined interests of other states. If Iran and Turkey want to expand their influences into former Soviet republics and Russia considers control over those territories essential to its national interests, then U.S. policies in those areas might reasonably be influenced by U.S. relations with each of the interested neighboring states.

Perhaps the U.S. will decide it has no vital interests in the independence of former Soviet republics and that U.S. interests are better served by the preservation of a Russian empire (i.e., a multinational state in which Russians dominate) which, however adversarial its behavior may sometimes be, is a "known" quantity and a fellow "great power." This idea, *mutatis mutandis*, was held by some Western diplomats when the Russian Empire disintegrated after World War I. It made them reluctant to support national independence movements. In the 1990s, the U.S. position, though perhaps not "a policy," has been close to this. It has the virtue of permitting U.S. analysts to focus exclusively on Moscow and let the Russians manage their "own" nationalities. Russia would surely welcome it. No one should be surprised, however, at the response from the republics who see themselves as following in American footsteps, finding an empire oppressive and deciding to "dissolve those political bonds" which bind them.

Selective support for, say, the Western or the Christian peoples, will surely lead to charges—already heard in some quarters—of Eurocentrism, neo–imperialism or, worse, that the U.S. is supporting a new Crusade.

If, however, the U.S. decides to use the basis of its own existence—the commitment to independence, democratic and republican government, rule of law, and guarantees of civil liberties and human rights—as the basis for its policies, then it is implicit in these values that they be applied as impartially abroad as they are meant to be domestically. It is not only when she stands in the Supreme Court that Justice must be blind.

## Conclusions

Armenian forces appear to have altered recognized boundaries by force of arms. Unless outside powers are prepared to force a withdrawal, which seems unlikely, these changes will be confirmed by treaty or by longevity. Some parallels to the former Yugoslavia suggest themselves. Because these territorial wars are rooted in national consciousness, Azerbaijan will not fundamentally acquiesce to the new "historical injustice," and the successful Armenians are likely to press for righting other "historical wrongs." With Nakhichevan further isolated, the next logical move would seem to be against it.

Russia is poised to reestablish its hegemony in Caucasus as Azerbaijan and a Georgia brought to its knees by Russian–backed Abkhaz separatists both accept CIS membership. The old Cold War ostensibly between "communism and democracy" may be over, but perhaps it was never actually ideological.

## Notes

This chapter should be regarded as a companion to my "Karabagh Case Study" to be published in a volume edited by Lee Walker, under the auspices of Women in International Security.

1. Walker Connor article: "A Nation is Nation, is a State, is an Ethnic Group is a" in *Ethnic and Racial Studies*, Vol. 1, No. 4 (October 1978).
2. The term "Azerbaijani" was first imposed as a national designation in 1937, replacing "Turk." Related were language policies that were meant to cut Azerbaijan off from other Turkic peoples of the USSR. In the tsarist period the natives of Azerbaijan

were misidentified as "Tatars" or called simply Muslims. The term "Azerbaijani Turk" first appears in the 1890s. Various historians of Azerbaijan consider it the most accurate term. "Azeri" is popular abroad, perhaps because it is short.

3. Alexandre Bennigsen and Chantal Lemercier-Quelquejay, *Islam in the Soviet Union*, trans G. Wheeler (London: Pall Mall Press, 1967), pp. 130–134 describe the steps in this division, but the more accurate description of the underlying aims is found in Edward Allworth, *The Modern Uzbeks* (Stanford, Ca.: Hoover Institution Press, 1990), pp. 201–209. These pages are a relatively concise segment of a volume that is often unclear and contains many errors and omissions.

4. J. V. Stalin, "Marxism and the National Question," *Collected Works of Stalin* (Moscow: Foreign Language Publishing House, 1953), Vol. 2, pp. 300–373. The essay was written in 1913 at Lenin's behest and apparently guidance.

5. The case of Azerbaijan is discussed in Audrey L. Altstadt, *Azerbaijani Turks: Power and Identity Under Russian Rule* (Stanford: Hoover Institution Press, 1992), Chapter 7. It is the topic of my forthcoming monograph *Culture Wars: Soviet Cultural Policies in Azerbaijan, 1920–1941*.

6. For an overview of the Georgian situation in the late 1980s, see Robert Parsons, "Georgians," in *The Nationalities Question in the Soviet Union*, edited by Graham Smith (London and New York: Longman Publishing Group, 1990), pp. 180–96; on later events, a good source is the Radio Free Europe/Radio Liberty (RFE/RL) Daily Reports.

7. The Party is described in Gerard J. Libaridian, "Revolution and Liberation in the 1892 and 1907 Programs of the Dashnaktsutiun," in Ronald G. Suny, editor, *Transcaucasia: Nationalism and Social Change* (Ann Arbor: Michigan Slavic Series, 1983). The movement is described in greater detail in Anahide Ter Minassian, "Nationalisme et socialisme dans le mouvement révolutionnaire arménien (1887–1912)," in the same volume.

8. Altstadt, "Azerbaijani Turks' Response to Russian Conquest," *Studies in Comparative Communism*, Vol XIX, Nos. 3–4 (Fall–Winter 1986), pp. 267–286.

9. The Baku population is incorrectly called "Tatar" but the Ganje population was called "Azerbaijani Turk." In later Baku city censuses of 1903 and 1913, the terminology changed.

10. The *jadid* movement, led by the Volga and Crimean Tatars, was intended to revitalize and modernize Islam. It began in the schools as a method for efficient teaching of reading and training of critical thinking. On this movement and its applications, see Azade-Ayse Rorlich, *Volga Tatars: A Profile in National Resilience* (Stanford: Hoover Institution, 1986).

11. This pattern is detailed in Altstadt, *The Azerbaijani Turks*, Chapter 4.

12. Muriel Atkin, *Russia and Iran, 1780–1828* (Minneapolis: University of Minnesota Press, 1980), Chapters 1, 3.

13. The imperial census of 1897 (*Pervaia vseobshchaia perepis' naseleniia rossiiskoi imperii 1897 g.* [St. Petersburg, 1897]) shows the many Armenians employed in "Administration" in the provinces of the region. The Armenian role in Oriental Studies of the empire is traced in Richard N. Frye, "Oriental Studies in Russia," in Wayne S. Vucinich, editor, *Russia and Asia: Essays on the Influence of Russia on the Asian Peoples* (Stanford: University of Stanford Press, 1972).

14. Audrey L. Altstadt, "The Baku City Duma: Arena for Elite Conflict," *Central Asian Survey* (Oxford) Vol. 5, Nos. 3/4 (1986).

15. Edmund M. Hertzig, "Armenians" in *The Nationalities Question in the Soviet Union*, p. 152.

16. Most recent English-language literature on Azerbaijan concerns this period, e.g. Ronald Grigor Suny, *The Baku Commune, 1917-1918: Class and Nationality in the Russian Revolution* (Princeton: Princeton University Press, 1972 takes a Marxist view and focuses on Russian and Armenian workers; Tadeusz Swietochowski, *Russian Azerbaijan 1905-1920: The Shaping of National Identity in a Muslim Community* (Cambridge: Cambridge University Press, 1985), and Altstadt *The Azerbaijani Turks*, Chapters 2-4 focus on this period.

17. Ismail's poetry has been published in Baku. The court language was recorded by 17th century travellers to Iran, quoted in Yagub Mahmudov, *Odlar Yurduna Säyahät* (Baku: Genchlik, 1980).

18. Described in Libaridian, "Revolution" and, in greater detail, by Anahide Ter Minassian, "Nationalisme et socialisme," both in Suny, editor, *Transcaucasia*.

19. Detailed descriptions of these events are given and analyzed by Richard Pipes, *The Formation of the Soviet Union, 1917-1923*, revised ed. (Cambridge: Harvard University Press, 1957).

20. Details can be found in Altstadt, *Azerbaijani Turks*, pp. 100-107. Related documents have been published in *K istorii obrazovaniia nagorno-karabakhskoi avtonomnoi oblasti Azerbaidzhanskoi SSR: Dokumenty i materialy* (Baku: Azerneshr, 1989), and *The Karabagh File*, edited by Gerard Libaridian, (Cambridge, Ma.: Zoryan Institute, 1988).

21. Azrevkom was a body that had been created by communist authorities on the eve of their take-over of Azerbaijan in April 1920. It constituted a control mechanism technically separate from the Party, but its members were all senior party members.

22. A. Sh. Mil'man, *Azerbaijan SSR-Suverenoe gosudarstvo v sostave SSSR*, (Baku: Azerneshr, 1971), pp. 233-4; S. V. Kharmandarian, *Lenin i stanovlenie zakavkazskoi federatsii, 1921-1923* (Erevan: Aiastan, 1969), p. 99 adds information.

23. *The Karabagh File*, p. 34.

24. Hertzig, "Armenians," p. 152.

25. *Kistorii obrazovaniia*, pp. 64-66.

26. Fighting continued in Karabagh, but whether against Bolsheviks or national enemies is not stated in available sources. This narrative is summarized from Altstadt, *The Azerbaijani Turks*, pp. 99-105, 125-128.

27. Under Soviet rule, a proposed railroad that would have bridged that gap across Zangezur was delayed for over a decade. See Altstadt, *The Azerbaijani Turks*, pp. 121-2.

28. Hertzig, "Armenians," p. 146.

29. Nicholas Adontz, *Armenia in the Period of Justinian*, translated with bibliography, notes and appendices by Nina Garsoian (Lisbon: Gulbenkian Foundation, 1970), p. 7.

30. His manuscript "Starye pesni i novye legendy" was provided to me several years after it was the written. I do not know whether Gambarov's reply was published.

31. Isa Gambar dropped the -ov ending from his name in 1993.

32. *Grakan Tert* (Erevan) attacked the dissertation of Ferida Mamedova on Caucasian Albania; the Azerbaijani response came in the *Khäbärlär/Izvestiia* of the Academy of Sciences, 1987, No. 4.

33. By October 1987, he had reportedly collected 75,000–100,000 signatures. P. H. Clendenning, "Armenian Unrest in the Caucasus," *Soviet Observer*, 1–16 March 1988, pp. 1, 3.

34. Atkin, *Russia and Iran 1780–1828*, Chapter 2, citing Russian imperial sources of the 19th century. It is also clear from George Bournoutian, "The Ethnic Composition and Socio-Economic Condition of Eastern Armenia in the First Half of the Nineteenth Century," in Suny, ed., *Transcaucasia*, pp. 69–86, that khans were not Armenian.

35. Atkin, *Russia and Iran*, pp. 149–50 describes the trends, based on imperial reports. By the end of the Russian conquest, there had been a net loss of population.

36. Bournoutian, "Ethnic Composition," pp. 78–79.

37. *Pervaia vseobshchaia perepis naseleniia rossiiskoi imperii, 1897 g.*, Vol. 63 for Elizavetpol *guberniia*. These data are summarized, with discussion of class structure and employment, in Altstadt, *The Azerbaijani Turks*, Chapter 3.

38. Kharmandarian, *Lenin i stanovleni*, pp. 280–1.

39. The phrase is the title of Lowell Tillett's fine monograph on Russian Soviet historiography on non-Russian minorities.

40. Mahmud Ismailov in *Azerbaijan*, 1986, No. 6.

41. Detail in Altstadt, *The Azerbaijani Turks*, Chapter 11.

42. Both phenomena are traced clearly in Ronald Grigor Suny, "Nationalism and Democracy in Gorbachev's Soviet Union: The Case of Karabagh," *Michigan Quarterly Review*, Vol. XXVIII, No. 3 (Summer 1989).

43. Suny, "Nationalism and Democracy," p. 484–5.

44. Clendenning, "Armenian Unrest in the Caucasus."

45. Clendenning "Armenian Unrest in the Caucasus."

46. This problem was outlined in "As the sparks fly upward from Nagorno-Karabagh," *The Economist*, 5 March 1988, pp. 49–50.

47. The "Letter to the Editor" by Vahabzade and Aliyarov, was in *Azerbaijan*, 1988, No. 2 (February); English translation by Altstadt in *Journal of the Institute of Muslim Minority Affairs* (London), Vol. 9, No. 2 (July 1988).

48. The speech was made in Paris at a gathering of Armenian war veterans; the report refers to Karabagh and Nakhjivan as "ancient Armenian lands" which Aganbegian says "ought to" belong to Armenia. *L'Humanité*, 18 November 1987, p. 17.

49. *Bakinskii rabochii* [Hereafter: *BR*], 11 March 1988, cited in *Sobytiia vokrug NKAO v krivom zerkale fal'sifikatorov* [Hereafter: *Sobytiia vokrug NKAO*] (Baku: Elm, 1989), p. 12. Despite the incendiary title and annotations, the slim volume reproduces published items from local newspapers and other sources. The data were reproduced with further discussion of conditions in the NKAR in *Azärbayjan Khalg täsärrüfaty/ Narodnoe Khoziaistvo Azerbaidzhana*, 1988, No. 7, pp. 8–16.

50. *Chislennost' i sostav naseleniia SSSR: Po dannym vsesoiuznoi perepisi naseleniia 1979 goda* (Moscow, 1984), Table 27.

51. Data in *Altynjı Chaghırısh Azärbayjan SSR Ali Sovetinin Ijlasları, 9ju sessiya (21–22 dekabr 1965-ji il); Stenografik hesabat* (Baku, 1966), pp. 107–11; *Bakinskii Rabochii*, 12 November 1988, reproduced in *Sobytiia vokrug NKAO*, p. 54

52. *Sovetskii Karabakh*, 15 March 1988; quoted in *Sobytiia vokrug NKAO*, p. 18.

53. Hertzig, "Armenians," p. 153 and Suny, "Nationalism and Democracy," p. 487–8, refer to "clashes," but Suny also refers to "violence against Armenians."

54. Wesselink, E. "Human Rights Violations in Azerbaijan and Armenia," *Soviet Refugee Monitor*, Vol.1, No. 2 (February 1992), p. 4.

55. Rauf Huseinov, "Refugees in the USSR: Facts, Situation, and a Search for the Way Out," was delivered in English during a lecture tour in 1991.

56. Wesselink, "Human Rights", pp. 5–6.

57. This they openly told authorities, as reported in *Pravda*, 4 April 1988; reproduced in *Sobytiia vokrug NKAO*, p. 29.

58. Wesselink, "Human Rights," p. 4.

59. "Spetszadanie," *Rabochaia gazeta*, 18 September, 1988, an interview with Soviet Internal Affairs troops in Armenia.

60. Initially, these were not in the official newspapers. A group called "People's Committee for Aid to Karabagh" was created in Baku. It started an unofficial newspaper called *Azerbaijan* in October 1989, which covered the attempts of convoys to supply the Azerbaijani population in the NKAR and other news.

61. Georgii Rozhonov, "Doroga bez kontsa," *Vyshka*, 11 February 1990. He had written the story the previous fall.

62. The Hojaly events were covered in the Western press: *Times* (London) on 1 (by Thomas Goltz), 3, March 1992, *New York Times*, 27 February, 4 March and *Washington Post*, 4 March (by Goltz), and others. I am grateful to Mr. Goltz for providing me the manuscript of his forthcoming book *Azadlik! A Year of War, Unrest and Revolution in the Former Soviet Republic of Azerbaijan* (working title).

63. Thomas Goltz reported the details of his conversations with the BBC and *Washington Post* in a report of 10 March 1992 to the Institute for Current World Affairs (New Hampshire) of which he was then a fellow, residing in Baku.

64. RFE/RL Daily Report No. 67, 7 April 1993. The Red Cross counted nearly 40,000 refugees when Kelbecher fell, according to the *New York Times*, 7 April 1993. The *Washington Times*, 9 April, estimated 50,000, but cited no source.

65. These efforts are summarized in Altstadt, "Karabagh Case Study," in a forthcoming volume of papers from a conference on ethnic conflict resolution sponsored by Women in International Security; it will be edited by Lee Walker.

66. Hasanov's speech was printed in the Azerbaijan Popular Front newspaper *Azadlik* 14 January 1990, then in *Vestnik Giandzhi*, 20 January, the day Russian troops stormed Baku, killing more than 100, and captured Popular Front headquarters. With other documents related to the Russian attack, it was reprinted in *Chernyi Ianvar': Baku 1990; Dokumenty i materialy* (Baku: Azerneshr, 1990), pp. 51–59.

67. Such incidents were reported in *Transcaucasus: A Chronology*, A Publication of the Armenian National Committee of America (Washington, D.C.); Vol. 1, No. 7 (1 July 1992) and Vol. 1, No. 9 (1 September 1992). Calls for resignation were repeated again in July 1993, reported ITAR–TASS (Moscow), excerpted in FBIS–SOV–93–128, 7 July 1993, p. 51.

68. Quoting *Yerevan Hayastan* 16 January 1992, in "Voices of Karabagh," pamphlet of the Central Intelligence Agency, June 1992 (LDA 92–13420).

69. Manukyan, former Prime Minister who had resigned due to disagreement with Ter–Petrossian, replaced Vazgen Sarkisyan by presidential decree of 14 September 1992. *Transcaucasus: A Chronology*, Vol 1., No. 10 (1 October 1992), p. 3. On Manukyan, see also RFE/RL Daily Report No. 203, 21 October 1992.

70. RFE/RL Daily Report No. 129, 9 July 1993.

71. RFE/RL Daily Report, No. 161, 24 August 1993. He was called "chairman of Karabagh Defense Committee" in the SNARK (Erevan) press service report of 26 July 1993, reported in FBIS–SOV–93–142, 27 July 1993, p. 61, and "Nagorno–Karabagh Republic" Defense Minister in an Armenpress (Erevan) report of 29 July, in FBIS–SOV–93–145, 30 July 1993, p. 54.

72. Jeyhun Mollazade, "On the Karabagh Problem," first delivered at the seminar on "Nationalism and minority issues in the CSCE Region: International Dialogue on Security and Cooperation in Transcaucasia," 28–30 April (Copenhagen), p. 27 of original paper. An extract was published in *Qarabag Quatre Ans Apres* (Paris: Azerbaycan Evi, 1992), pp. 24–31.

73. Former Popular Front member Etibar Mamedov, now leader of the National Independence Party, indicated he had such a discussion with a Russian journalist in November 1988, after the mass demonstrations in Baku. Private conversation, May 1991.

74. Thus one finds references by scholars to "The roots of prying Nagorno–Karabagh from Muslim control" as well as the view of Armenians in "Muslim eyes." Henry R. Huttenbach, "In Support of Nagorno–Karabagh: Social Components of the Armenian Nationalist Movement," *Nationalities Papers*, Vol. XVIII, No. 2 (Fall 1990), p. 5.

75. *Karabagh File*, p. xxvi. Rather than Islam, he blamed Turks, referring to "proto–fascist Young Turks." (p. xxvii)

76. Azerbaijan's law on religions was published, and issued with English translation, in late summer 1992.

77. The steps in this process are clearly outlined in Richard Pipes, *Formation of the Soviet Union*, Chapters 3–5.

78. Alexander Rahr, "Zhirinovsky's Plea for dictatorship," RFE/RL Daily Report No. 124, 2 July 1992. Zhirinovskii, also told *Rossiya* (No. 27), that "right–wing forces will come to power in Russia and Germany under the slogan of the protection of the white race and divide eastern Europe among themselves. He added that after the forthcoming demise of the United States, Alaska will also be incorporated into the Russian empire. He noted that, if elected president, he would strengthen the army and state security forces."

79. At a Conference on Ethnic Conflict Resolution, sponsored by Women in International Security, Prague, September 1992. Starovoitova had previously been a deputy to the USSR Supreme Soviet from Armenia.

80. RFE/RL Daily Report No. 230, 1 December 1992.

81. Serge Schmemann, "Yeltsin Suggests Russian Regional Role," *New York Times*, March 1, 1993.

82. RFE/RL Daily report No. 155, 16 August 1993.

83. So said Evgenii Ambartsumov, chairman of the Russian Congress of Deputies' Committee on International Affairs and Foreign Economic Ties. RFE/RL Daily Report, no. 145, 2 August 1993.

84. S. Enders Wimbush and Alex Alexiev, "The Ethnic Factor in the Soviet Armed Forces, Rand Corporation, R–2787/1 March 1982.

85. The use of the Oriental Institute in policy–making is traced in H. B. Paksoy, *Alpamysh: Central Asian Identity Under Russian Rule*, (Hartford, Conn: Association for the Advancement of Central Asian Research, 1989) and Wayne Vucinich, "The Structure of Soviet Orientology," in Vucinich, editor, *Russia and Asia*. The Institute has adjusted

to the post-soviet era, as its former Deputy Director Vitalii Naumkin and various staff members, formed the "non-governmental, non-profit" Russian Center for Strategic Research to provide the Russian government with "independent analysis." One wonders how such a "non-governmental non-profit" Center is funded. RFE/RL Daily Report No. 20, 13 January 1992.

86. Thomas Goltz, "Letter from Eurasia: The Hidden Russian Hand," in *Foreign Policy*, Number 92, Fall 1993, quotations from pp. 98–99. The six man was given a 15 year jail sentence.

87. CIS membership was rejected on 7 October 1992. The treaty with Russia was negotiated and signed in October, but was printed in Baku newspapers in November, including *Bakinskii Rabochii*, 19 November 1992.

88. Speaker of the National Assembly (until June 1993) Isa Gambar articulated these accusations, but the ideas were widely shared among Azerbaijani and foreign analysts. The monthly journal *Yeni Forum* (Ankara), August 1993, pp. 6–7 published a report, of undisclosed origin, summarizing an alleged meeting between the rebel leader Surat Huseinov, Azerbaijani opposition (to Elchibey) leaders and Russian military men in Moscow in April. If accurate, the report would confirm direct Russian planning and aid to the coup.

89. Elchibey was elected on 7 June 1992 in the first open elections since 1919. Still president at the time of writing, Elchibey is residing in his home in Nakhjivan while Aliyev rules in Baku. A brief summary of the coup can be found in the *AACAR BULLETIN*, publication of the Association for the Advancement of Central Asian Research, Vol. VI, No. 2 (Fall 1993).

90. Russian Ambassador to Azerbaijan portrayed Russian efforts as more fruitful and ignored those within the CSCE framework, reported in FBIS–SOV–93–128, 7 July 1993, p. 53.

91. Yakub Mamedov succeeded Ayaz Mutalibov after the latter's forced resignation on 6 March 1992. Mamedov remained in power until Mutalibov's abortive come-back attempt on 15–16 May. He resigned, then regained the post, only to resign again on 18 May. He was succeeded by Popular Front leader Isa Gambar. Gambar was Acting President until Elchibey's inauguration on 15 June.

92. In late June a Memorandum of Cooperation was signed and by 18 August, an agreement allowing Iran to explore Baku oil.

93. FBIS–SOV–93–156, 16 August 1993, p. 66. The route through Iran is currently favored over that through Armenia.

94. The Kars and Moscow Treaties of 1921 include guarantees of Nakhjivan's close association with Azerbaijan.

95. RFE/RL Daily Reports No. 157, 18 August, and No. 159, 20 August, 1993. Although Armenian officials have criticized Ankara, they also maintain lines of communication. See FBIS–SOV–93–160, 20 August 1993, p. 53.

96. See Wilson Nathaniel Howell, *The Soviet Union and the Kurds; A Study of National Minority Problems in Soviet Policy*. Ann Arbor, 1965.

97. Interviews with Armenian leaders by Agence France Presse, FBIS–SOV–93–156, 16 August 1993, pp. 63–4.

98. Hearings of 23 October 1991 included Baroness Caroline Cox (British House of Lords), Yelena Bonner and Alexander Arzoumanian (speaking on behalf of the Armenians); Nadir Mehtiyev from Azerbaijan and a US specialist on Turkey, Azerbaijan

and Central Asia, Dr. David Nissman. Hearings of 8 March 1993 included one representative each from the Armenian Assembly of America and the Armenian National Assembly of America; one from the Azerbaijan Embassy in Washington, and a specialist from the Rand Corporation who spoke on Georgia.

99. Reported in the Congressional CSCE *Digest* (Washington, D.C.), Vol 14, No. 6 (Summer 1991).

100. Different versions were passed by both the House of Representatives and the Senate in July and August. Among other things, this Amendment holds Azerbaijan responsible for the conflict and blocks humanitarian aid and Azerbaijani participation in U.S. education and other programs.

101. House Resolution 86, proposed by Rep. Bonior (D–MI), was never adopted.

102. "Tilting to Armenia," *Washington Post*, March 10, 1993.

103. Azerbaijan protested the reference to Azerbaijan's "blockade" being taken out of the context of the larger war.

104. e.g. *The Economist* of March 5, 1988; Clendenning, "Armenian Unrest in the Caucasus."

105. Several copyrighted UPI stories of October 1989 repeated this verbiage.

106. During the first year of the Karabagh conflict, Tamara Dragadze (University of London) described this problem and warned against taking too literally the Western media's coverage, "Le joug de la culture nationale en Transcaucasie," in *La Nouvelle Alternative*, No 13, March 1989, p. 14.

107. Isa Gambar made this argument from Azerbaijan's view point; private conversation, June 1992.

108. Armen Khanbabaian, "Territorial'nyi peredel kak razreshenie 'Karabakhskogo voprosa'?" *Nezavisimaia gazeta*, 24 June 1992, p.1.

# 5

# Central Asia: Prospects for Ethnic and Nationalist Conflict

*Malvin M. Helgesen*

The abortive August 1991 coup precipitated the collapse of the USSR and spawned a series of new states that have faced a painful process of national self–definition. Among them, the newly independent states (NIS) of Central Asia face the most difficult task shaping a distinct national identity. None of the Central Asian states had existed in anything like their present borders until the Soviet period, when Stalin carved them out as union republics during the 1920s and 1930s from the large Turkestan region, as Central Asia was known before the Revolution. The historical predecessors to these artificial entities were either city–state khanates or tribal confederations.[1] The region continued to lag in its nationalist consciousness long after the Baltics, Caucasus, and Ukraine—which all strove for independence after the Russian Revolution—seemed well on their way to splitting with Moscow in the late Gorbachev period. Communist leaders in Central Asia never embraced the independence cause until after the August 1991 coup, although they were happy to latch on to the concessions Moscow made to republic sovereignty as a way to recoup autonomy that had been curtailed after Brezhnev's death.[2] While Uzbekistan took the plunge in adopting independence soon after the coup collapsed, only lagging behind Ukraine by a few days, the others proceeded more cautiously and Kazakhstan was the last to give up efforts to create a reformed Soviet Union in December 1991.

Central Asia is a diverse region in terms of its history, culture, ethnography, and geography, especially when Kazakhstan is included as is customary among Western experts (Russians frequently treat it as a separate case). Western interest has focused most on Kazakhstan, with a population of over eighteen million people, because of the presence there of almost a thousand strategic nuclear weapons. It is also important for its large oil and gas reserves, stores of other strategic minerals like cobalt, zinc, and copper, and diversified agriculture; it is the only grain exporter in the region.  Uzbekistan has over twenty-two million people and a diversified resource base including cotton, gold, some gas and possibly substantial reserves of oil, making it an important competitor for regional importance despite its serious rural overpopulation and lack of water for its burgeoning population.  Turkmenistan has just over three and a half million citizens and is abundant in oil wealth and marketable cotton, but also faces water shortages and serious environmental and health problems. The last two states, Tajikistan and Kyrgyzstan, have five and a half and four million people respectively.  They are the most remote and the poorest among the NIS; both suffer from serious unemployment and a scarcity of most resources, with the exception of some rare earth minerals and water, which abundantly flows from their high mountain ranges in an area termed "the roof of the world."

The death of the Soviet Union posed immediate challenges for the leaders of these new states, who ranged from Eastern-style potentates in Turkmenistan and unvarnished Communist Party conservatives in Uzbekistan and Tajikistan, to Gorbachev-style party reformers in Kazakhstan and Kyrgyzstan.  Each leader shifted his base of political legitimacy from loyalty to Moscow to greater responsiveness to local needs in order to protect himself from political fallout following the coup's collapse.  The more reform-oriented leaders, Kazakhstan's Nursultan Nazarbayev and Kyrgyzstan's Askar Akayev, were on much firmer ground; both repudiated the coup publicly and aligned themselves with Yeltsin's efforts to resist it.  They had already been pursuing a political line that won broad support from the reformist elements in the Communist party and with moderate nationalists.  Uzbekistan's leader, Islam Karimov, also moved quickly after the failure of the coup to embrace the nationalist agenda in order to shift attention from his public support for the coup plotters.  The Turkmen party boss, Sapurmurad Niyazov, moved in the same direction over time, although his dominance of the old power structures in politically backward Turkmenistan allowed him to make the shift less abruptly than did Karimov.

Tajikistan's party leader, Kakhar Makhkamov, however, soon fell victim to his close association with the coup.  He was unseated by a coalition of Communist party rivals, representatives of competing regions, and increasingly vocal Tajik nationalist and Islamic forces.[3]  Not only was Makhkamov ousted as President, but the Communist Party was temporarily banned until late September 1991, when old guard communists staged a comeback and advanced a former party leader, Rakhman Nabiyev, to replace a moderate caretaker.  A compromise was reached in early October that set elections for an executive Presidency; Nabiyev won the closely contested election in late November amidst allegations of fraud.

Turkmenistan

## The Nationalist Factor

All the leaders have continued to move in a nationalist direction to broaden their base of legitimacy, but at rates determined mostly by internal political alignments. The Uzbek regime has been the most obvious in adopting nationalism as a new underpinning for its independence. Karimov has retained, but renamed the old Communist party, and sought to give substance to Uzbekistan's pretensions to regional leadership by maintaining a high international profile, visiting key regional states, and seeking to visit the United States. He has embraced a neo–populist agenda, talked about the need for

Kyrgyzstan

economic reform while reassuring the public that a social security net will be maintained.  He has, however, eschewed militant nationalism, fearing that it could undermine his control within Uzbekistan, with a sizeable Tajik minority, and foster regional instability by raising a series of border disputes involving Uzbek minorities in neighboring states.  At the other end of the spectrum have been the Kazakhstani and Kyrgyzstani regimes, which have been very cautious in brandishing nationalism.  These countries have large Russian minorities—about 35 and 20 percent respectively—who are deeply alarmed that nationalism

Tajikistan

will relegate them to a second class status. Nazarbayev and Akayev have both maintained that pursuing an unvarnished nationalist course would be disastrous for their countries.

Despite this fine tuning of the nationalist issue, all the states took steps as early as 1989—two years before the coup—to give ethnic majorities a special status. Most notably, the states have embarked on language reform that will eventually have the native language replace Russian as the language of administration and the economy. In the case of Tajikistan, the Nabiyev regime

Uzbekistan

even decided to move away from the Cyrillic script for Tajik to the Arabic script, which would make it virtually identical to Iranian Farsi. The status of this decision, however, is uncertain given the subsequent unrest in Tajikistan, which will be discussed at length below. In March 1993, educators from the Turkic Central Asian states—all but Tajikistan—appeared to commit themselves to adopting a Latin script to replace the Cyrillic script over the next several years; Azerbaijan, another nearby Turkic state, already took that decision about a year before. Given the level of concern in Kazakhstan and Kyrgyzstan for Russian sensitivities, however, this transition will probably be a slow process

Kazakhstan

and might even be challenged by the parliaments in both countries. Constitutions in the new states demand that the presidents are fluent in the native, state language and senior positions have increasingly gone to representatives of the titular nationality.

These moves have allowed the regimes to capitalize on the anti-colonial sentiment prevalent among the educated elite, but they have not developed into a full blown effort to force out Russians who remain vital to maintaining the economic and administrative infrastructure. None of the constitutions blatantly discriminate against minorities; all the constitutions—now approved except in Tajikistan—have granted citizenship to all inhabitants of the state. While not accepting dual citizenship, all five countries have tried to create a hospitable climate for those vital non-native personnel to remain. Regime leaders clearly aim to replace Russian cadres gradually with natives, many now being sent for training in the West, but want this process to be incremental and not disrupt the functioning of their states.

Information from the Russian press suggests that many Russians probably have left the region since 1989, with 1990 seeing a major exodus, 1991 a leveling off, and another upturn in 1992.[4]  The civil war in Tajikistan apparently forced over 50,000 Russians to flee, although the bleak economic situation in Russia probably has dissuaded many other Russians elsewhere, who are anxious about their eroding status in Central Asia, but see few good alternatives in Russia. Based on figures from the 1989 census, over 9.5 million Russians resided in Central Asia, and the total of European settlers—many Ukrainians and Germans in addition to the Russians—totaled over 12 million. The overwhelming majority of these Europeans remain in the region, making up about one fifth of its overall population. In areas like northern Kazakhstan, they make up a majority of the population.

## Nationalism as a Destabilizing Factor

Nationalism, or perhaps ethnic tension to be more precise, can become a serious destabilizing factor throughout Central Asia as events since 1989 have underscored. Several violent clashes in 1989 and 1990 signalled that even without a well-developed nationalist movement, the region had witnessed a potent emerging force. Clashes occurred between Uzbeks and Meskhetian Turks in Uzbekistan, Kyrgyz and Uzbeks in Kyrgyzstan, and Kyrgyz and Tajiks along the border of those states. Local reformers speculated that the local security forces may have goaded the confrontations to highlight the danger of democratization to the leadership in Moscow, but whatever their exact sponsorship, agitators found numerous willing participants. In the most serious clash, the battles between Kyrgyz and Uzbeks in Kyrgyzstan's Osh oblast, official reports indicated that over 200 people were killed. Pressure ran high on the Uzbek regime to come to the aid of Uzbeks who allegedly were being driven off the land by enraged Kyrgyz. The situation became so strained that the Uzbek and Kyrgyz party leaders had to meet to defuse the crisis. Eventually, the crisis led to the removal of the Kyrgyz leader and his replacement by the pro-reform head of the Kyrgyz Academy of Sciences, Askar Akayev.[5]

Since independence, nationalistic tensions have been generally muted, but the civil war in Tajikistan has taken on a somewhat ethnic cast. Following weeks of demonstrations by self-styled secular democrats, a coalition of Islamic groups organized around the Islamic Revival Party (IRP), and representatives of the Pamir regional clan, emerged to challenge the communists. In mid-May 1992, President Nabiyev conceded a power sharing arrangement and committed to new parliamentary elections initially scheduled for early December 1992. Within weeks, however, opponents of the new coalition from key regions—notably Khojend (earlier Leninabad) and Kulyab—began to contest the arrangement. By late June, large areas of southern Tajikistan were engulfed in a full-scale civil war between the factions, pitting neighboring villages or even groups within the same collective farms, who chose sides along regional-clan, ethnic, and religious lines. Tajikistan's large Uzbek minority—about a quarter of the population country-wide—sided increasingly with the Communist old guard elements centered in Khojend, Kulyab, and in the Hissar valley, west of Dushanbe. Proponents of the coalition government, strongly identified with the more Tajik, Islamic, and agricultural Garm region, retaliated increasingly by persecuting and attacking ethnic Uzbeks. Thousands of Uzbeks fled to Uzbekistan. The Uzbek regime, fearing a spillover of the unrest into heavily Tajik populated regions on the Uzbek side of the border, tried to keep many of the refugees out. The Karimov regime also appears to have stepped up harassment and surveillance of the Tajik cultural rights movement in Uzbekistan.

Some Tajik nationalists began to play explicitly on anti-Uzbek sentiment, much of it rooted in Stalin's decision in the 1920s to leave important ethnic Tajik cultural centers, Samarkand and Bukhara, within Uzbekistan. Anti-Uzbek propaganda reached a crescendo in late October, when regime media accused the Karimov government of direct involvement in an abortive attempt by old guard militia based in the ethnically Uzbek areas of the Hissar valley to eject the coalition government from Dushanbe.

Since the collapse of the coalition government in November—Nabiyev was forced to resign in September and was replaced as coalition head by a Pamir official, Akbarsho Iskandarov—and the military expulsion of the Islamic and "democratic" elements from Dushanbe in early December, the Uzbek regime has played a highly visible role in supporting the resurgent old guard forces. Tashkent has provided significant support, including some military support, to the old guard government of Ermakaly Rakhmanov.[6] The heavily Uzbek-populated Hissar region has also been pressing for an autonomous administrative existence. These developments have provided an increasingly nationalist cast to the Tajik civil war and could provide a rallying point for the Tajik opposition, which is trying to stage an insurgency from the Garm valley and Pamir regions.

None of the other inter-ethnic strains are as deep or volatile as the Uzbek-Tajik cleavage, but they do have the potential to generate unrest.

Uzbek–Kyrgyz strains are probably the most serious of the others and unrest in Tajikistan could also contribute to these problems. Tajik regime efforts to root out opposition forces in the Garm valley have driven them, and much of the civilian population, further into the upper regions adjacent to the Kyrgyz border. Renewed fighting could force many Kyrgyz across the border and add demographic pressure in Osh province, where Kyrgyz already resent the continued presence of a large number of Uzbeks. The fighting could obviously also reactivate Kyrgyz–Tajik tensions. Despite Dushanbe's desire to attain political, military, and economic support from Kyrgyzstan, Rakhmanov was unwilling to accept the legitimacy of current borders with that country when he visited there in February 1993; the borders have been contested in several areas during the last few years. Refugee flows from the Tajik civil war may also have raised tension levels elsewhere in the region—such as southern Kazakhstan—where Uzbeks and Russians seeking refuge have fled. Even in Turkmenistan, where the effects of the Tajik crisis have been muted, tensions have been simmering against the Uzbeks, whom many resent as potential imperialists.

Tensions between these ethnic groups and the neighboring states have, in fact, been strained by controversy over the use of Central Asia's limited water supply.[7] Tajikistan and Kyrgyzstan have an abundance of water. The headwaters of the region's two principle river systems, the Amu Darya and the Syr Darya, are situated on their mountainous territory. Both states have talked about charging the more populous downstream states for water, given their comparative poverty and lack of few alternate raw materials to make their own economies viable. By contrast, the much more populous downstream states of Uzbekistan and Kazakhstan and the comparatively wealthy Turkmen have been critical of pollution from upstream and resented the suggestion that Tajikistan or Kyrgyzstan would charge for water. Currently, the issue is largely moot. Tajikistan is so dependent on Uzbek support to control the Islamic insurgency that it is unlikely to press this issue. Similarly, Kyrgyzstan has not constructed the system of dams and reservoirs necessary to follow up on its threats to charge Uzbekistan for water and appeared hesitant to stand up to the Uzbek government, which provides critical gas supplies to southern Kyrgyzstan. Over the next decade, however, the water issue could become a major irritant within the region, particularly if more nationalistic regimes begin to emerge.

## Factors Reinforcing Nationalism

Several factors have intertwined with nationalism in ways that make the combination potentially more destabilizing. Chief among these factors is regionalism, but economic factors and Islamic identification can also work to reinforce nationalism.

On the surface, regionalism seems inherently at odds with nationalism, in fact, as its foremost competitor for allegiance. Regionalism within Central Asia, however, has sometimes aligned itself with nationalism among minorities concentrated in specific regions, sharpening inter-ethnic tensions within the new states. Separatist strains among the European groups in northern Kazakhstan are the clearest example of how regionalism and minority nationalism can intertwine. Tajikistan provides the clearest example of regionalism's divisive potential, having already resulted in the de facto fragmentation of the country. In some cases, this regionalism has an ethnic dimension, while in other cases it pits ethnically identical groups from different clans or regions against one another. In all cases, however, regionalism has been a major impediment for the new states seeking to create a broader, non-ethnic, national identity.

The concentration of ethnic Russian, and other Russian-speaking European settlers, in northern Kazakhstan has created the strongest linkage between regionalism and minority nationalism. The population of these regions fear that Kazakh nationalism, represented by the language law and moves to supplant Russians in key jobs, will erode their dominant position. Ukrainians, Germans, and other Europeans—most of whom rely on the Russian language—have strongly backed Russian opposition to burgeoning Kazakh nationalism.

Polls from the summer of 1992 indicate that three quarters of Russians in Kazakhstan agree that northern regions should remain an integral part of Kazakhstan, but Russian nationalism is apparently quietly growing.[8]  In December 1992, some 15,000 demonstrators in Ust-Kamenogorsk reportedly demanded that Russian have a co-equal status to Kazakh in the Constitution, and that the oblast control cultural and educational policy and manage all economic resources within the region.[9]  Cossack elements in northern Kazakhstan have also been an irritant, for instance provocatively celebrating the 400th anniversary of the Ural Cossack's allegiance to the Tsar in late 1991. Press revelations concerning the December 1992 alleged "political assassination" of a major industrial combine manager in Karaganda also suggested a linkage to Russian autonomous impulses. According to a report in *Komsomolskaya pravda*, the director encouraged some of this activity and had provided the funds for a new Orthodox church in Temirtau.[10]

If local leaders believe that they are not getting a voice in making policy—and most signs suggest they feel marginalized by the new structure—they may try to capitalize on discontent among the Russian populace to press for a federalist Kazakhstan, or even possibly outright separation, thus causing a major regional crisis. Russian activists are already calling for elections to give the local governments greater legitimacy and are likely to step up activities before expected national elections in 1994 or 1995.[11]  The Russian government has maintained cordial relations with the Kazakh government and supported President Nazarbayev's policy of maintaining close ties to Moscow, but is becoming more critical of the treatment of Russian minorities. Yeltsin would not welcome a separatist movement that could initiate another major crisis on Russia's periphery, threaten to generate a flood of refugees, or even embroil predominantly Russian-manned units of the Kazakhstan military in the north. It is less certain, however, that his government could successfully prevent private assistance, particularly from Cossack groups just across the Russian border, from reaching would-be separatists in northern Kazakhstan. In a similar situation in Moldova, the Yeltsin regime opted to maintain its military presence to pre-empt large-scale conflicts between the central government and Russian separatists.

Regionalism in Tajikistan has also played a politically volatile role, interacting with nationalism, and in the process undermining the unity of the fledgling Tajik state. Tajikistan, much like Kazakhstan, can be seen as an artificial creation, joining very diverse regions, ethnic and clan groups. In the pro-Communist Khojend and Kulyab regions, Tajik and Uzbek elements had frequently intermarried and adapted to one another's influences, forming a sort of amalgam, the so-called Sarts. By contrast, in the more remote regions, notably the Garm valley and the Pamirs, people viewed themselves as ethnically and linguistically pure Tajiks. These two sets of regional clans have been struggling for political ascendancy since almost immediately following the collapse of the USSR. The November 1991 presidential election pitted Khojend's favorite son, Nabiyev—who reportedly spoke better Uzbek than Tajik—against Davlat Khodonazarov, the former USSR Cinematographers' Union chairman—who is from the small Pamir ethnic group; it was no surprise that the former, representing the most powerful region, won handily. As Tajik politics has become more polarized, however, the country has begun to split along regional lines. Gorno-Badakhshan, which already had an active movement favoring autonomy within Tajikistan, is increasingly leaning toward independence, and Garm, the center of the insurgency, is only partially under Dushanbe's control.

Regionalism elsewhere in Central Asia is less strong, but it is beginning to play a visible role. In Kyrgyzstan, north-south tensions are coming to the fore and undermining efforts to forge strong allegiance to the national government rather than to local patronage networks. President Akayev had to replace the regional leader in Dzhalalabad in the fall of 1992, for instance, because he operated in his region like an independent potentate. In Turkmenistan, President Niyazov publicly alluded to his concerns about tribalism earlier this year, which could pit some of the smaller Turkmen tribes against Niyazov's dominant Teke tribe.[12] Similarly, Kazakhs are also divided in the greater, middle, and lesser hordes, with Nazarbayev and former long-time Communist Party boss Kunayev representing the greater horde. In all these cases, regionalism or tribal/clan divisions act as a competitor for nationalism. It underscores that allegiance to the Stalinist creation of nation-states in Central Asia has not fully taken root.

On the other hand, these strains can coexist and intensify minority nationalism and work to undermine national stability.

Islamic identification can similarly work in concert with nationalism among the majority Central Asians, alarming European minorities and undermining regime efforts to establish a non-ethnically based loyalty to the new secular states. Islamic consciousness varies sharply from state to state, with Tajikistan being the most Islamic, followed by Uzbekistan, Kyrgyzstan, Turkmenistan, and Kazakhstan in that order.

In several cases, local nationalists have tried to latch onto Islam—despite its inherently pan-national character—as a means of reinforcing local nationalism. In Tajikistan, Islamic groups and nationalist groups formed a close alliance in initially challenging and then ousting President Nabiyev. According to statements by the current Tajik government, they have continued attempts to overthrow the constitutional order since being driven into the insurgency.[13] Some other small groups, like the Alash party in Kazakhstan have also highlighted their Islamic agenda as a tool to increase Kazakh consciousness, which they apparently view as weak.[14]

The region's deepening economic crisis is another factor that can reinforce nationalism. The economies of all these states have taken a beating from the collapse of the USSR. Tajikistan has suffered most severely with its economy contracting by almost a third as a result of its fierce civil war. Kyrgyzstan, which ranked with Tajikistan as the poorest of the former Soviet republics, has also suffered from its isolation and dependence on uncertain trade links to Moscow. The other economies have contracted less sharply, but have also seen problems with key imports, growing unemployment, and steep inflation. Most are likely to contract further over the next two years because of declining trade and rising energy prices in their relations with Russia, their biggest trade partner, which are fueling inflation bordering on hyperinflation.

These woes have affected almost all segments of society, but have also magnified differences between various ethnic groups. Because they have generally been on the lower end of the socio-economic ladder vis-à-vis ethnic Russians, Central Asian people have been more concerned about the impact of price rises and the contraction of the social welfare net. Nationalist groups also worry that natives lack the resources to profit from privatization of land and businesses; they fear that Russians and largely Russified locals from the old Communist Party establishment will grab up the best resources. President Akayev in Kyrgyzstan has had to block several efforts by nationalists in the parliament to limit land ownership to ethnic Kyrgyz.[15] By contrast, Russians and other non-native groups are anxious that their earlier economic advantages are fading. They fear that the language competency laws will be used to ease them out from key jobs. Many are especially worried that budgetary stringencies, backed by pressure from the International Monetary Fund (IMF), will force the regimes to trim bloated labor rolls. In Bishkek, for instance, one press report suggested as many as 200,000 might lose their jobs and the overwhelming majority of these would be Europeans.[16]

Even economic good news, like Kazakhstan's expected revenue from its big oil and gas deals, could prove a political football between various regions and ethnic groups. Russified areas in the north are arguing that state revenues should be used to maintain the rust-belt and defense industries in the north, while Kazakh nationalists are pressing the government to invest in the areas with a fast-growing Kazakh population in the south. The regime can also expect to hear complaints about its generous help to resettle expatriate Kazakhs, especially from Mongolia, on land being vacated by Germans who are emigrating to Germany.[17]

## Prospects for Nationalist Unrest in Central Asia

Different Central Asian countries face different prospects for nationalist unrest over the next several years, with Tajikistan having the highest potential and only Turkmenistan unlikely to see serious problems. None, however, is entirely immune.

Tajikistan has already experienced some inter-ethnic conflict in the course of its civil war, and Uzbek involvement in propping up the Rakhmanov regime heightens the likelihood for more. Islamic and self-styled democrats fighting in the Garm valley and the remote Gorno-Badakhshan region will probably withstand the current regime's assault by adopting tactics similar to those that sustained the Afghan mujahedeen. By hiding in the hills and attacking only isolated regime outposts, they can conserve their strength and slowly win over a populace whose regime will be unable to adequately feed and protect them. The regime's hegemony can probably never be extended to the remote Pamir region. Without such control, the opposition will be able to receive arms and trained volunteers from Afghanistan, many probably recruited from the more than 60,000 who fled across the border in December 1992. Given this prospect, the regime is almost certain to continue its well-documented policy of regional cleansing and reliance on Uzbek and Russian military help. Their involvement will sharpen the nationalist dimension of the conflict and increase the chances for spillover, particularly into Uzbekistan but possibly also into Kyrgyzstan. Tajik nationalists that ousted Nabiyev rallied around the banner of the old Bukharan state—now in Uzbekistan—suggesting they already had a broader nationalist agenda. Moves by Uzbek dominated regions to play a more visible political role will also contribute to deepening inter-ethnic tensions in Tajikistan.

As happened in Afghanistan, the opposition may be able to rally broader support by relying both on Islam, with its antagonism to communism, and nationalism, highlighting Tajikistan's anti-colonial liberation struggle against Russia and Uzbekistan. Because of the similarity in their struggles and the involvement of the same ethnic groups on both sides of the borders, the Tajik and Afghan crises could increasingly become intertwined. Already, Afghanistan's ethnic Uzbek leader Dostam—the former mainstay of the Communist Najibullah regime—has aligned himself with Uzbekistan's neo-communist Karimov in trying to stem the "fundamentalist" threat represented by Afghanistan's Prime Minister, Gulbuddin Hekmatyar, and his chief rival in Kabul, ethnic Tajik Defense Minister Masood. Both of the latter two are being drawn into the Tajik conflict, perhaps even supplanting Yeltsin. Localist stirring in the north could emerge as a well-organized drive to demand a federalist Kazakhstan or even independence, as has already occurred in other ethnic hotspots like Nagorno-Karabakh and Trans-Dnestr.

Even Turkmenistan could face some nationalist strains over the next several years, stemming from tensions with its small but influential Uzbek minority. Uzbeks play a prominent role in the religious establishment; the Turkmen senior Islamic leader is Uzbek. The Turkmen and Uzbeks have also been at odds over control of scarce water resources, and some Turkmen probably fear that Uzbeks in Turkmenistan could become a fifth column for the stronger, more populous Uzbek state.

Events in Central Asia will have a broader regional impact. The West remains particularly concerned about Kazakhstan, where nearly a thousand strategic nuclear weapons await transfer to Russia. A crisis there could complicate this process and affect over six million ethnic Russians, whose fate Moscow would be unable to ignore. Nationalist and inter-ethnic conflict are also likely to delay the development of the region's substantial energy resources. While it is unlikely that an Islamic fundamentalist regime will arise in Central Asia over the next few years, the current jihad—Islamic holy war—will continue in Tajikistan and could spread to Uzbekistan, further alarming Russia and contributing to greater demands for humanitarian assistance and international involvement, including possible peace-keeping operations. Outsiders like the Iranians and Turks, who have been actively engaged in Central Asia, could also be drawn into any crisis.

## Notes

1. For a discussion of the incorporation of these regions into the Russian Empire, see Michael Rywkin, *Russia in Central Asia*, New York, Collier Books, 1963, revised edition, 1983, and Seymour Becker, *Russia's Protectorates in Central Asia, Bukhara and Khiva, 1965-1924*, Cambridge, Harvard University Press, 1968.

2. During the Brezhnev era, the process of nativization of the top ranks of the republic leaders continued apace, having begun under Khrushchev. Furthermore, local party leaders carved out increasing local control over personnel policy and even made inroads in coopting the local security services. These trends fostered a higher level of nepotism and corruption, overall characteristics of the Brezhnev era. When former KGB

chief Yuriy Andropov succeeded Brezhnev in November 1982, he began immediately to signal his intention to reverse that broad autonomy and corruption in the interest of greater efficiency, law and order, and social equity—an increasing concern given the recent rise of the Solidarity free trade union in Poland. For a discussion of Andropov's anticorruption campaign's implications for Uzbekistan, where it struck the hardest, see Donald Carlisle, "Uzbekistan and the Uzbeks," *Problems of Communism*, September–October 1991, pp. 23–44. Another important manifestation of this tendency cam in Kazakhstan, where under General Secretary Mikhail Gorbachev, an ethnic Russian, Gennadiy Kolbin, was installed in December 1986, touching off serious unrest. For discussion of this issue, see Martha Olcott, "Perestroyka in Kazakhstan," *Problems of Communism*, July–August 1990, pp. 65–77. For an assessment, of how nationality policy intertwined with the broader political agenda following Brezhnev's death, see Paul A. Goble, "Gorbachev and the Soviet Nationality Problem," in *Soviet Society Under Gorbachev, Current Trends and Prospects for Reform*, edited by Maurice Friedberg and Heyward Isham, Armonk, M.E. Sharpe, Inc., 1987, pp. 76–100.

3.    Makhkamov had come to power in 1985, but faced significant internal opposition within the party from both reformers, like Davlat Khodonazarov, and representatives of other clans, including the former Communist First Secretary, Rakhman Nabiyev. In February 1990, he had almost been overthrown when major demonstrations in Dushanbe were suppressed by the security forces. Many representatives of the opposition claim the entire incident was orchestrated by the KGB to discredit the opposition and Gorbachev's more tolerant policies toward democratization. See "The February 1990 Demonstrations in Dushanbe," *Report of the Helsinki Commission*, for a discussion of these events.

4.    Statistics published in *Literaturnaya gazetta*, October 9, 1991, substantiate a larger body of press reporting on this issue. Statements by the head of the Russian refugee committee, Tatiana Regent, indicates that refugee and emigration flows increased again last year. See p. 5.

5.    See the brief treatment of linkage between the riots and the removal of Absamat Masaliev, see Martha Olcott, "Politics in Five Central Asian Republics," National Council for Soviet and East European Research, February 12, 1992. Also see Guy G. Imart, "Fault or Hinge Line," September–October 1990, *Problems of Communism*, pp. 1–13 for a more detailed perspective on Kyrgyz nationalism.

6.    See *Izvestiya*, 12 January 1993, p. 5 for an interview with Rakhmanov confirming Uzbek military aid.

7.    See Gregory Gleason, "Water and Land Conflict Among the New States of Central Asia," *The National Council for Soviet and East European Research*, November 13, 1992, pp. 22–25.

8.    See "Kazakhstan Confident About National Security," *Opinion Research Memorandum*, December 1992, p. 3.

9.    See Bess Brown, "Central Asia: The First Year of Unexpected Statehood," Radio Liberty, vol. 2, no. 3, January 1993, p. 30.

10. See *Komsomolskaya pravda*, 3 February 1993, p. 2 translated in FBIS–USR–93–17, p. 84.

11. Public opinion polling indicates that local soviets do not command respect from many citizens. See "Kazakhstanis Support Nazarbayev, Miss Soviet Union," *Opinion Research Memorandum*, January 13, 1993, pp. 1 and 9.

12. See *Rossiyskiye vesti*, 12 January 1993, p. 2.

13. See FBIS–SOV 93–053, p. 85, 24 March 1993, for statements by Rakhmanov and the procurator's office leveling charges against the Islamic and democratic parties.

14. See Aleksandr Verkhovskiy, *Srednyaya Aziya i Kazakhstan, Politicheskiy spectr*, Moscow, 1992, p. 20 for a description of Alash's political agenda. According to press accounts, Alash activists tried to take control of the Kazakh mufti's mosque in December 1991, and during the incident, some allege that the mufti's arm was broken. See *Rossiyskaya gazetta*, 18 December 1991, p. 7.

15. See *Rossiyskaya gazeta*, 30 December 1992, p. 7.

16. See Moscow, "Programma Radio Odin, 1200GMT, 10 March 1993, LD1003165793 FBIS Wireservice.

17. See Graham E. Fuller, "Central Asia, the New Geopolitics," Rand, R–4219–USDP, pp. 60-61. Also see Nazarbayev's comments to Mongolia's Foreign Minister, where a total of 40,000 Kazakhs immigrating from Mongolia is mentioned. See FBIS–SOV–93–060, 31 March 1993, p. 71.

# 6

## Ethnic Relations and Conflict in the Baltic States

*Toivo U. Raun*

In view of the tragic developments in recent years in the former Yugoslavia, Nagorno (Mountainous)–Karabakh, Georgia, Tajikistan, and Moldova, it must be asked to what extent violent conflict will be the fate of other post–Soviet or post–communist countries and regions. This chapter will focus on the situation in the Baltic states of Estonia, Latvia, and Lithuania and assess the nature of ethnic relations and the prospects for conflict in the area. It is this author's contention that in the post–Soviet world this issue must be viewed in a clearly differentiated perspective, and each country or region must be examined in the context of its own distinctive ethnic composition and historical development. In particular, it should not be assumed that the Yugoslavian case is the norm for the future. Indeed, it will be argued here that the prospects for continued non–violent development and a gradualist solution to any ethnic problems in the Baltic states remain favorable.

It is almost axiomatic today to speak of the Baltic states as a distinctive region that began a parallel process of de–Sovietization during the Gorbachev years and then re–established independence in the wake of the failed August 1991 coup. However, it is important to bear in mind that Baltic regionalism is only a twentieth–century phenomenon that—ironically—developed most fully under Soviet rule.[1] In previous centuries Estonia and Latvia, under German domination in the main, showed differing patterns of development from Lithuania, which was historically tied to the Polish political and cultural world. In the second half of the nineteenth century national movements appeared among all three Baltic peoples, but the Lithuanian one was considerably delayed because of a special brand of tsarist repression aimed at the regions traditionally under Polish hegemony. It is really only with the Russian Revolution of 1905 and the parallel emergence of movements for cultural and political autonomy

Source: Romuald J. Misiunas and Rein Taagepera, <u>The Baltic States</u>: <u>Years of Dependence, 1940–1980</u> (Berkeley: University of California Press, 1983), p. xvi; copyright (c) 1983 by Romuald J. Misiunas and Rein Taagepera.

under tsarist rule that we can speak of the beginning of convergence in the history of the three peoples.[2] A key common historical experience for the Estonians, Latvians, and Lithuanians was the two decades of independence they enjoyed during the interwar era, a distinction that sets them apart from all other post–Soviet nationalities.[3] The political legacy of this period, as was the case elsewhere in East Central Europe, was mixed, but it signified the firm beginning of a modern civic culture that could not be eliminated by nearly fifty years of Soviet rule.

In all three cases the Baltic states began their first era of independence with liberal democratic regimes, lasting in the case of Estonia and Latvia to 1934 and in Lithuania to 1926. The new constitutions, reflecting the democratic idealism of the immediate postwar period, placed political power in the hands of broadly elected legislatures and ultimately in the newly enfranchised voters themselves through provisions for initiative and referendum. In view of their stunted political growth under tsarist rule, it was probably too much to expect that the Baltic peoples would make a smooth transition to democracy. Indeed, among the successor states in East Central Europe only Czechoslovakia and Finland did so. Nevertheless, significant experience with regular national elections and multiparty systems left a lasting legacy that was quickly tapped in the rebirth of the late 1980s. Although all three Baltic states succumbed to authoritarianism in the interwar era, the regimes were mild by the European standards of this period.[4] In any case in the Gorbachev years, Estonia, Latvia, and Lithuania were uniquely able among Soviet republics to build on major post–tsarist and pre–Soviet political precedents.

The secret protocols of the Molotov–Ribbentrop Pact in August 1939 sealed the fate of the Baltic states and ushered in a new era of parallel development: unwanted Soviet military bases in fall 1939; military occupation and forced annexation by the USSR in summer 1940; Sovietization, including mass deportations, in 1940–1941; German occupation in World War II; postwar Stalinism, including collectivization of agriculture and new deportations; and all the ups and downs of the post–Stalin era.[5] By the time Mikhail Gorbachev turned to *glasnost'* and *perestroika*, the homogenizing impact of Soviet rule in the Baltic was clear: the resolution of the status of Estonia, Latvia, and Lithuania in the late 1980s and early 1990s would involve a common fate for all three states. As if to symbolize their distinctive situation, the Baltic states were granted restoration of their independence in September 1991—*before* the collapse of the Soviet Union.

## Demographic Background

Tables 6.1 and 6.2 provide data on the population shifts in the Baltic states since the post–World War I era. For comparison with the Soviet era the first

TABLE 6.1
Major Ethnic Groups in the Baltic States (in 1,000's)

| Estonia | 1934[a] | 1959 | 1970 | 1979 | 1989 | 1989 as percent of 1934 |
|---|---|---|---|---|---|---|
| Estonians | 993.5 | 892.7 | 925.1 | 947.8 | 963.3 | 97% |
| Russians | 92.7 | 240.2 | 334.6 | 408.8 | 474.8 | 512% |
| Ukrainians | – | 15.8 | 28.1 | 36.0 | 48.3 | |
| Belorussians | – | 10.9 | 18.7 | 23.5 | 27.7 | |
| Finns | 1.1 | 16.7 | 18.5 | 17.6 | 16.6 | |
| Jews | 4.4 | 5.4 | 5.3 | 5.0 | 4.6 | |
| Germans | 16.3 | 0.7 | 7.9 | 3.9 | 3.5 | |
| Others | 18.4 | 14.4 | 17.9 | 21.9 | 26.9 | |
| Total | 1,126.4 | 1,196.8 | 1,356.1 | 1,464.5 | 1,565.7.5 | |

| Latvia | 1935[a] | 1959 | 1970 | 1979 | 1989 | 1989 as percent of 1935 |
|---|---|---|---|---|---|---|
| Latvians | 1,472.6 | 1,297.9 | 1,341.8 | 1,344.1 | 1,387.8 | 94% |
| Russians | 206.5 | 556.4 | 704.6 | 821.5 | 905.5 | 439% |
| Belorussians | 26.9 | 61.6 | 94.9 | 111.5 | 119.7 | |
| Ukrainians | 1.8 | 29.4 | 53.5 | 66.7 | 92.1 | |
| Poles | 48.9 | 59.8 | 63.0 | 62.7 | 60.4 | |
| Lithuanians | 22.9 | 32.4 | 40.6 | 37.8 | 34.6 | |
| Jews | 93.5 | 36.6 | 36.7 | 28.3 | 22.9 | |
| Germans | 62.1 | 1.6 | 5.4 | 3.3 | 3.8 | |
| Others | 15.3 | 17.8 | 23.6 | 26.9 | 39.8 | |
| Total | 1,950.5 | 2,093.5 | 2,364.1 | 2,502.8 | 2,666.6 | |

*(continues)*

column of figures in both tables includes census data from the interwar period when, in all three cases, the borders differed from those in place after World War II. In 1934, Estonia included the trans–Narva region and the Petseri district (about 5 percent of its territory); in 1935, the Abrene region was still part of Latvia (some 2 percent of its territory);[6] and in 1923, Lithuania included the Klaipėda (Memel) district, but not the Vilnius region.

As the tables suggest, there is a striking parallel between Estonian and Latvian demographic development whereas Lithuania has followed a distinctive path of its own. Two key trends should be singled out in the northern two Baltic states. First, the eponymous nationalities in both Latvia and Estonia have yet to recover from the demographic catastrophe of the 1940s (the result, mainly, of Soviet deportations, wartime deaths, and flight to the West); there are still fewer Latvians and Estonians today in their homelands than there were in the mid–1930s.[7] Second, there has been a precipitous decline—unique among

TABLE 6.1 *(continued)*
Major Ethnic Groups in the Baltic States (in 1,000's)

| Lithuania | 1923[a] | 1959 | 1970 | 1979 | 1989 | 1989 as percent of 1923 |
|---|---|---|---|---|---|---|
| Lithuanians | 1,739.5 | 2,150.8 | 2,506.8 | 2,712.2 | 2,924.3 | 168% |
| Russians | 50.7 | 231.0 | 268.0 | 303.5 | 344.5 | 679% |
| Poles | 65.6 | 230.1 | 240.2 | 247.0 | 258.0 | |
| Belorussians | 4.4 | 30.3 | 45.4 | 57.6 | 63.2 | |
| Ukrainians | – | 17.7 | 25.1 | 32.0 | 44.8 | |
| Jews | 154.3 | 24.7 | 23.6 | 14.7 | 12.4 | |
| Germans | 88.6 | 11.2 | – | – | – | |
| Others | 55.1 | 15.6 | 19.1 | 24.5 | 27.6 | |
| Total | 2,158.2 | 2,711.4 | 3,128.2 | 3,391.5 | 3,674.8 | |

[a]Prewar borders.

*Sources:* Egil Levits, "Die demographische Situation in der UdSSR und in den baltischen Staaten unter besonderer Berücksichtigung von nationalen und sprachsoziologischen Aspekten," *Acta Baltica*, 21 (1981), pp. 63, 90, 119; *Eesti arvudes 1920–1935* (Tallinn: Riigi Statistika Keskbüroo, 1937), p. 12; Riina Kionka, "Migration to and from Estonia, "*Report on the USSR*, vol. 2, no. 37 (1990) p. 20; Dzintra Bungs, "Migration to and from Latvia," ibid., p. 32; Saulius Girnius, "Migration to and from Lithuania," ibid., p. 25; Ilmārs Mežs, *Latvieši Latvijā* (Kalamazoo, Mich.: n.p., 1992), p. 7; Kalev Katus, "Rahvus: sakslane; elukoht: Eesti," *Aja Pulss*, no. 22 (1990), p. 10.

union republic nationalities in the former Soviet Union—in the proportion of the titular ethnic group in the total population. From the mid-1930s to 1989 the Estonian share of the population plummeted 26.7 percentage points while the Latvian one fell 23.7—and the drop would be even greater if postwar borders were used as the basis of comparison.[8] During the same period the ethnic Russian proportion more than tripled in both cases. The concentration of Russians and other non-Balts is greatest in the cities. In Tallinn, the Estonians lost their majority in the 1980s, comprising 47.4 percent of the population in 1989 while the Russian share reached 41.2 percent. In Riga, Russians began to outnumber Latvians already in the 1960s; in 1989, the proportions were 47.3 percent Russian and 36.5 percent Latvian.[9]

On the other hand, despite suffering the same kinds of repression as the Estonians and Latvians, the Lithuanians have shown a contrasting demographic dynamism based on higher birth rates and have maintained a strong 80–81 percent share of the population in their homeland in the past seventy years. Although in absolute numbers the ethnic Russian population of Lithuania increased markedly, the proportion in 1989 (9 percent) remained less than one-third of that in either Latvia or Estonia. Because of this strong ethnic

TABLE 6.2
Major Ethnic Groups in the Baltic States (%)

| Estonia | 1934[a] | 1959 | 1970 | 1979 | 1989 |
|---|---|---|---|---|---|
| Estonians | 88.2 | 74.6 | 68.2 | 64.7 | 61.5 |
| Russians | 8.2 | 20.1 | 24.6 | 27.9 | 30.3 |
| Ukrainians | – | 1.3 | 2.1 | 2.5 | 3.1 |
| Belorussians | – | 0.9 | 1.4 | 1.6 | 1.8 |
| Finns | 0.1 | 1.4 | 1.4 | 1.2 | 1.1 |
| Jews | 0.4 | 0.5 | 0.4 | 0.3 | 0.3 |
| Germans | 1.5 | 0.1 | 0.6 | 0.3 | 0.2 |
| Others | 1.6 | 1.2 | 1.3 | 1.5 | 1.7 |
| Total[b] | 100.0 | 100.1 | 100.0 | 100.0 | 100.0 |

| Latvia | 1935[a] | 1959 | 1970 | 1979 | 1989 |
|---|---|---|---|---|---|
| Latvians | 75.7 | 62.0 | 56.8 | 53.7 | 52.0 |
| Russians | 10.6 | 26.6 | 29.8 | 32.8 | 34.0 |
| Belorussians | 1.4 | 2.9 | 4.0 | 4.5 | 4.5 |
| Ukrainians | 0.01 | 1.4 | 2.3 | 2.7 | 3.4 |
| Poles | 2.5 | 2.9 | 2.7 | 2.5 | 2.3 |
| Lithuanians | 1.2 | 1.5 | 1.7 | 1.5 | 1.3 |
| Jews | 4.8 | 1.8 | 1.6 | 1.1 | 0.9 |
| Germans | 3.2 | 0.1 | 0.2 | 0.1 | 0.1 |
| Others | 0.8 | 0.9 | 1.0 | 1.1 | 1.5 |
| Total[b] | 100.2 | 100.1 | 100.1 | 100.0 | 100.0 |

*(continues)*

Lithuanian demographic base, Vilnius, which began the twentieth century as a virtually non–Lithuanian city, finally had a Lithuanian majority by the late 1980s (50.5 percent in 1989).[10]   Although Lithuania gained territory in World War II, this was not of any particular advantage from an ethnic Lithuanian point of view since much of the population in both the Klaipėda and Vilnius regions was non–Lithuanian.

## Roots of Ethnic Tension

Historically, ethnic conflict among the three indigenous peoples of the Baltic region has been very limited.  From the thirteenth to the twentieth centuries the Estonians and Latvians were under foreign rule, usually by the same powers or overlords, and in effect "partners in misery."  In the past 130 years, following the emergence of national consciousness and identity, there has been

TABLE 6.2 *(continued)*
Major Ethnic Groups in the Baltic States (%)

| Lithuania | 1923[a] | 1959 | 1970 | 1979 | 1989 |
|-----------|---------|------|------|------|------|
| Lithuanians | 80.6 | 79.3 | 80.1 | 80.0 | 79.6 |
| Russians | 2.3 | 8.5 | 8.6 | 8.9 | 9.4 |
| Poles | 3.0 | 8.5 | 7.7 | 7.3 | 7.0 |
| Belorussians | 0.2 | 1.1 | 1.5 | 1.7 | 1.7 |
| Ukrainians | – | 0.7 | 0.8 | 0.9 | 1.2 |
| Jews | 7.2 | 0.9 | 0.8 | 0.4 | 0.3 |
| Germans | 4.1 | 0.4 | – | – | – |
| Others | 2.6 | 0.6 | 0.6 | 0.7 | 0.8 |
| Total[b] | 100.0 | 100.0 | 100.1 | 99.9 | 100.0 |

[a]Prewar borders.
[b]Due to rounding off totals are not always 100.0%.

*Sources:* Egil Levits, "Die demographische Situation in der UdSSR und in den baltischen Staaten unter besonderer Berücksichtigung von nationalen und sprachsoziologischen Aspekten," *Acta Baltica*, 21 (1981), pp. 64, 91, 120; *Eesti arvudes 1920–1935* (Tallinn: Riigi Statistika Keskbüroo, 1937), p. 12; Riina Kionka, "Migration to and from Estonia," *Report on the USSR*, 2, no. 37 (1990) p. 20; Dzintra Bungs, "Migration to and from Latvia," ibid., pp. 32–33; Saulius Girnius, "Migration to and from Lithuania," ibid., p. 25; Kalev Katus, "Rahvus: sakslane; elukoht: Eesti," *Aja Pulss*, no. 22 (1990), p. 10.

some mutual recrimination regarding responsibility for the failure to resist foreign invasion in medieval times, but this has only been a minor irritant. In contrast, the Grand Duchy of Lithuania was territorially the largest state in Europe at the start of the fifteenth century, but its rather loosely ruled domains extended east and south to the East Slavic lands and did not include its northern Baltic neighbors. The Lithuanian elites, never very numerous, gradually became Polonized, and by the nineteenth century the position of the Lithuanian-speaking population, overwhelmingly peasant, was comparable to that of the indigenous peoples in Latvia and Estonia. In modern times these nationalities have been too small in numbers to have any imperial ambitions with regard to each other's territory. Indeed the much more pressing concern has been how to secure autonomy or independence from larger and more powerful neighbors.

Estonia and most of Latvia (with the exception of the eastern region of Latgale which remained Catholic) have been Lutheran since the Reformation. In the nineteenth century there was a minor trend toward conversion to Orthodoxy, but it remained limited in scope and was reversed beginning in 1905. In these two countries religious factors have not played a major role in shaping the ideology of nationalism, and despite a religious revival since the late 1980s, this generalization remains true today. In Lithuania, however, Catholicism has been the dominant religious force with minor exceptions since the conversion of the region to Christianity. In the nineteenth-century national movement, in interwar political life, and especially in resistance to Soviet rule, the Catholic Church in Lithuania had a significant impact. Still today, its presence—much as in Poland—lends a different tone to public life in Lithuania than that which prevails in Estonia or Latvia.[11] In none of the Baltic countries, however, does religious issues or divisions contribute significantly to ethnic tensions.

During the first era of independence in the 1920s and 1930s, the Baltic states proved to be highly protective of their newly established sovereignty and were reluctant to cooperate with each other. The Baltic Entente, established between the three countries in 1934, remained a paper alliance with no teeth in it, and Baltic diplomats and statesmen struck a remarkably cavalier tone toward each other.[12] They learned a hard lesson in the crisis of 1939–1940, and the rigors of Soviet rule, as noted above, brought them increasingly closer together. Baltic dissidents, for example, cooperated more and more as the Brezhnev era evolved. Most strikingly, when Gorbachev unleashed the possibilities of change, popular front movements in the three Baltic states moved quickly to learn from each other and work together, suggesting that the historical memory of events fifty years earlier was still fresh in their minds.[13] Thus, above all for historical and geopolitical reasons, there are virtually no prospects for any serious conflict among the indigenous Baltic nationalities.

The ethnic tensions existing in the Baltic states today are essentially a product of World War II and the period of Soviet rule. In Estonia and Latvia, the conflict is between the native Balts and Russians or the "Russian-speaking" population.[14] In the case of Lithuania the potential Lithuanian-Russian confrontation is muted because of the relatively small Russian presence, but a unique source of some tension here is the existence of a substantial Polish minority. Opinion differs today on how best to characterize the large contingent of ethnic Russians in Estonia and Latvia. They—or some of them—have been termed "colonists," "immigrants," "migrants," "occupiers," and "integrated Russians."[15] What is clear, however, is that it is not possible to view the great majority of the Baltic Russians as a traditional minority, i.e., one that has been settled in the region over a long period of time. They only began appearing en masse in the Baltic states under Stalin. Some came as part of the new political elite or the Soviet repressive forces ("occupiers"), others found their way to the Baltic mainly for economic reasons (the more permanent "immigrants" and the more coincidental "migrants"), and still others were sent to the Baltic under Stalin without knowing their final destination.[16]

The greatest source of tension in the Baltic states in the post-Soviet years has been the continuing, albeit declining, presence of ex-Soviet troops. Before its demise at the end of 1991, and even during the age of *glasnost'*, the Soviet Union remained tight-lipped with regard to any exact figures on its military in the Baltic region. This secrecy led to exaggerated unofficial estimates ranging as high as 600,000 as late as summer 1990. In fact, the troop strength must have been much lower, and a reasonable estimate for spring 1992 was 120,000 for all three Baltic states.[17] After that, a gradual decline took place, despite periodic suspensions and the absence of any formal agreements with Russia. The estimated overall figure fell to less than 30,000 by July 1993, and by the end of August, all troops had left Lithuania.[18] The issue of compensation for damages caused by the Soviet military presence, raised by the Lithuanian side, was left for future negotiation.

It is no accident that Lithuania became the first Baltic state to be rid of ex-Soviet armed forces. Its foreign and domestic policies were relatively acceptable to Moscow, and its Russian population was the smallest among the Baltic states and thus not a major issue. In Estonia and Latvia, in September 1993, there were probably just over 20,000 ex-Soviet troops left, but they were far from evenly distributed. Over three-fourths were concentrated in Latvia, presumably because it had served as the headquarters of the Baltic Military District and home to certain key installations such as the Skrunda radar station and the large submarine base in Liepāja. There is little doubt that external pressure has hastened the withdrawal process—in part from various international organizations and, most importantly, a U.S. Congressional resolution that threatened to cut off aid to Russia if its troops did not leave the Baltic in the near future. Under these circumstances the pullout will likely continue, and the resulting reduction of tensions should have a positive impact on ethnic relations in the Baltic states as well.[19]

The larger issue that the Baltic states are caught up in is the question of Russia's intentions as the main successor to the Soviet Union. To use Roman Szporluk's term, what is the role of an "empire-saving" mentality in Russian foreign policy today and for the foreseeable future?[20] Given the current state of flux in Russian politics, it is not possible to give any definitive answer to this question, but there is no doubt that a powerful imperial lobby, both civilian and military, remains in place. The widespread use of the term "near abroad" (*blizhnee zarubezh'e*) since early 1992 to refer to the ex-Soviet union republics, including the Baltic states, is only one indication of its strength. With increasing frequency in the latter part of 1992 and in the first half of 1993, the Russian Foreign Ministry and President Yeltsin linked the troop withdrawal issue to the question of Russian "minorities" in Estonia and Latvia, e.g., at the Vancouver summit in April 1993.[21] Various Western observers have pointed out that Stalin's presumed justification for seizing the Baltic states as a buffer zone or glacis is no longer relevant in a nuclear or post-nuclear age. As Karl-Guenther von Hase has asked: "who is going to attack the nuclear superpower Russia, and what difference will it make if it has bases in the Baltic or not?"[22] Still, as with the eclipse of earlier empires, old habits die slowly, especially since so much of the USSR/Russia's international prestige was based on its military might.

The strategic issue in the Baltic region is further complicated by the anomalous existence of the Kaliningrad oblast, physically separated from Russia by Lithuania and Belarus. Today, this small exclave is perhaps the most militarized piece of territory in the world, where close to an estimated quarter million ex–Soviet troops are stationed.[23] Comprising 15,100 sq km, the Kaliningrad (formerly Königsberg) area once formed the northern third of East Prussia and fell to Stalin as a result of World War II. According to the Soviet census of 1989, the 871,000 inhabitants of the Kaliningrad oblast were overwhelmingly East Slavic, consisting of 78.5 percent Russians, 8.5 percent Belorussians, and 7.2 percent Ukrainians, but there was also a small Lithuanian presence (2.1 percent). Historically, Lithuanians had lived in this region in considerable numbers from at least the fifteenth century. Although the German element increasingly dominated, there were still 61,000 Lithuanian–speakers in 1931.[24]

Originally, Stalin intended to annex northern East Prussia to the Lithuanian SSR, but dropped the idea by 1945. Instead, the Kaliningrad oblast became part of the RSFSR, and the ethnic composition changed dramatically, as noted above. The Soviet military presence dominated Kaliningrad throughout the postwar era, but the region has opened up to the outside world in the past few years. Various ideas to change its status have been floated, e.g., serving as a new home for Germans from other parts of the former USSR. It is highly unlikely, however, that the Russian government or military will relinquish this prize of World War II in the foreseeable future. Because of its historical ties to the region and the issue of land access, Lithuania is in a unique situation among the Baltic states in its relationship to Russia on this matter.[25] Kaliningrad's strategic impact remains ambiguous. On the one hand, the existence of a strong military base there may make the Russian leadership more flexible on troop withdrawals from the Baltic states. On the other hand, since Kaliningrad is physically separated from Russia, Moscow may be tempted to view the territory in between as strategically vital.

As noted above, an ethnic issue specific to Lithuania is the existence of a relatively compact Polish minority in the Vilnius region that was joined to the country only through the territorial gains made in World War II. The current tensions between Lithuanians and Poles in Lithuania must be seen in the entire historical context of Polish–Lithuanian relations. Although the Lithuanians were ostensibly not conquered in earlier centuries (unlike the Estonians and Latvians), over time the relationship with Poland became a subordinate one, and a strong undercurrent of resentment remains today. The hostility engendered by the issue of who should control the Vilnius (Polish Wilno) region was such that the two countries did not even have diplomatic relations for almost the entire interwar period.[26]

Thus, although the analogy is not entirely apt, the Polish role in Lithuania was comparable to the German, and later Russian roles in Latvia and Estonia. In this context it is not surprising that Sajudis, the Lithuanian popular front that led the movement for the restoration of independence from 1988, did not see fit to reach out to the Polish community in Lithuania, while the latter chose to ally itself with the local Russians rather than the Lithuanian majority in the country. Culturally, this tendency had already been favored by Lithuania's Poles since their knowledge of Russian is much stronger than that of Lithuanian (see Table 6.3 below). Lithuania's relations with Poland have been strained over this issue, but a major confrontation is unlikely. For example, tensions raised by Lithuania's dissolution of local councils in ethnic Polish areas for allegedly supporting the August 1991 Soviet coup gradually abated. Nevertheless, the historical legacy of the dispute over Vilnius/Wilno will probably continue to act as an irritant in Lithuanian–Polish relations for some time.[27]

In assessing ethnic tensions in the Baltic region a significant factor is the language issue and the entire question of communication among different nationalities. Table 6.3 provides an overview of language facility in both the majority language and Russian in each Baltic state by the major nationalities in 1989 (those numbering 10,000 or more). It is clear that the three Baltic peoples have all remained highly loyal to their mother tongues, but the Latvians are about twice as likely to be fluent in Russian as the Lithuanians and Estonians. On the other hand, Russians in Lithuania are more fluent in the local majority language by a factor of 2.5 than are Russians in Estonia with the Russians in Latvia falling in between these two poles, but closer to the Estonian one.

An important comparison can also be made regarding bilingualism among the eponymous Baltic nationalities and the Russians in each country. Here we find an almost exact correspondence in Lithuania (38 percent by both groups), but a huge disparity in Latvia (68 percent for Latvians vs. only 22 percent for Russians) and a substantial one in Estonia as well (35 percent for Estonians vs. 15 percent for Russians). These figures may be interpreted in several ways. Clearly, Lithuanian is the most dominant of the indigenous languages in the Baltic states, and Russians and others in the country feel relatively obliged to learn it. On the other hand, the greater role of Russian as a lingua franca in Latvia probably mitigates ethnic tensions there. It should also be noted that as Indo–European languages in the Baltic sub–group, Lithuanian and Latvian are easier languages for Russians to learn than is Estonian, a non–Indo–European tongue in the Finno–Ugric linguistic family. Among the smaller ethnic groups it is not surprising that only the Finns in Estonia and the Lithuanians in Latvia (i.e., speakers of languages related to the majority tongue in the country) know the dominant local language better than they know Russian.

The above data reflect the situation at the time of the last Soviet census, taken in January 1989. In the first five months of that year (January in Estonia and Lithuania, May in Latvia) all three Baltic republics, still part of the Soviet Union at the time, passed language laws that raised the status of Estonian, Latvian, and Lithuanian to state languages. Not all non–Balts were required to learn the local

TABLE 6.3
Language Choice and Competency
in the Baltic States, 1989 (%)

| Estonia Nationality | Estonian | | | Russian | | |
|---|---|---|---|---|---|---|
| | Native Tongue | Second Language[a] | Total | Native Tongue | Second Language[a] | Total |
| Estonians | 98.9 | 0.6 | 99.5 | 1.0 | 33.6 | <u>34.6</u> |
| Russians | 1.3 | 13.7 | <u>15.0</u> | 98.6 | 1.1 | 99.7 |
| Ukrainians | 1.2 | 6.9 | 8.1 | 54.5 | 39.7 | 94.2 |
| Belorussians | 0.7 | 6.1 | 6.8 | 67.1 | 29.9 | 97.0 |
| Finns | 40.8 | 33.3 | 74.1 | 28.1 | 38.9 | 67.0 |

| Latvia Native Nationality | Latvian | | | Russian | | |
|---|---|---|---|---|---|---|
| | Second Tongue | Language[a] | Native Total | Second Tongue | Language[a] | Total |
| Latvians | 97.4 | 1.3 | 98.7 | 2.6 | 65.7 | <u>68.3</u> |
| Russians | 1.1 | 21.1 | <u>22.2</u> | 98.8 | 1.1 | 99.9 |
| Belorussians | 2.5 | 15.5 | 18.0 | 64.8 | 29.7 | 94.5 |
| Ukrainians | 0.9 | 8.9 | 9.8 | 49.4 | 43.8 | 93.2 |
| Poles | 14.7 | 22.8 | 37.5 | 54.2 | 33.8 | 88.0 |
| Lithuanians | 23.8 | 40.3 | 64.1 | 11.9 | 36.0 | 47.9 |
| Jews | 1.9 | 27.0 | 28.9 | 74.9 | 17.5 | 92.4 |

| Lithuania Nationality | Lithuanian | | | Russian | | |
|---|---|---|---|---|---|---|
| | Native Tongue | Second Language[a] | Total | Native Tongue | Second Language[a] | Total |
| Lithuanians | 99.6 | 0.2 | 99.8 | 0.3 | 37.4 | <u>37.7</u> |
| Russians | 4.1 | 33.4 | <u>37.5</u> | 95.6 | 3.2 | 98.8 |
| Poles | 5.0 | 15.5 | 20.5 | 9.2 | 57.9 | 67.1 |
| Belorussians | 2.5 | 17.0 | 19.5 | 53.3 | 34.8 | 88.1 |
| Ukrainians | 3.0 | 16.8 | 19.8 | 45.3 | 42.1 | 87.4 |
| Jews | 6.7 | 38.0 | 44.7 | 56.8 | 22.2 | 79.0 |

[a] Self-stated fluency in given language

*Source:* Adapted from data in *Vestnik statistiki*, no. 1 (1991), pp. 70, 76; no. 6 (1991), p. 76.

languages, but in Estonia, for example, those in service positions that required social interaction with the population had to acquire a working knowledge of Estonian, the level dependent on the sophistication of the work they performed.[28] The restoration of independence in August 1991 provided still another boost to the status of the indigenous Baltic languages. Thus, there has been increasing incentive for Russians and other non–Balts to improve their knowledge of the Baltic languages, and there is evidence in Estonia, for example, that younger cohorts among the Russian population are adopting a considerably more favorable attitude towards learning Estonian.[29] A sign of the times is that there have been numerous complaints by Russians that Baltic language instruction is not readily available.[30]

Yet another crucial factor in evaluating the state of ethnic relations in the Baltic states is the question of citizenship, a particularly thorny issue that has been on the public agenda since the emergence of the independence movements in the late 1980s. Before the restoration of independence the Latvian and Estonian governments were reluctant to move hastily on the citizenship issue for fear of locking themselves into a long–term policy while the status of the large non–Baltic populations in their countries remained unresolved. In contrast, it was characteristic that Lithuania took the lead on this question since its demographic composition had been altered the least by the decades of Soviet rule, and in November 1989 it offered citizenship, after a two–year waiting period, to all permanent residents who declared loyalty to Lithuania. The great majority of non–Lithuanians exercised this option. In December 1991 a new, more restrictive citizenship law required ten years of residence, reading and speaking knowledge of Lithuanian, and knowledge of the constitution.[31]

Estonia took a more gradual approach, reinstating its 1938 citizenship law only in November 1991 and passing enabling legislation in February 1992. All citizens of Estonia in June 1940 and their descendants were automatically considered citizens. Naturalization required two years of residence (counting from March 30, 1990, when Estonia declared the beginning of a transition period to the restoration of independence) and an additional one–year waiting period, minimal competence in Estonian, and an oath of loyalty to the constitution. The post–Soviet Latvian parliament, elected in June 1993, was expected to pass a new citizenship law in early 1994, and there was every indication that it would be similar to the most recent Lithuanian and Estonian legislation described above.[32]

Lithuania's quick move to grant citizenship and voting rights to all permanent residents who sought them defused the issue in that country. However, Estonia and Latvia have been the subject of a heated international debate over the question of alleged discrimination against non–Estonians and non–Latvians. The most vociferous critic has been the Russian government, often led by Foreign Minister Andrei Kozyrev, who sought unsuccessfully in May 1993, for example, to block Estonia's entry into the Council of Europe for alleged violations of the human rights of its Russian population.[33]

The Russian government's campaign, however, has had considerable success in the U.S. where former presidents Richard Nixon and Jimmy Carter as well as various writers on foreign policy issues have accepted its view of the situation.[34] Why is this the case? As in the past, the U.S. feels more comfortable dealing with large states and nations, and Russia is correctly—if often one-sidedly—seen as the key to stability in most of the post-communist world. American reporting on the former Soviet Union since the latter's demise has also moved increasingly back to a Moscow-centered perspective. Furthermore, the intractable problems of the former Yugoslavia have colored much of the perception of the ex-Soviet world, leading to fear of more and more worst-case scenarios taking place.

The majority view among the indigenous nationalities in Estonia and Latvia, and among their political leaders, is probably expressed by the leading Estonian writer and member of parliament Jaan Kross. He has argued that citizenship cannot simply be granted to an "anonymous group," but rather each individual who seeks it must apply and be considered as an individual case. A minimal knowledge of the state language, he notes, is necessary for a democratic society to operate.[35] Worth noting is that fact-finding missions by representatives of international organizations such as the United Nations (UN), the Conference on Security and Cooperation in Europe (CSCE), and the Council of Europe have not found any significant violations of human rights in Latvia and Estonia, although the suggestion has been made that it would be in these two states' interest to facilitate the integration of non-Balts.[36] In Estonia, where a citizenship law has been in place since late 1991, some relaxation of the requirements, e.g., for the elderly and the handicapped or children of marriages in which one parent was a citizen of Estonia at the time of the child's birth, have been made since then.[37]

A minor factor, but one that cannot be ignored is the question of borders. As noted above, the territory of all three Baltic states changed during World War II. In 1945, Moscow arbitrarily transferred the entire area east of the Narva River in northeastern Estonia as well as about three-fourths of the Petseri (Russian Pechory) district in the southeastern corner of the country to the Russian SFSR. In three stages from 1945 to 1953 Moscow did the same with the town of Abrene (Russian Piatalovo) and the surrounding district in northeastern Latvia.[38] By an irony of fate, however, Lithuania regained both the Vilnius region (lost to Poland in 1920) and the Klaipėda district (lost to Germany in 1939). Probably because Estonia lost more territory (5 percent vs. 2 percent for Latvia) and some ethnic Estonians remain across the current border in Russia, it has made more of an issue of the border question in negotiations with Russia than has Latvia. The two sides have remained very far apart with Estonia using the Peace of Tartu (1920) as the point of legal departure while

Russia has wanted to go no further back in history than August 1991, rejecting responsibility for the actions of the Soviet regime.[39]

Nevertheless, it would be fair to say that both Estonia and Latvia see the border question as part of the larger framework of negotiations with Russia on a host of issues, and neither one would assign this particular item leading priority. In the Lithuanian case any potential problems are not with Russia, but Poland since it was Polish territory annexed by the Soviets in 1939 that was handed over to Lithuania in 1939–1940. However, Poland has not raised this issue—if for no other reason than it would encourage German pretensions to Poland's western territories.[40] There is also a possibility of Belorussian claims on border territory with Lithuania in the Vilnius region, but this issue should be resolvable through negotiation.[41] Thus, although border questions remain to be resolved in the Baltic states, they do not appear to be sources of serious regional conflict.

## Baltic Views of Russians and Russian Views of Balts

The popular ethnic stereotypes in the Baltic states are well known: Balts allegedly refer to Russians as "occupiers," and Russians call Balts "fascists."[42] Reality, however, is much more complex. Among most Balts it can be argued that a distinction is made between three groups of Russians (and non–Balts in general): (1) "integrated" Russians, a category of individuals best distinguished by their fluency in the Baltic languages (as noted in Table 6.3, in 1989 this included 38 percent of the Russians in Lithuania, 22 percent of those in Latvia, and 15 percent of those in Estonia); (2) economic immigrants or colonists who came to the Baltic mainly because of its relatively high standard of living; and (3) genuine "occupiers," i.e., those directly associated with the Soviet regime such as party officials and members of the military and KGB.[43] Only toward this third group can it be said that there is strong hostility. In the case of Latvia a complicating factor is the presence of an unusually large number of retired Soviet officers (a reasonable estimate is around 50,000, not including family members).[44]

Another measure of Baltic attitudes towards Russians can be gleaned from recent parliamentary elections in Estonia (September 1992), Lithuania (October–November 1992), and Latvia (June 1993). In the post–Soviet world all three Baltic states have become pluralistic societies with broad political spectrums. In the Estonian legislature (the *Riigikogu*) nine parties or electoral alliances are represented, ten in Lithuania's *Seimas*, and eight in Latvia's *Saeima*. If only major groupings are counted (those with ten or more seats in parliament), the total is five in Estonia, three in Lithuania, and four in Latvia.[45] The ideological sweep is broad, ranging from former communists to ex–dissidents and Christian–based parties. As might be expected, the right wing tends to be the most anti-Russian in its views while the left takes a more moderate position. There is no indication, however, that any Baltic political movement, including the so-called national radicals in each country, advocates the use of force as a solution to ethnic issues.

Given the similarity of the demographic situation in Estonia and Latvia, one might also expect parallel patterns in ethnic relations. In fact, however, there are significant differences. In Latvia the Russian and Latvian communities are considerably more integrated with each other than is the case with the Russian and Estonian populations of Estonia. This is evident, for example, in the more even distribution of Russians in Latvia in both urban and rural areas throughout the country and also in a substantially higher rate of ethnic intermarriage. In 1989, for example, 18.4 percent of ethnic Latvian men and 19.6 percent of women entered into ethnically mixed marriages in their home republic, while the comparable figures for ethnic Estonian men (8.0 percent) and women (8.3 percent) were less than half this rate. For ethnic Lithuanians, the proportion was even lower: 5.5 percent for men and 7.3 percent for women.[46] Probably a contributing factor to the higher Latvian rate of exogamy is the continuity of a much larger non-Baltic population in Latvia as compared to Estonia. In 1943, there were 168,000 Russians living within Latvia's postwar boundaries whereas the comparable figure for Estonia was only about 20,000 Russians in 1945.[47] Thus, the "colonist" factor in Estonia is considerably more significant than in Latvia and would suggest a more difficult process of integration.

In assessing the attitudes of Russians towards Balts it is important to distinguish which Russians are being referred to. According to the 1989 census, there were 145.1 million Russians in the Soviet Union of which 474,800 lived in Estonia, 905,500 in Latvia, and 344,500 in Lithuania. It is clear that many Russians living in the Baltic states or anywhere else outside Russia, depending on their length of stay and other factors, are affected by this experience and may develop differing values and attitudes from their co-nationals in Russia. One measure of non-Baltic public opinion in the Baltic states that occurred almost simultaneously in all three countries was the referendums on independence held in February-March 1991.

These polls were intended to preempt the Gorbachev-sponsored all-Union referendum scheduled for later in March 1991 and, in fact, successfully did so. As would be expected given the ethnic balance, voters in Lithuania supported independence by the largest margin: 90.5 percent "yes" vs. 6.6 percent "no" with 84.7 percent of the eligible voters participating. In Estonia the comparable figures were 77.8 percent "yes" and 21.4 percent "no" (82.9 percent voting), while in Latvia they were 73.7 percent "yes" and 24.7 percent "no" (87.6 percent participating).[48] It is nevertheless striking that Latvia and Estonia did not lag very far behind Lithuania, suggesting that a substantial proportion of non-Latvians (some 38 percent of the total) and non-Estonians (about 30 percent of the total) supported Baltic independence.[49] To be sure, some overwhelmingly non-Baltic areas such as the cities of Narva in Estonia and Daugavpils in Latvia or the Šalčininkai region of Lithuania voted much less than the average for independence, but these are special cases.

In the post-independence period public opinion polls have been increasingly used in the Baltic states, including for the measurement of perceptions of ethnic relations. In Estonia in February 1993, for example, both Estonians and non-Estonians found relations among nationalities to be much better than three to four years earlier. Compared to December 1988, the proportion of Estonians who assessed ethnic relations as "poor/very poor" declined from 55 percent to 12 percent while among non-Estonians this figure fell from 39 percent to 9 percent. In addition, by 1993 there was growing evidence that Russians and other non-Estonians were more and more reconciled to the existence of an independent Estonia.[50]

In terms of political attitudes and parties it is noteworthy that Russians in the Baltic states have remained relatively unorganized, especially in comparison to the Balts themselves. One of the hallmarks of the Baltic independence movements was a broad grass-roots base, and a strong nexus between the intelligentsia and the population at large. The Russian communities in the Baltic states have been relatively transient and heavily concentrated in the working class, lacking in particular a humanistic intelligentsia of any size or influence. This has rendered them much less cohesive or capable of mobilization. The most important political movements among Russians in the Baltic began in 1988 as reactions to the emergence of the indigenous popular fronts. Although called by different names (Intermovement in Estonia, Interfront in Latvia, and Unity in Lithuania), they all had the same social base—the old communist elite of party officials, military officers, and all-Union plant managers.[51] Initially, these groups enjoyed some success by playing on the fears of the Russian populations, but Moscow's heavy-handed policies (e.g., the economic blockade against Lithuania after March 1990 and the bloody crackdown in Lithuania and Latvia in January 1991) alienated significant numbers of non-Balts in the Baltic as well. Following the failed August 1991 coup and the restoration of Baltic independence, the position of Russian hardliners in the Baltic states was further weakened, leaving Russian populations who were most oriented toward economic questions (e.g., pensions, property rights, and the threat of unemployment) and who were relatively indifferent toward Baltic cultural and political agendas.[52]

## Prospects for Violent Conflict

At first glance it might appear that the Baltic states, especially Latvia and Estonia with their large Russian populations, would be probable candidates for a Yugoslav- or Transcaucasian-type scenario. However, a closer look at the situation suggests that there are key distinctive features in the Baltic case that make a continued non-violent solution to the region's ethnic tensions more likely. First, because Russians in the Baltic are overwhelmingly recent colonists or immigrants, the major ethnic issues in the region lack the deep-seated historical antagonisms associated with Serbs and Croats in the Balkans or with Armenians and Azerbaijanis in Transcaucasia. Moreover, the indigenous Baltic nationalities are currently at a historical high-point in terms of cooperation among themselves, and despite a post-communist desire to assert their individuality, it appears that this trend will gradually further develop. In essence, ethnic relations remain negotiable in the Baltic states and are not likely to pass the point of no return.

It might be objected that the more appropriate analogy for the Baltic states is Moldova, where violence has erupted between Russians and the indigenous Moldovans over the Trans-Dnestr region. However, the parallel has several flaws since the Soviet manipulation of borders in the Baltic was much less drastic than in Moldova and nothing comparable to the Gagauz problem exists in the Baltic states, except on a milder basis with the Polish issue in Lithuania.[53] Above all, it is crucial to bear in mind that Estonia, Latvia, and Lithuania were fully independent states in the 1920s and 1930s and not merely poor provinces of another state (Romania), as in the case of Moldova. In the interwar era the Baltic states established a precedent for constitutional government and representative democracy—however flawed in practice—that serves as a basis for gradualism in Baltic politics today. The use of violence and terror has never been part of Baltic political culture except for brief instances in the unstable 1930s.

The perspective of the recent past also suggests grounds for optimism. Since the onset of the Gorbachev era and the sweeping political changes and social upheaval it initiated, no one—to my knowledge—has been killed in the Baltic states for ethnic or political reasons, except by Soviet repressive forces. The two major instances of regime-sponsored violence occurred in Vilnius (15 dead) and Riga (6 dead) in January 1991 as part of Gorbachev's ill-fated crackdown in the Baltic and then in July 1991 at a Lithuanian border crossing (7 dead).[54] The credit for this record of non-violence in recent years should certainly go to Balts and non-Balts alike. Here is perhaps another instance in which Russians and other immigrants have to a considerable extent internalized values of the Baltic political environment.

The absence of violence does not mean the absence of issues that could lead to serious ethnic conflict. An example would be the city of Narva in northeastern Estonia with a population of 85,000 in 1989 of which only 4 percent was Estonian. According to the last census held in interwar Estonia in 1934, Narva's population of 23,500 was 65 percent Estonian.[55] What took place under Stalin's rule can only be termed a form of "ethnic cleansing" in which evacuated and otherwise displaced residents of Narva were not allowed to return after World War II. As an editorial in a Russian-language newspaper in Narva in 1950 put it, "Soviet Narva" did not want to see the return of "many White Guardists, spies, and exploiters."[56] In short, although Narva has always been a border region with a mixed population, it was deliberately turned into an overwhelmingly non-Estonian city by Soviet policy.

There has been some talk of secession in recent years and periodic discussion of the establishment of a special status for Narva and northeastern Estonia. In July 1993, a minor crisis occurred as the city councils of Narva and neighboring Sillamäe held referendums on the question of autonomy. The national government in Tallinn opposed the initiatives, but eschewed the use of force to stop them. The results were disputed. In both cities, although nearly all those voting supported autonomy, the turnout was low (54 percent in Narva and 60 percent in Sillamäe). More importantly, numerous irregularities were noted, e.g., questionable ballot box security, that raised the issue of whether half of the eligible voters in Narva actually participated. In August, the Supreme Court of Estonia declared the referendums invalid and unconstitutional, and this ruling was accepted by the local authorities in both cities.[57] Whatever its legality, the abortive vote suggested that about half or more of Narva's population had made its peace with an independent Estonia. As one opposition member of the Narva City Council, Aleksandr Gamazin, has suggested, the referendum is best explained as an attempt by Narva's traditionalist elite to hold on to political power in the face of impending local elections in October 1993. Thus, despite tensions and some misunderstandings cool heads have prevailed both in Narva and in the Estonian government in Tallinn. Because of the sense of historical injustice, Narva remains an emotional issue for many ethnic Estonians, yet one that can and should remain manageable.[58]

Another example of peaceful crisis resolution took place in June–July 1993 over adoption of a law on aliens in Estonia. In the face of international criticism from both Russia and the West and some internal opposition, President Lennart Meri declined to sign the bill already passed by parliament and sent it to the CSCE and the Council of Europe for expert assessment. The suggested changes proved to be minor, and Estonia's parliament accepted nearly all of them in an amended version that Meri promptly signed. In effect, Estonia had voluntarily accepted some limitation on its sovereignty, but it also succeeded in internationalizing this issue. Following the direct involvement of key European organizations in the matter and their approval of the amended law, it was much more difficult for Russia to continue its objections to the contents.[59]

A further perspective on the tradition of non-violence in the Baltic states is seen in their historical ties to Scandinavia and East Central Europe. In addition to their previous connections to the Baltic, the Scandinavian states served as important models for Estonia, Latvia, and Lithuania in the interwar period. Under Soviet rule the Balts were particularly impressed with the Prague Spring in Czechoslovakia in 1968 and the Solidarity movement in Poland throughout the

1980s. It seems clear that Solidarity's emphasis on grass–roots mobilization and non–violent resistance served as a key inspiration for the Baltic popular fronts in the late 1980s. These movements took a centrist position and acted as umbrella organizations that reflected the shift of public opinion from the more modest goal of autonomy to full independence. Especially striking is that the Popular Front of Latvia, having to deal with the greatest ethnic mixture in the Baltic, played a crucial role in mediating between the Latvian and non–Latvian populations.[60]

Finally, a pragmatic aspect of this question should also be noted. A glance at the 1989 census will recall that there were 145.1 million Russians in the former Soviet Union and only 5.3 million Balts in Estonia, Latvia, and Lithuania. Baltic advocacy or use of violence against local Russian populations clearly would be counterproductive. Here is another significant difference in comparing the situation to that in Transcaucasia. In any ethnic confrontation in the Baltic, Moscow would not be neutral or acting as some sort of mediator. Indeed, in the chaotic and shrill political atmosphere in Russia in spring and summer 1993, the Yeltsin government felt it incumbent to take an increasingly hard line on the Baltic situation. Nevertheless, neither Moscow nor the Baltic governments operated in a vacuum, and all of them had to take into account the consequences of their actions in the international arena. In view of their desperate need for economic aid and foreign investment, neither Russia nor the Baltic states could afford to alienate key international organizations or the major Western powers.

## The Baltic States and the International Community

Under Soviet rule and military occupation the Baltic peoples were cut off from membership in any significant international organizations. Their isolation eased somewhat in the post–Stalin era, but official contacts with the outside world were channeled only through Moscow. An oft–stated goal of the Baltic independence movements in the late 1980s and especially the newly restored Baltic states after August 1991 was to rejoin the international community and, in particular, the European family of nations. As the only members of the League of Nations—with the exception of Switzerland—who were not also in the United Nations, the Baltic states could and did appeal, with some success, to international law regarding the renewal of their independence. It is characteristic that in his inaugural address in February 1993 Algirdas Brazauskas, the first post–Soviet president of Lithuania, made the following statement: "I see Lithuania's future only in Europe. ... I am convinced that close and firm ties with...international organizations are a guarantee of our state's security and independence."[61] Other Baltic leaders would no doubt agree with Brazauskas's position, and they have perhaps taken a cue from

Finland's postwar experience in which that country sought a "multilateral solution" to its security problem by involving itself in a network of international connections intended to balance the imposing presence of the Soviet Union on its eastern border.[62]

Almost immediately after the restoration of independence the Baltic states were admitted to both the United Nations and the CSCE. Symbolically, the latter connection was the more important one since the Balts had felt most painfully the loss of their status as full–fledged participants in the European community of states. In March 1992, on the initiative of Germany and Denmark, the Baltic states joined with these two countries and Norway, Sweden, Finland, Poland, and Russia to become founding members of the Council of the Baltic Sea States. Finland chaired the council the first year, and in March 1993 Estonia was unanimously chosen to head the group during its second year. The organization's goals are to reduce tensions and foster cooperation, most concretely in the economic, technological, and cultural spheres. As a broad regional organization, the Council of Baltic Sea States holds significant potential for Estonia, Latvia, and Lithuania as a means to moderate any desire for domination in the area by the larger powers, i.e., Russia and Germany.[63]

Particularly gratifying for the Baltic states was the admission of Lithuania and Estonia, the latter despite the strong opposition of Russia, to the Council of Europe in May 1993. Indeed it appears that many member states found Russia's intervention, especially as a non–member itself, unseemly, and this action contributed to a near–unanimous vote of confidence in Estonia's application. Latvia held parliamentary elections in June 1993, and its bid for membership is to be considered in early 1994. Since the Council of Europe stresses the protection of human rights as one of its major goals, the clean bill of health Estonia received on this question must be seen as a major victory for its foreign policy.[64] In June 1993 the Baltic states also expressed strong interest in associate membership in the European Community with a view toward full integration into the organization in the future.[65] This wide range of activity suggests that Estonia, Latvia, and Lithuania are well on their way toward reintegrating into the international, and especially the European, community of states. There can be little doubt that the higher the international profile they can maintain, the greater are their chances for enhancing their security.

Since the re–establishment of their independence the Baltic states have also developed ties with the North Atlantic Treaty Organization (NATO) and the West European Union (WEU). All three are members of the NATO Cooperation Council, founded in 1991, and have raised the possibility of full NATO membership at some point in the future. In view of relations with Russia, of course, this is a sensitive issue that would require significant improvement in Baltic–Russian relations before it could be satisfactorily resolved. Baltic interest in the WEU is a military parallel to involvement in the

CSCE, the Council of Europe, and developing ties to the European Community.[66]

In terms of external powers the key question for the Baltic states remains relations with and developments in Russia. Although the collapse of the Soviet Union was a relatively gradual process, Russia—its main successor state—showed great difficulty in coming to terms with its changed status. Even Boris Yeltsin, who stated at the end of 1992 that "'the imperial period in Russia's history has ended,'" proved ambivalent on this question in the following months.[67] The internal power struggle in Russia preoccupied its leaders to the extent that it seemed incapable of redefining its relations with the ex–Soviet republics, including the Baltic states, and fell back on a generic approach—showing strong continuity from the past—to the "near abroad."[68] In these circumstances the avoidance of serious conflict in the Baltic region depended on several factors, including, above all, the stability of Russia and its fitful evolution toward a democratic system, Baltic *and* Russian involvement in international organizations, and the role of other outside powers in the area.

Among other former republics of the USSR, Ukraine can play a potentially significant role for the Baltic states, especially as a counterweight to Russia. For example, during a period of tense Estonian–Russian relations over Estonia's proposed law on aliens in July 1993, Ukrainian Prime Minister Leonid Kuchma and several other members of his cabinet made a conspicuous visit to Tallinn, signing several agreements. Kuchma also publicly expressed his satisfaction with the treatment of ethnic Ukrainians living in Estonia.[69]

Other than Russia, the major external players in the Baltic are the Scandinavian states, Poland, Germany, and the U.S. The small countries of Finland, Sweden, Denmark, and Norway have provided important economic and diplomatic support for the Balts, in striking contrast to the situation during the decades of Soviet rule. Poland's main interest is its traditional ties with Lithuania, including the ethnic Polish minority there, and in the problem of the Kaliningrad oblast. Germany has had an historical presence in all three Baltic countries, but its involvement in the post–Soviet era is limited by its commitments to the former East Germany and central Europe in general.

The role of the U.S. in the region can and should be a major one, but it must be coordinated with an overall policy toward the former Soviet bloc. The goal should be to encourage a post–imperial mentality in Russia and ease its transition to a redefined role as an international power, more through the medium of international organizations rather than any unilateral U.S. action. As Paul Goble has argued, it does not make sense to single out the ethnic Russians for human rights concerns since that would only encourage Russian chauvinism and the "empire–savers." What is needed is an even–handed approach that includes all nationalities equally.[70] The West must also recognize that self-determination is not an inherent evil. Left to their own devices, many—if not most—parts of the former Soviet bloc, including the Baltic states, could evolve into stable and well-functioning members of the international community.

## Conclusion

In sum, the argument presented above suggests that a non-violent scenario is most likely in the Baltic states and that ethnic relations will not deteriorate to the point of no return. Why should the Baltic region be different from the southern tier of the former Soviet Union or Yugoslavia? First, we should note the role of location and previous historical development. Situated on the Baltic Sea, Estonia, Latvia, and Lithuania have had strong previous ties to Scandinavia and East Central Europe and an awareness of political and cultural pluralism. A key element is the tradition of non-violence in the political culture of these countries, both earlier in the twentieth century and in the recent past. Second, in a real sense there is not a "minority" problem in Latvia and Estonia today, but an "immigrant" or "colonist" problem. The Russians in the Baltic states are overwhelmingly newcomers, and the issues associated with, say, Nagorno-Karabakh or the former Yugoslavia, do not exist there. Third, as suggested by the two years since the restoration of independence, time in the Baltic case is on the side of non-violent development. With minor flare-ups now and then, emotions have generally cooled since August 1991, and this trend can be expected to continue.

The main factor of uncertainty in the Baltic question is, in fact, a non-Baltic one: the role of Russia and its foreign policy in the region. By meddling in Baltic affairs and asserting an imperial right to intervene in the "near abroad," Russia is certainly capable of artificially raising ethnic tensions. However, as Carl Bildt, the Swedish Prime Minister, has argued, it would be in Russia's long-term interest, economic and otherwise, to promote stability rather than conflict in the Baltic states.[71]

## Notes

1.  Some observers questioned the validity of the concept of Baltic regionalism as late as the latter part of the 1980s. See, for example, the following collection of papers from a conference held in Kiel, West Germany in June 1987: Dietrich A. Loeber, V. Stanley Vardys, and Laurence P. A. Kitching, eds., *Regional Identity Under Soviet Rule: The Case of the Baltic States* (Hackettstown, N.J.: Association for the Advancement of Baltic Studies, 1990).

2.  For the late tsarist era, see the sections on Latvia and Estonia, respectively, by Andrejs Plakans and Toivo U. Raun in Edward C. Thaden, et al., *Russification in the Baltic Provinces and Finland, 1855-1914* (Princeton: Princeton University Press, 1981)

and Manfred Hellman, "Die litauische nationale Bewegung im 19. und 20. Jahrhundert," *Zeitschrift für Ostforschung* 2 (1953): 66–107.

3. For this period, see Royal Institute of International Affairs, *The Baltic States* (London: Oxford University Press, 1938) and Georg von Rauch, *The Baltic States: The Years of Independence, 1917–1940* (Berkeley: University of California Press, 1974). The latter volume, however, is marred by a poor translation, and it is advisable to consult the German original: *Geschichte der baltischen Staaten* (Stuttgart: W. Kohlhammer, 1970).

4. On interwar domestic politics, see the following two articles by V. Stanley Vardys: "Democracy in the Baltic States, 1918–1934: The Stage and the Actors," *Journal of Baltic Studies* 10 (1979): 320–36 and "The Rise of Authoritarian Rule in the Baltic States," V. Stanley Vardys and Romuald J. Misiunas, eds., *The Baltic States in Peace and War, 1917–1945* (University Park: Pennsylvania State University Press, 1978), pp. 65–80.

5. On the Soviet period, see especially Romuald J. Misiunas and Rein Taagepera, *The Baltic States: Years of Dependence, 1940–1990* (Berkeley: University of California Press, 1993). For developments in Estonia, see Toivo U. Raun, *Estonia and the Estonians*, 2nd ed. (Stanford: Hoover Institution Press, 1991).

6. On the border question and territorial losses during and after World War II, see Edgar Anderson, "How Narva, Petseri, and Abrene Came To Be in the RSFSR," *Journal of Baltic Studies* 19 (1988): 197–214. On the Petseri region, see Toivo U. Raun, "The Petseri District of the Republic of Estonia," *Jahrbücher für Geschichte Osteuropas* 39 (1991): 514–32.

7. For a useful introduction to Baltic population losses in the 1940s, see Misiunas and Taagepera, *Baltic States*, especially Tables 1–5 in Appendix B.

8. It is estimated that the Estonians comprised fully 97 percent of the population of Estonia in 1945 (Luule Sakkeus, *Post-War Migration Trends in the Baltic States*, RU Series B, no. 20 [Tallinn: Estonian Interuniversity Population Research Centre, 1993], p. 5) and in 1943, the Latvian share of the population of Latvia (in postwar borders) was 82 percent (Ilmars Mežs, *Latvieši Latvijā* [Kalamazoo, Mich.: n.p., 1992], p. 7).

9. Mikhail Guboglo, "Demography and Language in the Capitals of the Union Republics," *Journal of Soviet Nationalities* 1, no. 4 (Winter 1990–1991): 17–19.

10. Ibid., pp. 14–15.

11. On Catholicism in Lithuania, see V. Stanley Vardys, *The Catholic Church, Dissent, and Nationality in Lithuania* (Boulder, Colo.: East European Quarterly, 1978).

12. Edgar Anderson, "The Baltic Entente: Phantom or Reality?," Vardys and Misiunas, *Baltic States in Peace and War*, pp. 126–35.

13. See Alfred Erich Senn, "Lithuania's Path to Independence," *Journal of Baltic Studies* 22 (1991): 245–50; Toivo U. Raun, "The Re-establishment of Estonian Independence," ibid., 251–58; Andrejs Plakans, "Latvia's Return to Independence," ibid., 259–66.

14. The term in Russian is *russkoiazychnyi* and refers collectively to Russian-speakers, including many non-Russians who have accepted Russian as their habitual means of communication. It is not appropriate, however, to equate the *russkoiazychnyi* population with ethnic Russians, as is often carelessly done. Although this issue has not been studied in depth, many Russian-speaking individuals of Ukrainian, Belorussian, or Jewish origin, for example, plausibly retain a different ethnic consciousness than those of solely

Russian background. Nevertheless, it is noteworthy that non–Russian and non–Baltic ethnic groups such as Ukrainians and Belorussians have shown little evidence of political initiative in the Baltic states.

15. "Colonists" is used by Rein Taagepera in *Estonia: Return to Independence* (Boulder, Colo.: Westview Press, 1993), pp. 218–21. The other four terms are used by Andrejs Pantelejevs, head of the Latvian Supreme Council's Human Rights and National Affairs Commission, as cited in Richard J. Krickus, "Latvia's 'Russian Question,'" *RFE/RL Research Report* 2, no. 8 (1993): 31–33.

16. Many aspects of the early years of Soviet rule in the Baltic states remain a "blank spot." A thorough study of Soviet population policy in the late Stalin era remains to be done.

17. Dzintra Bungs, "Soviet Troops in Latvia," *RFE/RL Research Report* 1, no. 34 (1992): 19; Douglas L. Clarke, "Former Soviet Armed Forces in the Baltic States," ibid., 1, no. 16 (1992): 43. According to Kalev Katus, an Estonian demographer, in the post–Stalin era (before Gorbachev) there were about 300,000 troops stationed in the Baltic states altogether (private communication, July 1993).

18. Riina Kionka, "Estonia: A Difficult Transition," *RFE/RL Research Report* 2, no. 1 (1993): 91; *The Baltic Independent*, May 28–June 3, 1993, p. 3; *RFE/RL Daily Report*, no. 162, August 25, 1993; *New York Times*, August 24, 1993, p. A4.

19. Clarke, "Former Soviet Armed Forces," pp. 46–47; Bungs, "Soviet Troops in Latvia," pp. 20, 24; Saulius Girnius, "Progress in Withdrawal of Troops from Lithuania?," *RFE/RL Research Report* 1, no. 34 (1992): 29–33; Dzintra Bungs, "Progress on Withdrawal from the Baltic States," *RFE/RL Research Report* 2, no. 25 (1993): 57–59; *Helsingin Sanomat*, July 28, 1993, p. B2; *Postimees*, July 23, 1993, p.2; August 14, 1993, p. 1.

20. Roman Szporluk, "Dilemmas of Russian Nationalism," *Problems of Communism* 38, no. 4 (1989): 17.

21. John Lough, "The Place of the 'Near Abroad' in Russian Foreign Policy," *RFE/RL Research Report* 2, no. 11 (1993): 21–29; Krickus, "Latvia's 'Russian Question,'" p. 30.

22. Jan Arveds Trapans, ed., "Conference in Salzburg," *RFE/RL Research Report* 1, no. 49 (1992): 18, 22.

23. Amos Elon, "The Nowhere City," *New York Review of Books* 40, no. 9 (1993): 29.

24. *Itogi vsesoiuznoi perepisi naseleniia 1989 goda*, 12 vols. (Moscow: Goskomstat, 1991–), VII, p. 392; Alfred Erich Senn, *The Emergence of Modern Lithuania* (New York: Columbia University Press, 1959), pp. 13–15; Misiunas and Taagepera, *Baltic States*, p. 336.

25. Misiunas and Taagepera, *Baltic States*, pp. 336–37, 344–45; Anatole Lieven, *The Baltic Revolution: Estonia, Latvia, Lithuania and the Path to Independence* (New Haven: Yale University Press, 1993), pp. 210–13.

26. On the Vilnius (Vilna) question, see Royal Institute of International Affairs, *Baltic States*, pp. 89–93. For more detail, see Alfred Erich Senn, *The Great Powers, Lithuania and the Vilna Question 1920–1928* (Leiden: E.J. Brill, 1966).

27. Jan B. de Weydenthal, "The Polish–Lithuanian Dispute," *Report on Eastern Europe* 2, no. 41 (1991): 20–23; Stephen R. Burant, "International Relations in a Regional Context: Poland and Its Eastern Neighbors—Lithuania, Belarus, Ukraine,"

*Europe–Asia Studies* 45 (1993): 402–05. For useful overviews, see Stephen R. Burant, "Polish–Lithuanian Relations: Past, Present, and Future," *Problems of Communism* 40, no. 3 (1991): 67–84, and Richard J. Krickus, "Lithuania's Polish Question," *Report of the USSR* 3, no. 48 (1991): 20–23.

28. Rein Taagepera, "Estonia's Road to Independence," *Problems of Communism* 38, no. 6 (1989): 24; "Language Law of the Estonian Soviet Socialist Republic," Advig Kiris, ed., *Restoration of the Independence of the Republic of Estonia* (Tallinn: Estonian Information Institute, 1991), pp. 7–16. For a brief comparison of the Baltic language laws, see Riina Kionka, "Are the Baltic Laws Discriminatory?," *Report on the USSR* 3, no. 15 (1991): 21–22.

29. See a recent interview with the new rector of Tartu University, Peeter Tulviste, in *Helsingin Sanomat*, July 11, 1993, p. A4.

30. Philip Hanson, "Estonia's Narva Problem, Narva's Estonian Problem," *RFE/RL Research Report* 2, no. 18 (1993): 19.

31. Dzintra Bungs, Saulius Girnius, and Riina Kionka, "Citizenship Legislation in the Baltic States," *RFE/RL Research Report* 1, no. 50 (1992): 40.

32. Ibid., pp. 38–39; *Riigi Teataja*, no. 7 (1992): 175–76.

33. *Helsingin Sanomat*, May 12, 1993, p. A8; May 14, 1993, p. C2.

34. Krickus, "Latvia's 'Russian Question,'" p. 29; Charles William Maynes, "Containing Ethnic Conflict," *Foreign Policy*, no. 90 (Spring 1993): 5; Robert Cullen, "Human Rights Quandry," *Foreign Affairs* 71, no. 5 (Winter 1992/1993): 80–81; Francis Fukuyama, "Trapped in the Baltics," *The New York Times*, December 19, 1992, p. 15.

35. *Helsingin Sanomat*, October 26, 1992, p. C4.

36. *The Baltic Independent*, May 21–27, 1993, p. 1; *Helsingin Sanomat*, March 22, 1993, p. A2; Commission on Security and Cooperation in Europe, *Russians in Estonia: Problems and Prospects* (Washington, D.C.: n.p., 1992).

37. *The Baltic Independent*, February 12–18, 1993, p. 10; *Riigi Teataja*, no. 17 (1993): 395.

38. Raun, *Estonia and the Estonians*, 2nd ed., p. 169; Anderson, "Narva, Petseri, Abrene," p. 207.

39. Riina Kionka, "Armed Incidents Aggravate Russian–Estonian Relations," *RFE/RL Research Report* 1, no. 34 (1992): 36–37.

40. *Helsingin Sanomat*, July 24, 1993, p. A7; Burant, "Polish–Lithuanian Relations," pp. 83–84.

41. Stephen R. Burant and Voytek Zubek, "Eastern Europe's Old Memories and New Realities: Resurrecting the Polish–Lithuanian Union," *East European Politics and Societies* 7 (1993): 386–88.

42. *Wall Street Journal*, February 4, 1992, p. A1.

43. Krickus, "Latvia's 'Russian Question,'" pp. 31–32.

44. Bungs, "Soviet Troops in Latvia," p. 20; *The New York Times*, November 22, 1992, p. 11.

45. *The Baltic Independent*, September 25–October 1, 1992, p. 9; November 27–December 2, 1992, p. 8; Dzintra Bungs, "Moderates Win Parliamentary Elections in Latvia," *RFE/RL Research Report* 2, no. 28 (1993): 1–2.

46. O. Krastiņš, "Jauktās laulības, vecāku un bērnu tautības problēma," *Latvijas Zinātņu Akadēmijas Vēstis*, no. 6 (1992): 6; *Narodnoe khoziaistvo SSSR v 1990 g.* (Moscow: Finansy i Statistika, 1991), pp. 84-85.

47. Mežs, *Latvieši Latvijā*, p. 7; Kalev Katus, "Rahvus: venelane; elukoht: Eesti," *Aja Pulss*, nos. 5/6 (1991): 8.

48. *Ekho Litvy*, February 13, 1991, p. 4; *The Estonian Independent*, February 14, 1991, p. 1; March 7, 1991, p. 3.

49. B. Zepa, "Sabiedriskā doma pārejas periodā Latvijā: Latviešu un citlatviešu uzskatu dinamika (1989-1992)," *Latvijas Zinātņu Akadēmijas Vēstis*, no. 10 (1992): 23; Raun, *Estonia and the Estonians*, 2nd ed., p. 239; Taagepera, *Estonia*, p. 194.

50. Aksel Kirch, Marika Kirch, and Tarmo Tuisk, "Russians in the Baltic States: To Be or Not To Be?," *Journal of Baltic Studies* 24 (1993): 178, 182-83.

51. Anatol Lieven, "Baltic Notebook," *Encounter* 74 (May 1990): 66; Rein Ruutsoo, "Transitional Society and Social Movements in Estonia, 1987-1991," *Eesti Teaduste Akadeemia Toimetised: Humanitaar- ja Sotsiaalteadused* 42 (1993): 211.

52. See, for example, Hanson, "Estonia's Narva Problem," p. 20.

53. On Moldova, see Daria Fane, "Moldova: Breaking Loose from Moscow," in Ian Bremmer and Ray Taras, *Nations and Politics in the Soviet Successor States* (Cambridge: Cambridge University Press, 1993), pp. 121-53.

54. *The Baltic Independent*, August 16-22, 1991, p. 1.

55. Raimo Pullat, *Linnad kodanlikus Eestis* (Tallinn: Eesti Raamat, 1978), p. 137; Raun, *Estonia and the Estonians*, 2nd ed., pp. 207, 235.

56. *Sirp*, October 11, 1991, p. 1.

57. Philip Hanson, *Local Power and Market Reform in the Soviet Union* (Munich: RFE/RL Research Institute, 1993), p. 50; *The Baltic Independent*, July 23-29, 1993, p. 1; *RFE/RL Daily Report*, No. 153, August 12, 1993.

58. *Sirp*, August 6, 1993, p. 4; *Izvestiia*, July 31, 1993, p. 8. For a discussion of the relations between the national government in Tallinn and the city of Narva, see Hanson, "Estonia's Narva Problem."

59. *The Baltic Independent*, July 9-15, 1993, p. 1; July 16-22, 1993, p. 1; *Rahva Hääl*, July 8, 1993, p. 3; *Suomen Kuvalehti*, July 16, 1993, pp. 14-15.

60. Eric Rudenshiold, "Ethnic Dimensions in Contemporary Latvian Politics: Focusing Forces for Change," *Soviet Studies* 44 (1992): 620-21, 626, 634.

61. *Lithuania Today: Politics and Economics*, March 1993, p. 6.

62. George Maude, *The Finnish Dilemma: Neutrality in the Shadow of Power* (London: Oxford University Press, 1976), pp. 142-43. Estonian President Meri's handling of the law on aliens in July 1993, discussed above, is an example of this "multilateral solution."

63. *Postimees*, May 8, 1993, p. 1; *Rahva Hääl*, May 3, 1993, p. 3; *Helsingin Sanomat*, January 25, 1992, p. A8; Eve Kuusmann, "Estonia and Cooperation in the Baltic Sea Region," Pertti Joenniemi and Peeter Vares, eds., *New Actors on the International Arena: The Foreign Policy of the Baltic Countries* (Tampere: Tampere Peace Research Institute, 1993), p. 83.

64. *Helsingin Sanomat*, May 12, 1993, p. A8; May 14, 1993, p. C2.

65. *RFE/RL Daily Report*, No. 105, June 4, 1993.

66. *The Baltic Independent*, March 20-26, 1992, p. 1; *Päevaleht*, May 21, 1993, p. 1.

67. John Lough, "Defining Russia's Relations with Neighboring States," *RFE/RL Research Report* 2, no. 20 (1993): 53.

68. Ibid., pp. 53–60.

69. *Helsingin Sanomat*, July 7, 1993, p. B1.

70. Paul Goble, "The Russians Aren't Going," *Washington Post*, July 19, 1992, p. C4.

71. *The Baltic Independent*, August 6–12, 1993, p. 3.

# Conclusion: The Implications of Post–Soviet Conflicts for International Security

## W. Raymond Duncan
## and G. Paul Holman, Jr.

As our case studies on ethnic conflict in the former Soviet Union and Yugoslavia illustrate, the international community faces an enormous security challenge in devising ways to deal with intrastate conflict in the pursuit of peace and stability. Yugoslavia is afire, armed conflict has escalated in the Caucasus Mountains, Central Asia has seen serious ethnic and communal turbulence, and the Baltic states face economic pressures from Moscow and disputes over Russian troop withdrawals and rights of ethnic Russians. Russia and Ukraine, meanwhile, must deal with a number of ethnically–driven issues, not made easier by extreme nationalists, nuclear weapons, and deteriorating economies on both sides.

The regions explored in this study by no means have lagged in attention from the international community, far from it. The United Nations, EC, NATO, WEU and CSCE have pursued efforts to dampen the turmoil and strife as they spread in the Balkans. From peace negotiations and fact–finding missions to humanitarian aid, cease–fires, peace conferences, border settlement plans, economic sanctions and "no–fly" zones, the United Nations and other international organizations have tried to stop the fighting and bring humanitarian aid into war–torn Croatia and Bosnia.

Events in these parts of the world indicate that the stakes are high in intrastate crises arising from the Balkans to Central Asia. Ethnic wars in former Yugoslavia have demonstrated that neither traditional United Nations (UN) peace–keeping—let alone collective security—nor the collective defense system of the North Atlantic Treaty Organization (NATO) has had any significant impact on easing Balkan wars.[1] Equally irrelevant have been the economic integration of the European Community (EC), conflict management efforts by the Conference on Security and Cooperation (CSCE), and activities of the

Western European Union (WEU). Ineffective conflict management by the international community suggests that ethnic tensions in the Balkans and former Soviet Union may well spread regionally and internationally—certainly that was one effect of insufficient international attention to the widening conflict in former Yugoslavia from 1990 onwards.

In the former Soviet Union, the international community has taken even fewer steps to try to soften ethnic conflict. As the longest-running of current Caucasus conflicts, Nagorno-Karabakh has been the subject of the greatest number of peace initiatives in that region, with notable lack of success.[2] Successive cease-fires were brokered by Russia and Kazakhstan (September 1991 and September 1992) and by Iran in February and May 1992. The United Nations and CSCE have sent fact-finding missions to Georgia and Abkhazia in 1992, and CSCE missions travelled to troubled South Ossetia—but such efforts have proceeded with agonizing slowness. Ethnic frictions in the Baltic have drawn CSCE fact-finding missions and placed the region on the CSCE security agenda; the foreign ministers of the CSCE agreed to admit Estonia, Latvia and Lithuania as CSCE participating states in late 1991 in the aftermath of the attempted coup. NATO meanwhile has expressed displeasure with Russian pressure on the Baltic states.

Yet the need for a clearer political framework to address the types of crises discussed in our case studies is underscored by the lack of international consensus on how to cope with intrastate wars and ethnic tensions. Lack of agreement led the Western community to eschew military force and walk away from political commitments in Bosnia, ineffective UN efforts to create a workable division of labor with the CSCE in dealing with the Nagorno-Karabakh crisis, and divided interests among NATO members regarding places like former Yugoslavia. Russia's insistence on going easy on Serbian "ethnic cleansing" in Bosnia against more forceful U.S. proposals dramatically highlights disagreement among United Nations Security Council members on the causes of conflict—just as Germany's early recognition of Croatia illustrates political differences among NATO members.

Because ethnic turmoil in the Balkans, Caucasus and Central Asia especially has generated so much discussion on the costs and benefits of military intervention, we will examine the nature of this debate. Toward these ends, we assess ethnic nationalism in the former Soviet Union and Yugoslavia as it has shaped:

- Post-Cold War international politics;
- Capabilities of international organizations to cope with regional civil wars;
- Long-term regional insecurity;
- Lessons learned about crisis prevention;
- U.S. foreign policy implications.

## Transforming the International System

As ethnic tensions in our case studies illustrate, the post-Cold War global setting is far from the "new world order" postulated by President George Bush. In rallying a UN-sanctioned coalition against Saddam Hussein's reckless invasion of Kuwait in August 1990, President Bush envisioned a global setting of respect for international law protected by an effective UN collective security system along the lines envisaged by President Woodrow Wilson at the conclusion of World War One.[3] The Gulf War did not bear out this premise, because the allied powers against Iraq had keen interest in oil—not merely in suppressing aggression as the ultimate priority.[4]

In contrast to President Bush's vision, the world today seems more like that portrayed by the new director of the Central Intelligence Agency, James Woolsey, during his confirmation hearings in the U.S. Senate. He observed that after slaying the Soviet dragon, "we live now in a jungle filled with a bewildering variety of poisonous snakes. And in many ways, the dragon was easier to keep track of."[5] Among the poisonous snakes must be included the ethnic strife underscored in our case studies—frequently of genocidal dimensions. As Daniel Patrick Moynihan observes, it was the collapse of the Soviet Union and end of superpower rivalry that opened the door to ethnic violence.[6] The key force shaping ethnic turmoil, however, appears to be the seventy-five-year-old Wilsonian principle of self-determination, giving ethnic groups the right to self-government, in other words, their own state.[7] The international system, as our case studies indicate, is changing rapidly in directions difficult to predict.[8] Some basic characteristics of global politics, to be sure, remain in place. We still do not have an international sovereign power that can make and enforce laws and agreements. Key forces causing conflict still drive world politics, such as religion, economic rivalries, striving for prestige, and hostile nationalism—although states continue to cooperate when their interests mesh.[9] As in the past, democratic states will not likely attack democratic states. Developed and developing countries share a growing economic, financial, and information-sharing interdependence; and technological change has made possible increased interaction of the world's people on a larger scale than in previous decades. Call it globalization.

Still, change has been enormous since the collapse of the Soviet Union and communism, with wide-ranging implications for international order and stability. How is the post-Cold War international system so different from previous years, and how is ethnic nationalism affecting such change? First, bipolarity has collapsed, and with it the competing alliance systems that created a kind of strategic balance of power—and a discipline of bloc politics that tended to hold the passions of ethnic nationalism in check. As Richard Falk notes, there is "no longer an enemy to serve as a focus for unified purpose."[10]

Second, what has replaced bipolarity depends upon one's reference point: unipolarity in terms of U.S. military power; tripolarity when defined as economic and financial influence divided among Europe, Japan and the United States; and multipolarity when defined as diplomatic links between the West and the formerly communist countries. Today, the United States overall is the key remaining power center with the potential for global effectiveness in addressing ethnic issues and regional crises, although just how long that situation will remain is an issue of considerable debate.[11] This situation places a heavy burden of leadership in international crisis—prevention efforts on the shoulders of U.S. leaders—a point explored in greater detail below.

Third, while the developed countries are drawn together in limited types of cooperation—symbolized by the Group of Seven leading industrialized states—major threats to international security proliferate within the developing countries. As the EC Commission President Jacques Delors stated in his March 1991 address to the International Institute for Strategic Studies: "All around us, naked ambition, lust for power, national uprisings and underdevelopment are combining to create potentially dangerous situations, containing the seeds of destabilization, aggravated by the proliferation of weapons of mass destruction."[12] Atrocities in Bosnia, Nagorno-Karabakh, Abkhazia, South Ossetia and Tajikistan dramatically underscore Delors' observation.

Zbigniew Brzezinski notes that this view could be appended with a list of specific factors generating instability in the developing countries. The list would include long-lasting regional conflicts stemming from the residue of imperialism, others stirred by the emergence of regional hegemons, and still others inherent in the nature of inequality, poverty and population growth.[13] Generally speaking, Brzezinski and other scholars like Samuel Huntington argue that despite global economic, financial, commercial, technological and informational interdependence among the developed countries, the emerging system in many developing countries lacks the order and predictability of the Cold War system.[14]

Fourth, within the changing international system ethnic nationalism has become a key driving force—as our case studies attest.[15] Its pressures have led to an international system increasingly characterized by rising intrastate conflict, nationalism against the state, and assertion of group rights as opposed to individual rights—a key factor implicit in democratic systems of government. As animosity among ethnic groups has erupted and self-determination movements proliferated, the international system has seen a break-down in state sovereignty—giving rise to over twenty new states, often weakened by civil wars, and large numbers of refugees, migrations, abused minorities and terrorism.[16] Huntington's observation that the future will see an increase of such conflicts as Western, Confucian, Japanese, Islamic, Hindu, Slavic- Orthodox, Latin American and possibly African civilizations clash, captures the essence of this situation.[17]

Ethnic conflict in places like the former Soviet Union and Yugoslavia, where disciplined bloc politics has collapsed, should not, however, come as a surprise. Scholars for years have stressed the importance of ethnic national identity submerged under communist ideology and party politics.[18] Indeed, observers like Walker Connor and Daniel Patrick Moynihan for a long time have stressed that ethnic identity is not likely to disappear under the pressures of modernity, that ethnic identity formed one basis of national identity, that nations were different from states, and that states quite likely could break up along ethnic lines.[19] More surprising has been the genocidal violence and defiance of international peace-keeping efforts in regions such as former Yugoslavia, Caucasia and Central Asia.

Fifth, the intensity of ethnic tensions varies from region to region. In former Yugoslavia they have created a bloodbath of horrific proportions, defying efforts of the international community to bring order and stability. In Caucasia, as Audrey Altstadt argues, ethnic nationalism's chances of escalating into an even more expanding regional war are chilling. Indeed, by July 1993 two Caucasus regions were sinking deeper into civil war with Armenia's advance into Azerbaijan and Abkhazia's drive for independence inside Georgia.[20]

Then we have Central Asia. As Malvin Helgesen points out, it is the scene of large ethnic minorities, inter-ethnic tensions, inter-clan frictions and local allegiances. Although ethnic nationalism seems at present less virulent here than in former Yugoslavia, Russia, Ukraine, or Caucasia, it is growing, and in Tajikistan communal violence has exploded.[21] Compared to all these areas, prospects for both peace and democracy look more positive in the Baltic, as Toivo Raun discusses, barring a shift toward the radical right in Russia and potential territorial designs. Still, how Baltic relations with Russians inside and outside the region will play out remains an issue of debate.[22]

Russia has numerous geopolitical and demographic interests in the former Soviet republics—not least the 25 million Russians living in surrounding countries. Moscow continues to battle brushfires in bordering states.[23] Russian soldiers at outposts on the Tajik–Afghan border have been attacked more than once. Russia is involved in an ongoing dispute with Estonia over the status of Russians living in that Baltic republic, which could easily lead to claims upon Estonian territory (475,000 ethnic Russians living in Estonia alone, of whom the great majority do not hold Estonian citizenship). Russo–Ukrainian conflict festers over territorial issues in Crimea and ownership of nuclear weapons. Within Russia there is a plethora of tensions. Should right-wing nationalists come to power in Russia, they could become acute.

Ethnic conflict has raised key questions regarding international security in the post-Cold War era. What is the appropriate use of military force to stem the tide of a spreading ethnic conflict—as in South Ossetia, Abkhazia, Nagorno-Karabakh and Tajikistan? How can international and regional security organizations like the UN and NATO avoid "too little, too late" actions to prevent widening turmoil in such regions? Is it possible in situations of ancient ethnic animosities to engage in multilateral military peace-enforcement—to physically interpose armed forces to separate ongoing combatants and thus create a cease-fire that does not yet exist? How willing is the international community to execute peace-enforcement operations that violate traditional definitions of state sovereignty? Under what conditions are civilized states prepared to defend the rights of groups and individuals within states when they are abused by their own governments?[24] William Safire asks, "When do the world's responsible leaders have a right to intrude on what used to be an impenetrable sovereignty?"[25]

## Intergovernmental Security Organizations

Ethnic tensions in the former Soviet Union and Yugoslavia have posed serious challenges for intergovernmental security organizations designed essentially for interstate conflict. As Yugoslavia's crisis spread step by step—from the very beginning a classic case for early collective intervention—first European Community efforts, then UN humanitarian and peace-keeping operations, simply did not work.[26] Although preventive diplomacy could have gone into gear during the early stages of the crisis in 1991, no serious effort at conciliation or mediation occurred—while the U.S. essentially tossed the ball into the Europeans' court.

As for the West European community, the EC was greatly divided. France preferred to activate the Western European Union. Great Britain objected to sending in troops, owing to its problems in Northern Ireland. Germany cited constitutional impediments to such military involvement. As the crisis spread, such actions—coupled with UN peace-keeping, which called for neutrality *vis-à-vis* the belligerents—produced a public renunciation of the threat or use of force, in other words a green light for Serbian aggression.[27] Indeed, as the crisis deepened, UN forces became virtual hostages and their sponsoring governments worried more about their safety than about ending the tragedy. Crisis prevention became a non-starter.

The ill-fated international organizational efforts in Yugoslavia illustrate the lack of a clear policy blueprint for when and where to use force in what has become, in the words of one observer, "a more anarchical and competitive world order,"[28] following the end of the Cold War. The U.S. and other great powers have approached each post-Cold War crisis on an *ad hoc* basis—from operations on behalf of the Kurds in 1991 to help in southern Iraq, Somalia and Bosnia in 1992. Such *ad hoc* U.S. and UN interventions—which in Iraq and Somalia represent challenges to the Westphalian principle of state sovereignty—have produced much debate on the merits of military intervention in Yugoslavia to stop the fighting. As an aside, it should be noted that daily television-monitoring of the siege of Sarajevo—as earlier in Vietnam—has played a key role in escalating public debate on the costs and benefits of a U.S.-led, UN-legitimized military intervention in Yugoslavia, ostensibly against the Serbs.

## The United Nations and Other International Organizations

The United Nations, under the leadership of Secretary General Boutros-Ghali, has attempted to adapt itself to intrastate wars and ethnic conflict situations represented by Yugoslavia and the Caucas—for sound reasons. Of the 27 United Nations operations mounted within the last 45 years—with 13 still running—nine were begun during 1991-1993.[29] In the overwhelming majority of UN Security Council operations today, a strong element of civil war and ethnic/communal conflict characterizes the struggle.[30] Boutros-Ghali's efforts are part of the larger scholarly and policy-making debate now emerging from turmoil in the former Yugoslavia and Soviet Union over the UN's capability to support peace-keeping with stronger military enforcement—and whether or not the UN should intervene in places like the Balkans and Caucasia in the first place.

Boutros-Ghali published his *Agenda for Peace* in 1992, a coherent rationale for stepped-up UN peace-keeping efforts under the new conditions emerging in the post-Cold War era. This optimistic and pioneering effort among other things responds to the notion that since ethnic conflicts are on the rise and likely to get worse, and since the old antagonism between Russia and America has waned with the passing of the Cold War, why not create a system of global collective security as the framers of the UN charter originally intended?[31] In tackling this assumption, the UN Secretary General advances a series of new steps, including the call for creation of a small, standing UN force.

The *Agenda for Peace* recognizes challenges posed by ethnic nationalism and intrastate conflict and the need to rethink old notions of state sovereignty—given the break-down of central authority in settings where the UN seeks to implement humanitarian remedies and forge long-term political solutions.[32] While the foundation of UN operations, in Boutros-Ghali's view, must remain the state, his *Agenda for Peace* notes a number of shifts in the international context of security in which the UN must operate, including the break-down of state governments and maltreatment of minority populations. Places like former Yugoslavia, among others, in Boutros-Ghali's words, illustrate that in the post-Cold War era:

The time of absolute and exclusive sovereignty ... has passed; its theory was never matched by reality. It is the task of leaders of states today to understand and to find a balance between the needs of good internal governance and the requirements of an ever more interdependent world. ... If every ethnic, religious or linguistic group claimed statehood, there would be no limit to fragmentation, and peace, security and economic well-being for all would become ever more difficult to achieve.[33]

On traditional concepts of state sovereignty, he argues that "The dynamics and priorities of a new era, along with the difficulties in working with local authorities, have raised profound questions about the absolute need for consent from the parties in the first place."[34]

The *Agenda for Peace* recognizes that new thinking is called for if UN peace-keeping is to keep pace with change in the post-Cold War international system:

> There is another aspect to the end of the Cold War. The thawing of its frozen political geography has led to the eruption of savage conflicts in, and sometimes between, newly emerging independent states. The former Yugoslavia has become the United Nations' largest peace-keeping commitment ever. Ethnic conflict across borders and the brutal killing of civilians there are reminiscent of the ordeal that United Nations peace-keeping forces faced in the 1960s in the then Congo. United Nations forces again are taking an unacceptable level of casualties. It is difficult to avoid wondering whether the conditions yet exist for successful peace-keeping in what was Yugoslavia."[35]

Boutros-Ghali's thoughts were prophetic, for by July 1993 UN aid efforts in former Yugoslavia were on the verge of collapse, owing to a paucity of funding and the tendency of the Western powers to "walk away" from their political commitments on Bosnia, especially the defunct Vance-Owens peace plan. The West essentially retreated from its threats to impose the plan by force. Such a retreat created a political vacuum in which President Slobodan Milosevic of Serbia, his Croatian counterpart, Franjo Tudjman, and Serb and Croat proxies in Bosnia devised their own plan to divide Bosnia along ethnic lines.[36]

Boutros-Ghali calls for traditional peace-keeping efforts to be complemented by more forceful operations, including preventive diplomacy and peace enforcement—as in enforcing the "no fly zone" over Bosnia.[37] In meeting the challenges of new forces at work in the international security setting, the *Agenda for Peace* focuses on four types of actions:

- *Preventive diplomacy*, by which is meant "action to prevent existing disputes from arising between parties, to prevent existing disputes from escalating into conflicts and to limit the spread of the latter when they occur."[38]
- *Peace-making*, defined as "action to bring hostile parties to agreement, essentially through such peaceful means such as those foreseen in Chapter VI of the United Nations Charter." Mediation, as in the case of Cyrus Vance in former Yugoslavia is a classic example of peace-making. The

> *Agenda for Peace* includes taking a new look at the use of military force—by peace enforcement units—as stipulated by Article 42 of the Charter.[39]

- *Peace-keeping*, which is the "deployment of a United Nations presence in the field, hitherto with the consent of all the parties concerned, normally involving United Nations military and/or policy personnel and frequently civilians as well. Peace-keeping is a technique that expands the possibilities for both the prevention of conflict and the making of peace."

- *Post-conflict peace-building*, which is meant as "action to identify and support structures which will tend to strengthen and solidify peace in order to avoid a relapse into conflict." [40]

These steps and other remarks by the UN Secretary General represent strong initiatives to reshape the UN for more assertive influence when individual and group rights are egregiously violated by state governments, as in Bosnia, or when central authority completely breaks down, as in Somalia. The *Agenda for Peace* recognizes that we have moved into a new era of weak states, intrastate wars, civil strife and ethnic self-determination movements in many parts of the globe. As for the UNs' role in the Balkans, regional leaders in that part of the world see it as crucial to stability. In the view of Milan Kucan, who led Slovenia's secession from Yugoslavia: "Only the UN can protect this state (Bosnia). The only way to save the Muslim state is as a UN-guaranteed protectorate. The alternative is partition, which will amount to UN acceptance of a military power (Serbia), which will dominate and destabilize the whole region. That can prove catastrophic for Europe."[41]

## The Case For Military Intervention

In making a case *for* more forceful UN-sanctioned intervention in regional conflicts, Boutros-Ghali argues that the UN is fully prepared and capable of peace-keeping with teeth—to overcome situations like Bosnia where lightly-armed peace-keepers look helpless. Ethnically-spawned regional conflicts increasingly call for muscular actions, and the UN Charter affords the legal basis to pursue them.[42] In the words of Kofi A. Annan, UN Under-Secretary for Peace-Keeping Operations:

Today's conflicts in Somalia and Bosnia have fundamentally rearranged the parameters of peace-keeping. It is no longer enough to implement agreements or separate antagonists; the international community now wants peace-keepers to demarcate boundaries, control and eliminate heavy weapons, quell anarchy and guarantee the delivery of humanitarian aid in war zones...tasks that call for "teeth" and "muscle." ... Further,...many...believe...the future will demand an even greater involvement in conflicts occurring within borders, as well as a wider use of force.[43]

Bosnia's turmoil has generated other calls for more forceful UN-sanctioned intervention, based upon thoughtful policy prescriptions and analytic formulas. In line with Boutros-Ghali's framework, policy analysts stress that Iraqi persecution of the Kurds and the anarchic situation in Somalia justified UN Security Council (UNSC) decisions affirming the right of the international community to intervene in internal affairs in support of human rights, minority rights and the survival of populations.[44] Using Iraq and Somalia as precedents, valid criteria for collective security intervention in Bosnia and, say, Nagorno-Karabakh, arguably are: (1) potential for wider regional conflict; (2) impact of the conflict on international norms; (3) moral considerations, as in Bosnia's "ethnic cleansing" and killing of innocent civilians; and (4) danger to democratic governments.[45] Indeed, Pierre Hassner makes the case that by most accepted criteria in the international community, the issue in the former Yugoslavia is not being whether intervention is legitimate, but rather who should do it and to what regional and international end.[46]

As to who should intervene, observers emphasize the UN—in cooperation with other international organizations, such as the CSCE, NATO and WEU—as the natural candidate:

> Chapter VII of the United Nations Charter confers major responsibility on the Security Council for peace-enforcement. There is nothing comparable at present in the charters of other relevant international organizations. For this reason, the United Nations is likely to become the premiere legitimizing authority for Eurasian collective security operations.[47]

This line of thinking stresses that the UN need not take on the job of peace enforcement alone. It can work in tandem with such organizations as the CSCE, which has sent investigative and rapporteur missions to former Yugoslavia, Albania, Armenia, Azerbaijan, Ukraine, Moldova, Belarus, Turkmenistan, Uzbekistan, Tajikistan, Kazakhstan and Georgia.[48] NATO represents another cooperative partner with the UN, illustrated by its enforcing the naval blockade of Serbia and Montenegro to bolster the early UN sanctions on strategic goods the first time NATO used its forces in an authorized military operation in Europe.[49] Some regional leaders in the Balkans strongly urge a U.S.-led NATO intervention.[50] The WEU, as we have seen, also has entered peace-keeping and peace-enforcement operations, participating in the United Nations-mandated blockade against former Yugoslavia by dispatching a fleet to the Adriatic.

Additional reasons for the international community to intervene with military force in places like former Yugoslavia and hot spots in the former Soviet Union include:

- Deterring attempts to change borders by force.
- Preventing the rise of expansionist regimes (e.g., Serbia today but perhaps Russia after Yeltsin).

- Easing tensions between Muslim and Christian states.
- Punishing Serbian brutality to deter other potential ethnic cleansers.
- Reinforcing hope in the weaker states of Central and Eastern Europe that they can count on the West, not the "rogue states," for help.
- Preventing a widening of the war in the Balkans.
- Bolstering liberal elements in Serbia and elsewhere as opposed to allowing a drift toward xenophobic dictatorships.
- Setting up conditions for a UN trusteeship, first in Bosnia, later perhaps elsewhere.[51]
- Preventing or delaying proliferation of weapons of mass destruction.
- Allowing Cold War alliances and security structures to experiment with new solutions to ethnic conflicts.

The failure to intervene with some kind of multilateral use of force in former Yugoslavia (better to have engaged in early crisis prevention measures through a multilateral division of labor) arguably runs the risk of creating more Yugoslavias on an ever widening scale, drawing increasing numbers of countries into the conflict. The trick is to figure out how to translate force into policy and to mobilize a sufficient number of states to pull it off. An alternate theory, less well articulated, is the forest fire analogy: let the ethnic conflicts burn themselves out.

## The Case Against Military Intervention

Ethnic conflict in former Yugoslavia and the Caucasus has generated strong arguments for non-intervention. Not least among the negative views must be included the European Community member states' pronounced reluctance to commit military forces, the U.S. military community's distinct distaste for such endeavors, and precedent-setting effects of military intervention in a world loaded with ethnic conflicts that neither the United Nations nor United States is prepared to take on.[52] The case against military intervention rests essentially on the argument that places like former Yugoslavia and Caucasia vividly illustrate the lack of international security mechanisms required to control ethnically-induced civil violence.[53] As one observer notes, to create such a structure would call for the World War Two solution: total defeat of the sanctioned country or group, imposition of a new political order in that region, and a lengthy occupation until the new order took hold sufficiently to guarantee peace and stability.[54] As Donald Snow argues, the case for nonintervention rests on the intractability of these ethnic conflicts—basically political and cultural in substance, not military, in ways that outside military force cannot address.[55] Force will not provide a quick fix for centuries-old ethnic disputes; indeed, it might suppress one form of violence only to replace it with another.[56]

The case against military intervention objects to undermining state sovereignty at the expense of protecting rights of the oppressed ethnic groups.  By such a precedent, then all states would leave themselves open to intervention by other states.[57]  West European and U.S. reaction to Bosnia, in Snow's view, suggests a reluctance to adopt the duty, right or obligation to protect individuals and groups from the atrocious behavior of their own governments, because it would redefine the purposes for which the international community will use force in the future.  Snow worries about Boutros-Ghali's *Agenda for Peace*, with its new thinking on individual and group rights versus the traditional Westphalian view of state sovereignty.

Indeed, intervention may entail problems so severe that they stack the deck overwhelmingly against the benefits as opposed to the costs.  Defeat of Serbian and perhaps the other militias in Bosnia, followed by military occupation, would require an estimated 500,000 men to separate the warring factions.  We would have to negotiate with numerous local commanders whose control over their own personnel is frequently incomplete.  Some would resist disarmament and likely cause even more bloodshed—not only to combatants but to many innocent civilians caught up in the fighting.[58]  Once the fighting ceased, any established government would have to be bolstered indefinitely by an occupying multilateral force, with consequences likely to far overshadow UN problems with mob violence and shootings in Somalia during the summer of 1993.

While the UN has achieved a few successes in Bosnia under arduous conditions, it could be said that even the UNPROFOR—designed not to impose peace on warring factions, but to mitigate the tragedy—has produced counterproductive consequences.  Admittedly, by Christmas 1992 UNPROFOR had delivered some $750 million worth of assistance and aided thousands of refugees.  Yet, when the UN placed its neutral troops in Bosnia, it may have signalled to aggressor militias that it would not intervene in their operations, because its own troops became hostage to revenge.  European resistance— notably by France and Great Britain—to U.S. efforts to back the "No–Fly Zone" with more muscle illustrates this point.  In this sense, some would argue that UN efforts actually helped Serbian aggression—with rules of engagement prohibiting forceful action, insistence on remaining neutral, and pursuit of policy without force.[59]  Perhaps worst of all, the UNPROFOR presence deceived many into believing that the tragedy was almost over.  It may also have emboldened the Bosnians to continue fighting, rather than accept a dictated peace.

Whether or not the UN can rearrange its operations to gear up for true collective security in places like the Balkans, Caucasia and elsewhere in the former USSR remains highly debatable.  Indeed, some scholars question the advisability of using UN collective security in the absence of a clear state aggressor, where instability *per se* is the issue.[60]  In cases where intrastate war has fired up, central authority broken down, and ethnic conflict escalated, the UN simply may not have the resources to:

- Develop a consensus among Security Council members that instability must cease—as in the case of Russo-American disagreement over Serbian actions in Bosnia.
- Mobilize sufficient force and devise an effective strategy to stop violations of cease-fires.
- Avoid taking sides during a military intervention.
- Compel local militia leaders to lay down arms.
- Arrange a satisfactory long-term political solution to avoid future outbreaks of ethnic violence.

On top of such problems, worth noting in this respect is the large-scale growth in demands for the services of the UN and the transition in types of activities in which the UN has become involved—owing to the changing character of conflict.[61] As opposed to interstate war—the kind the framers of the UN Charter had in mind—civil war and ethnic conflict form the overwhelming majority of UNSC operations today. As Adam Roberts notes:

> The collapse of large multinational states and empires almost always causes severe dislocations, including the emergence or re-emergence of ethnic, religious, regional and other animosities. The absence of fully legitimate political systems, traditions, regimes and state frontiers all increase the likelihood that a narrowly ethnic definition of 'nation' prevails. These difficulties are compounded by the fact that, for the most part, the geographical distribution of populations is so messy that the harmonious realization of self-determination is impossible. Conflict-ridden parts of the former Yugoslavia and the former Soviet Union are merely the two most conspicuous contemporary examples of imperial collapse leading to inter-ethnic war.[62]

As a result of the changing nature of conflict, UN, CSCE, EC, NATO and WEU activities are clearly in a process of transition. The UN now has far more military responsibilities than ever before, and it seems quite possible that the level of activity may well increase.[63] Most operations undertaken by the UN today are long-term in nature and involve larger numbers of military personnel bringing more firepower than we think of in the UNs' earlier efforts in observer and interposition activities.[64] Nor do many recent UNs' activities conform to the "theology" normally identified with peace-keeping. One can no longer assume that such operations are conducted with the consent of all involved, that UN personnel are lightly armed, that they avoid force except in self-defense, and that they do nothing to raise the question of UN impartiality in the dispute.[65] Indicative of change in UN actions is that recent and expected United Nations activities have been generally initiated in response, not entirely to international aggression, but to the disintegration or breakup of states and associated human tragedies.[66]

United Nations activities have been generally initiated in response, not entirely to international aggression, but to the disintegration or breakup of states and associated human tragedies.[66]

## Long–Term Regional Insecurity

Apart from international security organizations, worth looking at is the impact of ethnic nationalism and regional conflict on international security in the long term.    Our case studies underscore how ethnic tensions can undermine economies and prospects for democracy, spawn the spread of nuclear and conventional weapons, and in other ways erode regional stability and peace. Our intent here is not to go into depth on this issue, but to suggest in broad brush strokes how, and in what ways, ethnic nationalism and regional conflicts negatively affect regional and international security.

## Economic Dislocation

It would be difficult to overstate the negative economic effects of regional upheavals such as those examined in our case studies.[67]  Croatia is a prototype of the economic catastrophe created by ethnic war, where about 40 percent of the country's economic capacity was destroyed during 1991 alone, a percentage representing an estimated $13 billion.[68]  As to the infrastructure so vital to economic development, 38 percent of the total road network was badly damaged, dozens of key bridges destroyed, and port and air facilities shelled heavily.  Serbian attacks also targeted thousands of public buildings, such as schools, hospitals, churches and cultural centers—a situation replicated in Bosnia—and the oil industry in Baranja and Eastern Slavonia have been greatly damaged.  Beyond the physical damage, Croatia's tourist industry—the biggest source of foreign currency before the war—has suffered greatly, shrinking in 1991 to around one tenth of its previous level.

Serbia has not escaped the economic pitfalls of ethnic aggression.  Only a minority of Serbia's 10.5 million people can afford the prices of goods smuggled in from abroad or the lower–priced basic commodities, owing to hyper–inflation.[69]  Prices have risen sharply, around 2.6 million out of a work force of 3.4 million are unemployed; the average monthly income fell to $25.00, and production declined 40 percent during 1992–1993.  More than three million people are living below the official poverty line of $11 per month; the average monthly wage is $17.00.[70]  Although the United Nations–imposed sanctions on Serbia and Montenegro undoubtedly have contributed to Serbia's economic woes, additional causes likely stem from unrestricted printing of dinars, the local currency, failed efforts to apply Western–style market reforms and the huge economic costs of the war. There has also been a brain drain of the best and the brightest owing to the war, economy and lack of educational opportunities.[71]

In Croatia—as well as the economies of Western European countries—additional burdens have been created by the enormous number of refugees. By 1993 Croatia's population of under five million citizens had received an additional 700,000 refugees—about half Croatians and the other half Muslims from Bosnia.[72] Refugees create huge economic demands for already scarce housing and food, in addition to ethnic frictions as has been seen in Germany. Thousands have fled Sarajevo, supposedly one of the "safe havens" designated by the UN for Bosnian Muslims, where by summer 1993 the Serbian siege had produced severe deprivation—fuel, water and bread shortages and growing health problems that included dysentery.[73] As a result of such economic pressures, Croatia turned to printing money, which in 1992 produced rising inflation (250 percent), declining salaries, and increasing unemployment.

It takes no great intellectual effort to imagine future economic threats faced by Croatia—not to mention Serbia, Bosnia and similar situations in Caucasia and other regions of the former Soviet Union. Once unifying factors of war have passed, one foresees undermined political viability and internal instability as Croatia and its counterparts struggle with rebuilding a war-torn infrastructure, coping with debt and unemployment, and trying to move toward privatization (which tends to generate unemployment initially). It would seem hardly the setting for flowering democratic institutions and a market economy—even less the once great income-generating haven for tourists. Ethnic wars produce pyrrhic victories at best.

Such economic difficulties do not augur well for the future, because they set up conditions for a vicious circle of more protracted ethnic conflict. As research on social conflict underscores, protracted ethnic tensions have enduring features "such as economic and technological underdevelopment, and unintegrated social and political systems."[74] Ethnic conflict also stems from distributive injustice, which can only be eliminated by a substantial shift in economic and social disparities in "levels of political privilege and opportunity."[75] Any "solutions" that do not come to grips with these features are solutions that must rest on law enforcement, threat, or control by the more powerful party to the conflict. Conflict is likely to erupt once again as soon as there is any change in the balance of forces, in leadership, or in some other significant ecopolitical conditions.[76] Key sources of conflict are deeply rooted in the economic, social and political conditions—underdevelopment and distributive injustice—in which multi-ethnic and communal groups find themselves living. Research suggests that the fundamental source of conflict is denial of basic human needs common to everyone: "security, distinctive identity, social recognition of identity, and effective participation in the processes that determine conditions of security and identity and other such developmental requirements."[77]


## Weapons Proliferation

Ethnic tensions and ethnic wars lead naturally to weapons proliferation—and to a loss of control over existing weapons.  First, in the case of nuclear weapons, the break-up of the Soviet Union into ethnically conscious new republics left the nuclear arsenal in new hands—not only Russia, but Ukraine, Belarus and Kazakhstan.  An obvious problem of control over the nuclear weapons immediately emerges—not least the potential breakdown of administrative control and possible smuggling and illegal sales of some of the 27,000 nuclear warheads under guard by outlying military units.[78]  Another problem is getting such missiles and warheads back under central control.  In Kiev a growing number of parliamentary deputies argue that Ukraine should retain some of the 176 strategic missiles, 30 nuclear bombers, and over 1,600 warheads to deter any ultranationalist Russian government that might come to power and attempt to reimpose control over Kiev.[79]

Second, ethnic self-determination movements—as Slovenia, Croatia and Bosnia breaking away from former Yugoslavia—mean more armies and militias—and more weapons in competing hands.  The pattern is similar in Nagorno-Karabakh, Abkhazia, and elsewhere in the former Soviet Union. Instead of a central military, as in Yugoslavia under Tito for example, we find Slovenian, Croatian, Serbian and Bosnian military forces—in addition to numerous militias (notably Serbian militias in Bosnia) frequently reporting to no higher authority.

More weapons in the hands of competing ethnic groups, used to combat perceived victimization, point toward a social and political setting hardly conducive to ethnic harmony.  The efforts of one group to try to enforce its security, distinctive identity and effective participation in political processes, can victimize other groups—setting up conditions for more protracted social conflict. Weapons proliferation in multiethnic societies certainly reduces the sense of trust among distinct groups, opportunity for cooperation, and setting for acceptable compromises over priority interests.[80]

More weapons in competing hands also mean complex negotiating problems for UN and other international officials trying to reach consensus among battling military groups, arrange cease-fires and negotiate long-term political solutions, given the number of armed actors able to destabilize such agreements.  Serbian militias in Bosnia, for example, time and again have undermined cease-fires. From a regional and international perspective, prospects for long-term peace in the region may be undermined by such widespread proliferation of weapons and armed groups with grudges to settle, let alone the burdens placed on newly independent economies struggling with the costs of weapons.

Third, once independence has been achieved, ethnically conscious states typically begin to think about building their own armed forces, which adds to weapons proliferation, more independently militarized actors in the region, and economic costs. As new republics were formed out of the Soviet Union, for example, declarations on "nationalization" of the ex-Soviet armed forces' property deployed in the territories of the former republics became the name of the game, followed by separate oaths of allegiance taken by the servicemen, and replacement of Russian officers by natives.[81] New armed forces in the former Soviet Union likely will move toward different alignment—European republics like the Baltic states looking toward Western Europe, Turkey and Iran vying with Russia for influence in Central Asia, and the Caucasus potentially sliding into anarchy in the Nagorno-Karabakh conflict, Armenian-Azerbaijanian border war, South Ossetian-Georgian war, and civil war in Georgia itself.

Fourth, ethnic conflicts accentuate weapons proliferation forces previously at work within societies—pressures that do not augur well for conflict resolution and social and political stability. The Caucasus region, for example, has been known for many years as the spawning ground for criminal organizations similar to the Sicilian Mafia, with an influence that has spread beyond the region itself.[82] Powerful Armenian, Chechen and Azerbaijani Mafias have been competing and fighting each other on the whole territory of the former USSR—a trend exacerbated by the breakdown in central authority occasioned by regional ethnic conflict. As Andrei Kortunov of the USA-Canada Institute in Moscow has observed:

> These criminal structures that have accumulated a lot of additional wealth and power are in no way interested in stabilizing the situation and can successfully confront regular troops. There already are a lot of reports about criminal groups stealing weapons from the military garrisons, killing military personnel or taking their family members hostage. It (ethnic conflict) cannot but aggravate the general situation even more.[83]

Fifth, the Balkans and Caucasus have long-standing traditions of private citizens having their own guns. In the former Soviet Union, Soviet authorities consistently fought the Caucasian tradition of private ownership of guns, but the tradition has outlived Soviet power and with ethnic wars raging now has an extremely powerful impetus. In the chaotic setting there, citizens seek to purchase guns—Kalashnikov rifles, machine guns, whatever they can acquire—to protect themselves against criminals and semi-criminal groups. The same weapons can of course be used in riots, social disorder and anti-government protests.[84] Similar patterns have been reported in Bosnia, with a clear consequence: weapons out of control.[85] Ethnically-centered communities and weapons proliferation go hand in hand in places like Bosnia and Georgia.

## Transition to Market Economies

Ethnic tensions hold the potential for undermining a transition toward democratic market economies, as suggested above, a point worth fleshing out in greater detail. The problem is not only the deleterious economic effects of ethnic war—damaged infrastructure, undermined capacity to absorb capital, brain drain, a weakened and uneducated work force, political instability that drives away foreign investors, and the overall cost of rebuilding human and physical capital. A parallel problem is real and latent tensions among ethnic groups that hinder government economic planning, cooperative industrial projects and efficient investment in various geographical regions of the state, that is, ethnic minorities living inside the state or in neighboring states that are candidates for economic integration. Russia and the Commonwealth of Independent States (CIS) is a good case in point.

In the CIS, Russia has the largest number of ethnic minorities, with over 27 million non-Russians residing in the Russian Federation. Many such minorities living in Russia have been asserting their independence, raising the long-term prospect of possible disintegration of the Russian Federation, while in the short term posing problems for a cohesive political and economic union.[86] At a time when Boris Yeltsin is trying to move toward Western-style democracy and market economy reforms, he faces a situation within the Russian Federation where some of its 20 ethnic republics have demonstrated sharp independence from Moscow. These include Karelia, on Russia's northwest border with Finland, the vast Siberian Republic of Sakha—rich in gold and diamonds-Tuva, which borders Mongolia, and Bashkiria, a gas-producing region south of the Ural mountains.[87]

Although ethnically distinct autonomous republics account for less than 20 percent of Russia's total population, they control a much larger proportion of the country's natural resources.[88] As observers note, they hold the key to Russia's territorial integrity and geopolitical cohesiveness—foundations for economic growth and stability. Many fear that Yeltsin's demise could lead to neoimperialist policies in Moscow, a continuing source of tension between the capital and outlying republics which greatly complicates political reform and economic recovery. Unemployment, inflation, crime, corruption and environmental pollution are likely to exacerbate ethnic differences in the struggle for scarce resources.

Meanwhile, as the decade of the 1990s began, around 25 million Russians lived outside the Russian Federation in neighboring republics (some have been returning to Russia). Pressures from Russian right-wing nationalists to protect the Russian diaspora—as in Estonia—can lead to policies not conducive to economic cooperation with Russia's neighbors, as in shutting down oil supplies, as well as discouraging aid and investment in Russia itself. The point is that a resurgent Russian nationalism in defense of Russian minorities abroad is not conducive to Russian and CIS economic cooperation—at a time when reformists in the various republics will be under pressure to protect their own economies and ethnic groups at home and in other republics. Russo–Ukrainian relations vividly underscore this problem.

Obstructing economic recovery through closer cooperation among CIS members, then, will be a number of driving forces stemming from separate ethnic identities: historically suppressed ethnic antagonisms, competing economic interests among the different national groups, difficulty in assimilating ethnic minorities within the states (notably Russia), disparities in economic wealth, and pressure to take unilateral political actions in defense of perceived ethnic interests. Most of the former Soviet Union was in economic difficulty before the break–up; since then, the new states have endured a deepening crisis. Because deteriorating economic conditions tend to accentuate ethnic tensions, a potential future for Russia and the CIS is exacerbated ethnic friction and difficulty in finding long–term solutions to economic recovery.[89]

## Social Disintegration and
## Undermined Political Development

Ethnically–driven social disintegration in the Balkan, Caucasian and Central Asian conflicts does not augur well for developing institutions to facilitate a stable political environment meeting the needs of a state's population. Underlying social institutions that allow democratic self–determination to work are not facilitated in settings where crime, mass rape (as in Bosnia), and social disintegration become the norm rather than the exception. Indeed, the trauma and psychological dislocation of Bosnia's inhabitants may be so entrenched that rebuilding social and political institutions compatible with democratic self–determination will take years.[90]

In Bosnia, political development and future stability will be especially complicated by the patchwork of rival Serbian groups consumed by lawlessness and economic collapse, months of near anarchy, families burned out of their homes, and civilians killed in reprisal for deaths of relatives at the front.[91] U.S. and UN efforts to invoke a war crimes tribunal indicate the severity of barbarity in Bosnia, which has convicted its own war criminals.[92] Such crimes as terrorism (bombing, beatings and killings of innocent civilians), mass executions and mass killing of family members will make a transition to political stability difficult in Bosnia—unless the country simply disappears into new territory acquired by Croatia and Serbia.[93]

A psychology of fear is likely to reinforce authoritarian cultures and strong–man leadership as opposed to self–government and democratic institutions. In Serbia, for example, a criminal has run for parliament on a platform of intense nationalism, although the U.S. has said he should face a war-crimes tribunal on charges of participating in the killings and forcible expulsion of thousands of Muslim civilians from Bosnian towns.[94] Strong-man Milosevic, meanwhile, remained in power in Serbia; the tougher economic conditions became, the more dictatorial his rule.[95] Lack of participatory democracy and emphasis on centralized control under Milosevic—in some ways like his old communist days—foreshadowed a setting of protracted conflict ahead. Yugoslavia's crisis erupted in the first place owing in part to an inadequate economic performance and one-party monopoly of power.[96] His brand of centralized rule reinforced the political alienation of Serbia's urban educated sectors, eroded their declining trust in government and increased their victimization for not backing a "Greater Serbia."[97]

## The "Spread Effect" of Regional Conflict

In regions where state boundaries do not represent ethnically homogeneous populations and where deteriorating economic conditions exist—as in Central Europe, Southeast Europe and much of the former Soviet Union—ethnic conflict naturally spreads to adjoining states, as our case studies illustrate. At the time of this writing, ongoing ethnic conflict in Bosnia, Caucasia and Central Asia threatens to draw other countries into the conflict.

Bosnia's conflict could spread into Kosovo, a province of Serbia. Should the Serbs move into Kosovo, 90 percent of which is populated by Albanians, Albania likely would come to their aid, while a large Albanian minority in neighboring Macedonia also could rise in support. This could lead Serbia to invade Macedonia, which it perceives as "South Serbia," leading Greece and Bulgaria to invade as well, because they think of Macedonia as their own. Enter Turkey. Turkey, a traditional enemy of the Serbs and with long-standing frictions with Greece, could feel compelled to intervene on the side of the Albanians. One consequence could be that Russian nationalists might intervene to aid the Serbs.[98] In one observer's view: If fighting envelops Kosovo and Macedonia, neighboring states will become involved in the fighting. Such a final step—a true Balkan War—can be expected in the next decade or so as long as there is no large international peace-keeping presence in those regions.[99]

Spread effects of ethnic conflict are potential outcomes in several areas of the former Soviet Union. In addition to the scenario of Russia coming to the aid of Russians in outlying republics, as on the Tajik-Afghan border, Turkey is becoming impatient, not only with Serbian treatment of Bosnian Muslims, but also with "Armenian oppression of the Azeri people." Armenia is party to a security pact among the former Soviet republics, including Russia, that requires all signatories to help defend any member that is attacked. Turkey is, of course, a NATO member.[100] Enmity between Georgia and Russia has been on the increase over the Black Sea region of Abkhazia, while Central Asia has gained increased attention from Iran and Turkey, and to a lesser extent Pakistan. Tajikistan's troubles could spill over into neighboring Uzbekistan, where most of the 1 million Tajiks who live in other Central Asian republics reside.

## How Should Other Nations Respond?

While many international relations specialists have tended in the past to leave the issue of ethnic conflict untouched, our case studies illustrate how ethnic identity impacts on the interstate system, especially when one ethnic group is spread over more than one state. Ethnic nationalism has become a major driving force of regional conflict and perhaps the single most divisive force in the late twentieth century. It has defied efforts of the international community to bring it under control. More than ever, new thinking on how the international community can act in ways to moderate its dark potential for instability or to channel it toward constructive activity merits attention.

The case studies suggest a number of conclusions learned about crisis prevention as it has played out in the former Soviet Union and Yugoslavia. A look at such conclusions will set the scene for examining ethnic conflict's implications for the United States and the international community.

### *Political Elites and Self-Determination*

The role of political leaders in spawning ethnic conflict as a means to personal power is impressive. Tudjman and Milosevic shifted from communist ideology to nationalist ideology in the twinkling of an eye, using their persuasive powers to ignite old feuds and glorious dreams of the future. They utilized the rhetoric of nationalism—under conditions of declining living standards, unemployment and low productivity—to promote their political careers. Yeltsin and Kravchuk also shifted from communism to nationalism rather late in their careers, but their moderation stands in sharp contrast to Balkan intolerance. Political leaders, in serving as catalysts of brewing discontent, may become leaders of sharply different revolutions.

Western leaders have fallen victim to the illusion that "nationalist" leaders like Croatia's Tudjman sought self-determination in order to pursue "democratic" governments. When Tudjman pressed for Croatia's independence, he was portrayed as a "democrat" and "statesman" and his republic a Western look-alike democracy. The point here is that nationalist leaders may mouth democratic platitudes in the quest for personal power, when in fact they adhere to authoritarian principles. In recognizing new states, the international community should pay close attention to their political and moral character.[101]

The role of political leaders in encouraging (or restraining) ethnic conflict suggests two points. First, the international community needs to watch for early warning signs of political elites on the verge of launching ethnic conflict. Secondly, in dealing with ethnic conflict, the international community needs to concentrate not so much on negotiating agreements with power–seeking and volatile, often unreliable, political leaders, but on trying to alter the economic and social conditions under which groups live and the relationships between groups in conflict.[102] This goal suggests an active role for developed countries in promoting democracy abroad through creative economic and political development programs designed to foster more harmonious relations among contending ethnic groups inside states.

The disintegration of the former Soviet Union and Yugoslavia—with their wake of secessions—raises serious questions about the validity of self–determination as an enshrined legal right in international relations. Increasing numbers of ethnic nationalist, breakaway movements within states complicate relations among the great powers, intensify regional conflicts, and confuse conflict management as we enter the twenty–first century. In tracking ethnic conflicts from the Balkans to Central Asia, there is much evidence to support those who say self–determination for every ethnic group on the face of the earth should give way to accommodating ethnic groups inside sovereign states.[103]

### Early Action

The most effective period for the international community to react decisively to ethnic conflict is in the early stages of the game. The Balkan wars illustrate how quickly ethnic conflict can spread across state boundaries as ancient rivalries and new power–oriented political elites capitalize on past feuds. Once the conflict spreads, decisive international action becomes more problematic, owing to the complexity of issues, difficulty of management, and risks of intervention. An exploding crisis makes enforcing a cease–fire extremely difficult, even if combatants sign it. The costs of intervention mount rapidly over time.

An ongoing ethnic war creates staggering problems for decision–makers in the U.S. and elsewhere to determine how and under what conditions to define and protect their interests in terms of the regional conflict. Confusion is compounded in an ethnic war, as opposed to traditional wars of aggression, by the multiplicity of competing groups, blurred battle lines, and unclear lines of command and control. Situational uncertainty tends to result in delayed or ineffective action by the international community.

### Avoiding Mixed Signals

Yugoslavia unravelled in violence, owing in part to the mixed signals communicated by the international community.[104] Beginning as early as 1991 the EC, notably Germany, supported a policy of disintegration; the U.S. opposed Croatian and Slovenian secessionist movements, yet tossed the ball into the Europeans' court. This miscommunication strengthened Serbia's resolve to hold Yugoslavia together and bolstered Croatia's and Slovenia's drives for independence. Later the international community disagreed sharply over enforcing policies, emboldening Serbia to press on with its brand of "ethnic cleansing." Observers have noted that disputes between the U.S. and its European allies over Bosnia have aided Milosevic.[105]

The record of U.S.-European operations in the Balkan crisis illustrates the security conflicts the alliance faces in the absence of the Soviet threat. Underscoring the lack of a common vision have been the early and evolving differences over how to treat the ethnic conflicts in the Balkans, notably Serbian "ethnic cleansing" in Bosnia from 1991 onwards. European states may have, in the words of Leon Brittan, the EC's commissioner for external trade relations, "no real definition" of their own security.[106] While the Europeans balked at backing U.S. urging for more forceful efforts in Bosnia, no European state appears ready and able to replace U.S. leadership—as in NATO. A new vision is needed for U.S.-European cooperation on security in Central and Southeastern Europe.

### Economic Sanctions Rarely Work

A look at the record of events in Bosnia suggests that economic sanctions rarely, if ever, lead ethnic aggressors to cease and desist from their actions. In the case of Serbia's Milosevic, several reasons account for this state of affairs. In circumventing sanctions, Milosevic set up a war economy, made use of militia groups financed by hard currency reserves maintained in Cyprus, and engaged in smuggling networks in which citizens of surrounding states have participated.[107] Porous borders impeded the sanctions, and Serbia's backward peasants, Milosevic's main supporters, were unaffected. For the region as a whole, sanctions did much harm by exacerbating the economic woes of old Yugoslav trading partners, such as Romania.

### The Un-United Nations

Weaknesses of UN peace-making and peace-enforcement stem not only from the structure of the UN itself, but also from perceived national interests of its members. Until a sufficient number of members—especially on the Security Council—decide that they want an organization that can act effectively, rather than basing their support on direct national advantage, UN peace-keeping operations will be *ad hoc* and improperly financed, while peace-enforcement is not likely to take flight.[108] The ethnic crisis in former Yugoslavia has revealed the lack of consensus on how to use the UN in ways compatible with distinct state interests.   In this respect, we have entered a period of great uncertainty.

## Implications for U.S. Foreign Policy

How should U.S. foreign policy address the post–Cold War international security environment, with its multiplicity of ethnic, tribal, religious and national conflicts emerging today?  Is there any way the U.S. can prevent, control and resolve these conflicts—and the spread of weapons they spawn—to foster a more orderly and peaceful world?  Implications from our case studies point in at least five directions.

First, a new age of internationalism is not guaranteed, especially under conditions of low economic growth, overloaded domestic agendas, and lack of a common adversary as characterized the Cold War years.  Differences among the allied powers on how to deal with former Yugoslavia's break–up and ethnic wars illustrate this point, as does the low level of international attention to preventing or controlling ethnic conflicts in Caucasia and Central Asia.  The UNs' inability to craft effective peace enforcement measures in Bosnia illustrates that key international actors are far from agreeing on a common threat to national interests posed by geopolitically proximate ethnic nationalist conflict and intrastate wars.  How to devise an effective UN policy on the use of force remains an open issue.

Secondly, the U.S. remains a dominant military power, but questions remain as to how it will use its power.  Will it work toward, and take the leadership in building, a UN–based collective security organization?  Will it move to strengthen NATO's response to regional crises in places like the former Yugoslavia?  How much blood and treasure should America contribute to multilateral intervention in the internal affairs of another country?

If U.S. leaders decide to intervene with force in an ethnic crisis, they should take the lead in *crisis prevention* through some kind of UN–sanctioned multilateral force and do it early, before the crisis spreads.  In the case of Yugoslavia, the U.S. did too little too late; the best chance to stop it was at its beginning, the summer and fall of 1991.  Intervention, however, was not proposed, and ruling out direct application of force against Serbia undermined the power of diplomatic persuasion.  Squabbling and lack of clear consensus in the ranks of the Bush and Clinton administrations, as well as among U.S. allies in Europe, undermined decisions and actions.[109]

U.S. forces sent to Macedonia in July 1993, to supplant 700 UN–sanctioned Scandinavian troops deployed in Macedonia earlier in 1993, were a step in the right direction.  This marks the first–ever UN operation mounted to stop a war before it begins.[110]   The key point is that we now face intrastate conflict situations for which we never have had a satisfactory answer.  What we do know, however, is that the old form of collective security did not work in former Yugoslavia nor the former USSR. Today's world calls for new thinking in terms of crisis prevention.

Third, U.S.-led, multilateral crisis prevention, peace enforcement or peace-keeping will be made difficult by the ambiguity of ethnic conflicts and their capability to drag down any intervenors in quagmires resembling Lebanon and Vietnam. The U.S. military memory of Lebanon and Vietnam is vivid in this respect, as reflected in former Chairman of the Joint Chiefs of Staff Colin Powell's publicized opposition to imposition of U.S. military force in Bosnia without clear political objectives and popular support. President Clinton's hesitation about using American military force in Bosnia reflects the Beirut frame of reference—eschewing intervention in places where political and military objectives remain elusive.[111] In this sense, President Clinton's policy may reflect a new kind of realism—matching capabilities to interests.[112]

Fourth, ethnic conflicts like Bosnia, Caucasia and Central Asia will make consensus-building within U.S. policy-making circles difficult owing to the nature of bureaucratic infighting and organizational differences. The wisdom of using force has led to sharp, public conflicts between the Defense and State Departments, with the former arguing against military intervention and the latter pressing for the U.S. military to take more forceful action against the Serbs. In April 1993 the State Department's top experts on the Balkans sent Secretary of State Warren Christopher an impassioned letter calling Western diplomacy a failure and recommending military action against the Serbs.[113]

This controversy was more or less settled by the West Europeans, who rejected in May President Clinton's proposal to arm Bosnian Muslims and threats to mount air strikes on Bosnian Serb targets. European foot-dragging, coupled with a growing number of congressional lawmakers opposing attacks on Serbia and an American public distinctly unfavorable to risking U.S. lives in Bosnia, led the U.S. to declare that Bosnia was not a vital U.S. interest.[114] Indeed, the Bosnia imbroglio may have inspired a senior State Department official to remark to reporters that the Clinton administration expected to withdraw from many foreign policy leadership roles normally played by the U.S. owing to its limited resources—a position Clinton officials raced to deny. Yet when Christopher spelled out new American foreign priorities in November 1993, ending the war in Bosnia was not on his list.[115]

Fifth, asserting world leadership will require cooperation with Russia, and the big question is the extent to which, and under what conditions, such cooperation will occur. Russia will be a vital partner in addressing problems in the former Soviet Union; Moscow has been a vital key in trying to craft an international policy for the Balkans. Russia desires to play a world role—in the UN and elsewhere—which adds to its part in the future drama of crisis prevention and peace enforcement. As a critical partner in future cooperative crisis prevention with the U.S., it will be interesting to watch closely Russia's position on the nuclear weapons issue dividing Moscow and Kiev, its response to Estonian and other former Soviet republic pressures on the Russian diaspora, and its role in local wars along its borders.

Complicating Russia's future foreign policy on such issues is the political make-up of Moscow's new parliament. In the December 1993 parliamentary elections, Vladimir Zhirinovsky, head of the misleadingly named Liberal Democratic Party, scored strongly and emerged as a major political figure. As a populist with a xenophobic nationalist message, he has written of the day when Russian soldiers will "wash their boots in the warm waters of the Indian Ocean and change into summer uniform for good."[116]  He has stated that the independence of the former Soviet republics is a temporary aberration, soon to be corrected by cutting off their aid and trade—after which they will come begging.[117]  His blatant appeals to racism bear a striking resemblance to those of Serbia's Milosevic.

As our case studies illustrate, the U.S. and international community face enormously complex problems in the post–Cold War period. Whether the U.S., Western Europe and Russia will craft effective policies to meet ethnic challenges to international security remains one of the larger questions today. If collective security is to be made effective, the international community, including the U.S., probably will have to agree that its members share a number of vital interests such as:

- Protecting the norms of international legality and political order.
- Reaffirming the unacceptibility of changing internationally recognized borders through force.
- The obligation of national groups to observe basic human rights, as defined by the UN Charter, Geneva Convention and Helsinki accords.
- Supporting those forces that enhance democratic determination and opposition to those that seek fragmentation and tribalism.

The more basic issue, however, is to work toward alleviating the very forces that enhance ethnic tensions in the first place: poverty and ineffective political institutions.

## Notes

1.  See James E. Goodby's insightful essay, "Collective Security in Europe After the Cold War," *Journal of International Affairs*, Vol. 46, No. 2, (Winter 1993), pp. 299–319.

2.  See Elizabeth Fuller, "Mediators for Transcaucasia's Conflicts," *The World Today*, Vol. 49, No. 5, (May 1993), pp. 89–92.

3.  See Richard Falk, "In Search of a New World Model," *Current History*, Vol. 92, No. 573, (April 1993), p. 145.

4. See Laurence Martin, "National Security in a New World Order," *The World Today*, Vol. 48, No. 2, (February 1992), pp. 21–26. While President Bush intervened in Iraq to help the Kurds in the aftermath of the Gulf War, he made clear that he would not risk a single soldier's life in trying to build a new Iraq, nor commit ground forces to Bosnia to become entangled in civil strife. Intervention to remove an aggressor state from the territory of another state was one thing, intervention in another state's domestic affairs to end oppression—as a general guideline for foreign policy—quite another. Martin, p. 22.

5. Falk, p. 145.

6. See Daniel Patrick Moynihan, *Pandaemonium: Ethnicity in International Politics* (Oxford: Oxford University Press, 1993).

7. Morton H. Halpern and David J. Scheffer, with Patricia L. Small, *Self—Determination in the New World Order* (Washington, D.C.: Carnegie Endowment for International Peace, 1992).

8. On the difficulties of predicting future events in world politics, see Robert Jervis, "The Future of World Politics: Will It Resemble the Past?" *International Security*, Vol. 16, No. 3 (Winter 1991–1992), pp. 39 ff.

9. Jervis, "The Future of World Politics," p. 46.

10. Falk, "In Search of a New World Order," p. 148.

11. See Christoph Muhlemann, "Clinton's America and Clinton's World," *Swiss Review*, March 1933, pp. 2–3; also Christopher Layne, "The Unipolar Illusion: Why New Great Powers Will Rise," *International Security*, Vol. 17, No. 4 (Spring 1993), pp. 5–51.

12. As quoted by Zbigniew Brzezinski, "Selective Global Commitment," *Foreign Affairs*, Vol. 70, No. 4 (1991), p. 6.

13. Brzezinski, "Selective Global Commitment," p. 6.

14. This point is made by Donald M. Snow, "Peacekeeping, Peacemaking and Peace-Enforcement: The U.S. Role in the New International Order," a paper presented at the Fourth Annual Conference on Strategy, "Strategy in Periods of Transition," Carlisle Barracks, Pennsylvania, February 1993, p. 1.

15. See James Mayall, "Nationalism and International Security After the Cold War," *Survival* (Spring 1992), pp. 18–35; Stephen R. Bowers, *Conflict Studies*, No. 248 (March 1992), pp. 1–25; Charles William Maynes, "Containing Ethnic Conflict," *Foreign Policy*, No. 90 (Spring 1993), pp. 3–21; Donald L. Horowitz, *Ethnic Groups in Conflict*, Berkeley: University of California Press, 1985; and Moynihan, *Pandemonium*.

16. See Gerald B. Helman and Steven R. Ratner, "Saving Failed States," *Foreign Policy*, No. 89 (Winter 1992–1993), pp. 3–20; and Amitai Etzioni, "The Evils of Self-Determination," *Foreign Policy*, No. 89 (Winter 1992–1993), pp. 21–35.

17. Samuel P. Huntington, "The Clash of Civilizations?" *Foreign Affairs*, Vol. 72, No. 3 (Summer 1993), pp. 22–49.

18. See the work of Walker Connor, Cynthia Enloe, Donald L. Horowitz, John F. Stack, Jr., Daniel Patrick Moynihan and Nathan Glazer.

19. See Daniel N. Posner, "Fighting Ethnic Demons: A Review of Senator Moynihan's 'Pandaemonium,'" *Harvard International Review*, Vol. XV, No. 4, pp. 62–63.

20. See *The New York Times*, (July 5 and 6, 1993).

21. Anthony Hyman observes that "ethnic nationalism, not various brands of Islam, constitutes the main potential threat to regional security. The governments all support the status quo in state borders. But in nationalist intellectual circles there is an enthusiasm to bring about alterations in the 1924 borders drawn around the new republics and unite with their ethnic brethren living as minorities in neighboring states." Hyman goes on to point out that "Border disputes in the former USSR as a whole vary greatly in their immediacy: Daniel Franklin ranked them in a recent article on a scale of one to five, from the dead, dormant and awakening to the wide awake and hyperactive. The 'hyperactive' disputes are all in the Caucasus (Nagorno-Karabakh, South Ossetia, Chechen-Ingushetia), while the 'wide awake' disputes are in the Russian Federation (Tatarstan, Bashkiria and the Kuriles). On this scale, Central Asian border disputes are 'awakening' or 'dormant.'" Anthony Hyman, "Moving Out of Moscow's Orbit: The Outlook for Central Asia," *International Affairs*, Vol. 69, No. 2 (April 1993), pp. 296–297. See also Daniel Franklin, "International Boundaries: Ex-Soviet Union and Eastern Europe," *The World Today*, London: RIIA, 1992, pp. 38–40.

22. For a different view, one less optimistic about Baltic security in terms of issues involving Russia, see Stephen J. Blank, *Russia and the Baltic: Is There A Threat To European Security?* Strategic Studies Institute, U.S. Army War College, (March 31, 1993).

23. See Justin Burke, "Russia Battles 'Brushfires' in Bordering States," *The Christian Science Monitor*, (July 16, 1993), p. 8.

24. See Snow, "Peacekeeping, Peacemaking, and Peace-enforcement: the U.S. Role in the New International Order," p. 13.

25. William Safire, "Right to Intervene," *The New York Times*, (November 30, 1992), p. A11.

26. Goodby, "Collective Security in Europe," p. 301.

27. Goodby, "Collective Security in Europe After the Cold War," p. 302.

28. William Pfaff, "Redefining World Power," *Foreign Affairs*, Vol. 71, No. 5 (Winter 1992/93), p. 36.

29. See Kofi A. Annan, "The Path of Peace-Keeping," *Harvard International Review*, Vol. XV, No. 4 (Summer 1993), pp. 32–35. Kofi A. Annan is the United Nations Under Secretary-General for Peace-Keeping Operations.

30. Adam Roberts, "The United Nations and International Security," *Survival*, The ISSS Quarterly, Vol. 35, No. 2 (Summer 1993), pp. 3–30.

31. See Maynes, "Containing Ethnic Conflict," p. 6.

32. Boutros-Ghali, *An Agenda for Peace*, New York: United Nations, (1992).

33. Boutros-Ghali, *An Agenda for Peace*, p. 9.

34. Boutros-Ghali, "United Nations Peace-Keeping in a New Era: A New Chance for Peace," *The World Today*, Vol. 49, No. 4, p. 68.

35. Boutros-Ghali, "Empowering the United Nations," *Foreign Affairs*, Vol. 72, No. 5 (Winter 1992/93), p. 91.

36. *The Christian Science Monitor*, (July 14, 1993).

37. Roberts, "The United Nations and International Security," p. 6.

38. Boutros-Ghali, *Agenda for Peace: Preventive Diplomacy, Peace-Making and Peace-Keeping*, New York: United Nations, (1992), pp. 11–19.

39. Boutros-Ghali, *Agenda for Peace*, pp. 25–26.

40. Ibid.

41. Interview with *The Christian Science Monitor*, (July 16, 1993).

42. Annan, "The Path of Peace-Keeping," p. 34.

43. Ibid.

44. Goodby, "Collective Security in Europe after the Cold War," p. 309.

45. Ibid.

46. Pierre Hassner, "Beyond Nationalism and Internationalism: Ethnicity and World Order," *Survival*, Vol. 35, No. 2 (Summer 1993), pp. 49-65. Hassner writes that, "Today, the prevailing international consensus accepts that intervention may be legitimate in three types of cases: in cases in which aggression is committed against an internationally recognized state (the Iraqi invasion of Kuwait); in cases in which states massacre their own citizens, whether for ideological or ethnic reasons (Cambodia); and in cases in which a breakdown in law and order leads to anarchy and massive suffering (Somalia). The former Yugoslavia fits all three categories." Hassner, "Beyond Nationalism and Internationalism," p. 62.

47. Goodby, "Collective Security in Europe After the Cold War," p. 313.

48. See "CSCE Missions," a summary prepared by the staff of the Commission on Security and Cooperation in Europe of the U.S. Congress, (September 1992).

49. Goodby, "Collective Security in Europe After the Cold War," p. 314.

50. Albania's President, Sali Berisha, is a case in point. Berisha fears Serbian intervention in Kosovo and pressure for a "Greater Serbia." See his interview with *The Christian Science Monitor*, (July 16, 1993).

51. See Jane M.O. Sharp, "Intervention in Bosnia: The Case For," *World Today*, Vol. 49, No. 2 (February 1993), pp 29-31; Eric Grove, "UN Armed Forces and the Military Staff Committee: A Look Back," *International Security*, Vol. 17, No. 4 (Spring 1993), pp. 172-179.

52. See Maynes, "Containing Ethnic Conflict," pp. 10-11.

53. A 1992 Brookings Institution study, as reported by Maynes, "Containing Ethnic Conflict," p. 10.

54. Maynes, "Containing Ethnic Conflict," p. 11.

55. Snow, "Peacekeeping, Peacemaking and Peace-Enforcement: The U.S. Role in the New International Order," pp. 11-12.

56. See Nikolaos A. Stavrou, "The Balkan Quagmire and the West's Response, " *Mediterranean Quarterly: A Journal of Global Issues*, Vol. 4, No. 1 (Winter 1993), p. 27.

57. Snow, "Peacekeeping, Peacemaking," p. 13.

58. See Michael Dewar, "Intervention in Bosnia: The Case Against," *The World Today*, Vol. 49, No. 2 (February 1993), p. 33.

59. For other problems with UNPROFOR, see Alan James, "The UN in Croatia: An Exercise in Futility?" *The World Today*, Vol. 49, No. 5 (May 1993), pp. 93-96.

60. Maynes, "Containing Ethnic Conflict," pp. 7-8.

61. See Adam Roberts' perceptive essay, "The United Nations and International Security," pp. 3-30; and Donald M. Snow, "Peacekeeping, Peacemaking and Peace-Enforcement: The U.S. Role in the New International Order," (February 1993).

62. Roberts, "The United Nations and International Security," p. 10.

63. See the paper resulting from the Conference on Options for U.S. Participation in United Nations Sanctioned Military Operations, Strategy and Campaign Department, Research Memorandum 2-93, Naval War College, Newport, Rhode Island, (May 17,

1993), p. 2. By April 1993, the UN had organized 13 new peace–keeping operations since 1988—as many as the whole 1948–1987 period. As opposed to the 10,000 blue helmets operating two years ago, by 1993 many thousands of civilian aid workers were joined by over 53,000 United Nations troops deployed all over the world—at an annual cost of $3 billion, a sixfold increase since 1988. See Nikos Tzermias, "The Bloom Is Off the UN Rose—Again," *Swiss Review*, (April 1993), p. 2.

64. Research Memorandum 2–93, p. 2.

65. Ibid.

66. Ibid.

67. On economies and ethnic conflict, see S.W.R. de A Samaralsinghe and Reed Coughlan, eds., *Economic Dimensions of Ethnic Conflict: International Perspectives*, New York: St. Martin's Press, (1991).

68. These statistics are from *The Croatian Economy in Times of War*, Report of the Ministry of Information, Zagreb, 1992, as cited by Ian Kearns, "Croatia: The Politics Behind the War," *The World Today*, Vol. 49, No. 4 (April 1993), p. 63.

69. These statistics on Serbia's economic conditions are from Jonathan S. Landay, "Serbia's Economy Falters, But Not From Sanctions," *The Christian Science Monitor*, (June 2, 1993), p. 1.

70. Jonathan S. Landry, "Plunging Living Standards Test Milosevic's Strategy," *The Christian Science Monitor*, (July 19, 1993), p. 1.

71. Christine Spolar, "Serbian Brain Drain," *The Washington Post*, (January 6, 1993), p. A 20. On Serbia's wasteland characteristics in Bosnia, see John F. Burns, "Bosnian Serbs Begin to Question the Price of Victory," *The New York Times*, November 14, 1993, p. A1.

72. Kearns, "Croatia: The Politics Behind the War," p. 63.

73. Jim Muir, "With Fuel and Water Cut, Siege of Sarajevo Worsens," *The Christian Science Monitor*, (July 13, 1993), p. 1.

74. See Edward E. Azar, "Protracted International Conflicts: Ten Propositions," in Edward E. Azar and John W. Burton, eds., *International Conflict Resolution: Theory and Practice*, Boulder, Colorado: Lynne Rienner Publishers, (1986), p. 28.

75. Azar, "Protracted International Conflicts: Ten Propositions," in Azar and Burton, *International Conflict Resolution*, p. 28.

76. Azar, "Protracted International Conflicts," pp. 28–29.

77. Ibid, p. 29.

78. Bruce W. Nelan, "Fighting Off Doom," *Time*, (June 21, 1993), p. 38. CIA Director James Woolsey has testified that Russia does not yet have an effective system for controlling exports of sensitive military equipment and technologies related to the development of nuclear, chemical or biological weapons. *The Washington Post*, (February 25, 1993), p. A18.

79. Bruce W. Nelan, "Fighting Off Doom," *Time*, (June 21, 1993), p. 37. Ukraine moved all of its tactical nuclear weapons to Russia between January and May 1992, but none of its strategic nuclear weapons have been transferred to Russia. That force is aimed at the U.S., but could be reprogrammed to strike Russia. At a minimum 130 SS–19s (6 warheads each), 46 SS–24s (10 warheads each), and 30 Bear–H and Blackjack bombers (together carrying 416 bombs), making a total of 1,656 nuclear weapons. See John F. Mearsheimer, "The Case for a Ukrainian Nuclear Deterrent," *Foreign Affairs*, Vol. 72, No. 3 (Summer 1993), p. 52. Mearsheimer argues that nuclear weapons are

the only reliable deterrent to Russian aggression. Some observers, however, fear that Ukraine is 12–18 months away from cracking the Russian computer codes that prevent Kiev from retargetting or firing the nuclear missiles. Should they succeed, they will gain control of the world's third largest nuclear arsenal of nuclear weapons. While Moscow has not said that it would attack Ukraine to prevent Kiev from gaining control, they have suggested at high levels that this could happen. Nelan, "Fighting Off Doom," p. 37. For this and other reasons, the argument against Ukraine possessing nuclear weapons is strong. See Steven E. Miller, "The Risks of Nuclear Proliferation," *Foreign Affairs*, Vol. 72, No. 3 (Summer 1993), pp. 67–79. By November 1993, Ukraine continued to cling to its nuclear weapons. See Lee Hockstader, "Ukraine is Clinging to Nuclear Arsenal Despite U.S. Prodding," *The Washington Post*, October 31, 1993, p. A25.

80. Note that the Baltic states are splitting on acquisition of weapons and training. Estonia is looking West and has bought arms from Israel ($ 50 million worth), while Lithuania is getting arms from Russia.

81. Observations by Andrei Kortunov, USA–Canada Institute, at the National Defense University, Washington, D.C., May 23, 1993.

82. Ibid.

83. Ibid.

84. Ibid.

85. Ibid.

86. See Bohdan Pyskir, "Russia Has No Special Minority Rights Claim," *The Christian Science Monitor*, (April 14, 1993), p. 19.

87. Note that the term "ethnic republics" may be misleading here, in that many, if not most of these entities are not all that "ethnic." Karelia was only 11 percent Karelian in 1989. What we are seeing is a decentralization of power and in most cases the old nomenklatura (mainly Russians) asserting their claims for local power.

88. See Michael Dobbs, "Russian Regions Resist Yeltsin Decree," *The New York Times*, (March 23, 1993), p. A1.

89. As to Russia's alternate futures, see David K. Shipler, "Four Futures for Russia," *The New York Times Magazine*, (April 4, 1993), pp. 28 ff.

90. See Roger Cohen, "The Tearing Apart of Yugoslavia: Place by Place, Family by Family," *The New York Times*, (May 9, 1993), p. 4.

91. Chuck Sudetic, "Serbs' Gains in Bosnia Create Chaotic Patchwork," *The New York Times*, (August 15, 1992), p. A1.

92. See Elaine Sciolino, "U.S. Names Figures to Be Prosecuted Over War Crimes," *The New York Times*, (December 17, 1992), p. A1. Serbia's leader Milosevic topped the list.

93. On social disintegration in Bosnia, see "The Relentless Agony of Former Yugoslavia," *Foreign Policy Bulletin* (January–April 1983), pp. 57–75.

94. Chuck Sudetic, "A Shady Militia Chief Arouses Serbs," *The New York Times*, (December 20, 1992), p. A12.

95. In early 1993, the number two man in Serbia, Vojislav Seselj, was a former fanatical communist turned fanatical Serb nationalist, who carried an automatic pistol in his pants and kicked protestors who got in his way. Seselj told a Belgrade magazine in February 1993 that he wanted power—"very much with all our souls" and that he was cleverly heading toward the realization of that aim. In Azerbaijan, meanwhile, the parliament elected rebel leader Suret Guseinov as prime minister, less than two weeks

after his forces chased popularly elected President Abulfaz Elchibey from power. Guseinov also gained direct control of the defense, interior, and national security ministries. In Central Asia, however, people worry more about prices, food, work and political stability than about democracy, hence democratic institution–building is not of high priority among the rank and file. See *The Christian Science Monitor*, (July 1, 1993), p. 7.

96.  See Vasil Tupurkovski, "The Dissolution of Yugoslavia: An Insider's View," *Mediterranean Quarterly*, Vol. 4, No. 2 (Spring 1993), p. 14.

97.  A major proposition stemming from research on ethnic and social conflict is that "protracted social conflicts in multi–ethnic societies are not ameliorated peacefully by centralized structures." Azar, "Protracted International Conflicts," pp. 33–34.

98.  For a good background on this issue, see Brian Hall, "A Holy War in Waiting," *The New York Times Magazine*, (May 9, 1993), pp. 22 ff.

99.  Daniel N. Nelson, "A Balkan Perspective," *Strategic Review* (Winter 1993), p. 36.

100.  Justin Burke, "Former Soviet Republics Beset by Power Struggles," *The Christian Science Monitor*, (April 6, 1993), p. 7.

101.  See Nikolaos A. Stavrou, "The Balkan Quagmire and the West's Response," p. 35.  As Stavrou notes, "What the West seemingly failed to notice in the Balkans, however, was that prewar elites and opportunistic elements leapt to the front with old scores to settle. In some countries, these opportunistic elements succeeded in hijacking the bandwagon of democratization and moved to pursue their age–old agendas." p. 33.

102.  See Harold H. Saunders, "A Political Approach to Ethnic and National Conflict," *Mediterranean Quarterly*, Vol. 4, No. 1 (Winter 1993), p. 15.

103.  See Donald L. Horowitz, "Ethnic Conflict: The Known and the Unknown," paper presented at the Defense Intelligence College Conference, "Ethnic Conflict: Challenge to U.S. Security?," Washington, D.C., (June 23, 1992), p. 25.

104.  See Vasil Tupurkovski, "The Dissolution of Yugoslavia: An Insider's View," pp. 23–25.

105.  Jonathan S. Landay, "Milosevic's Maneuvers Solidify His Reign in Serbia," *The Christian Science Monitor*, (June 14, 1993).

106.  William Drozdiak, "U.S.–European Alliance Plagued by Trade, Security Conflicts," *The Washington Post*, (February 13, 1993), p. A20.

107.  Misha Glenny, "Bosnia: The Last Chance?," *The New York Times Book Review*, Vol. XL, No. 3 (January 28, 1993), p. 5.

108.  On these and related points, see R.J.G. Merrills, *International Dispute Settlement*, Cambridge: Grotius Publications Limited, 1991, 2nd ed., p. 247.

109.  See Don Oberdorfer, "A Bloody Failure in the Balkans," *The Washington Post*, (February 8, 1992), p. 1.

110.  See Jonathan Landay, "US Troops in Macedonia to Keep Watch on Serbian Border," *The Christian Science Monitor*, (July 7, 1993), p. 1.

111.  Thomas L. Friedman, "Leading the U.S. into the Balkans, on Tiptoes," *The New York Times*, (February 28, 1993), p. 4–1.

112.  Heinz A. J. Kern, "The Clinton Doctrine: A New Foreign Policy," *The Christian Science Monitor*, (June 18, 1993), p. 19.

113.  Michael R. Gordon, "12 in State Dept. Ask Military Move Against the Serbs," *The New York Times*, (April 23, 1993), p. A1.

114. Steven A. Holmes, "Backing Away Again, Christopher Says Bosnia Is Not a Vital Interest," *The New York Times*, (June 4, 1993), p. A12.

115. See *The New York Times*, November 5, 1993, p. A8.

116. The Washington Post, December 13, 1993, p. A17.

117. Ibid.

# About the Editors and Contributors

**Audrey L. Altstadt** is associate professor at the University of Massachusetts-Amherst. She holds a Ph.D. from the University of Chicago and is author of *The Azerbaijani Turks: Power and Identity Under Russian Rule* (1992) and of many articles on Azerbaijan and Central Asia published in the U.S., Canada, Europe, and former USSR.

**W. Raymond Duncan** is Distinguished Teaching Professor of International Relations at the State University of New York (SUNY), College at Brockport. He is author of *Moscow and the Third World* (Westview Press, 1990)—with Carolyn McGiffert Goodman—and he has published a number of other studies of Soviet-Third World relations. During 1992-93, he served as a Secretary of the Navy Fellow at the Naval War College, Newport, Rhode Island, teaching in the Department of National Security Decision-Making.

**Malvin M. Helgesen** has a Ph.D. in Soviet History from State University of New York (SUNY), College at Stony Brook. He has taught at several universities in the Washington, D.C., area as well as at the Naval War College. He has also served as an analyst of Soviet and post-Soviet issues at the Central Intelligence Agency.

**G. Paul Holman, Jr.** currently is professor of national security in the Department of National Security Decision-Making, Naval War College, Newport, Rhode Island. A career intelligence officer, he has a Ph.D. in Russian history from Georgetown University. His teaching interests include force planning, economics, and the armed forces of Russia and Eurasia.

**Wayne P. Limberg** is currently chief of the Western Division, Office for the Analysis of the Commonwealth of Independent States and East Europe, Bureau of Intelligence and Research, U.S. Department of State. He has taught at American University, Georgetown University, Loyola University of Los Angeles, the University of London's School of Slavonic and East European Studies, and the National War College. He received his Ph.D. in Russian history from Georgetown University.

**Toivo U. Raun** is a professor of Central Eurasian studies and adjunct professor of history at Indiana University, Bloomington. He is the author of *Estonia and the Estonians,* 2nd ed. (1991) and numerous other studies on Baltic history. During 1992–94, he is president of the Association for the Advancement of Baltic Studies.